WHAT HAPPENED TO MILLENNIALS

To Soon-Hee Ingrum

WHAT HAPPENED TO MILLENNIALS

IN DEFENSE OF A GENERATION

CHARLIE WELLS

ABRAMS PRESS, NEW YORK

Library of Congress Control Number: 2024951584

ISBN: 978-1-4197-7081-4
eISBN: 979-8-88707-144-2

Printed and bound in the United States
10 9 8 7 6 5 4 3 2 1

Abrams books are available at special discounts when purchased
in quantity for premiums and promotions as well as fundraising
or educational use. Special editions can also be created to specification.
For details, contact specialsales@abramsbooks.com or the address below.

Abrams Press® is a registered trademark of Harry N. Abrams, Inc.

ABRAMS The Art of Books
195 Broadway, New York, NY 10007
abramsbooks.com

CONTENTS

YOU THINK YOU KNOW

There was a time when they called us "Generation Y." There was an actual article in a prestigious national newspaper that suggested calling us "the Tamagotchi Generation."[1] We were, briefly, the Net Generation, which sounds so dated now that it hurts to type. We were The Thumbs, because texting and video-gaming had made ours the strongest parts of our hands, rather than the fingers of our forbears.[2] We were Generation Me, we were the Echo-Boom.[3] We were even called Generation 9/11.

"Millennials" won out. It is a hefty word. Unlike the term for the previous generation, marked by a simple X, "Millennial" connotes a moment in history. It wraps a thousand years around what you might call fin-de-siècle twentieth-century America. With a label like that came high expectations. But over time, what other people said about us changed. There were magazine cover stories written about our unnatural need for self-affirmation and self-esteem. There were experts warning the public that we weren't growing up. Now there are suggestions that we are irrelevant, out of date in the face of Gen Z. The purpose of this book is to defend us against these claims. This defense will help craft a better understanding of us—Millennials—twenty-five years after the new millennium began and the first of us started to become adults. It will do so by exploring our particular slice of history, on levels both cultural and personal. It will document the changes that occurred around us as we were growing up, the world events shaping who we would become.

I am a reporter at one of the country's largest news organizations. I have been writing stories about Millennial life for my entire career. I have interviewed hundreds of us from all parts of the country for stories in newspapers and on blogs, websites, television, radio, Instagram, Snapchat, and TikTok. I call fellow Millennials almost every day of my life to talk about theirs: their sex lives, home lives, financial lives, digital lives, the lives they thought they would be living by now but aren't. And when I want to get down to the heart of the matter when I'm interviewing strangers about their stories, I need a little bit of an icebreaker. The question I ask to loosen things up sounds completely unserious. But it takes most of us back to a formative period, and beyond that is itself surprisingly revealing. The question is this: *What was your AIM screenname?*

The answers are usually single words. Or rather, compound-word/ things. Mine was gigawells. I hate that I'm revealing this, but I named myself that on America Online because at one point in the late 1990s, I was a caretaker for no less than nine Tamagotchis and Gigapets, all beeping and pooping themselves and needing to be fed at the same time. (I think digital pets prepared me to be good at attending to smartphone notifications.) Also, my last name is Wells. Another person you will meet later in this book went by CoolBlue91. "Cool" because she was, "Blue" after that Eiffel 65 song about the color, and "91" because of the year she was born. Of course, not everybody had AIM, and if they didn't, that's telling, too.

Back when we were our AIM names, the so-called World Wide Web was fun. It wasn't for work. The consumer internet was growing up alongside us in the late 1990s, giving us this new, secret, fast way to communicate. It was like a lush valley to explore. But it changed, and so did we as we moved through it. AIM gave way to Gchat which gave way to BBM which gave way to iMessage which gave way to Slack and then suddenly everything was a messaging app from Discord to Telegram to WhatsApp to even LinkedIn, where you can talk to people using AI prompts now. Communicating at the speed of silent, human-generated text, we seemed—or at least felt—faster, smarter, savvier and wiser than those who came before.

But the old tricks aren't working any longer. The return on these new technologies has declined. AOL discontinued AIM in 2017. There is a new generation growing up beneath us, raised on video snippets and disappearing photos. Millennials, to put it bluntly, are starting to be old. A fair few of our children have drivers' licenses now. They don't know what landlines were. The translucent, tangerine sheen of the 1990s feels like a lifetime ago. Sometimes, it's hard to believe it's been a quarter century since the first of us turned 18. Sometimes it's easier, the years feeling like they've blitzed by. The work nights get heavier, the dishes sit still undone in the sink, the laundry somehow crumples even more where it lies unfolded on the couch. Nights like this, I get the possibly unhealthy urge to sink into the blue light of my phone and look at old pictures of myself and my friends on dumb apps. We are allegedly the most nostalgic generation. That is convenient, because many of our memories are stored in our pockets—which is to say, in social-media data centers deep in the Nevada desert. But it feels as if something is missing. Which is what makes it hard not to ask another revealing question: *What happened to Millennials?*

The data answering that question is not pretty. In one nationally representative poll of Americans, nearly one out of every three Millennials said they have zero best friends.[4] We report being lonely "often" or "always" at higher rates than Baby Boomers and Gen Xers. Our rates of suicide are higher than they were for previous generations.[5] We are having less sex than older people did at our age.[6] We have more student debt. A slight majority of us finally own homes, but it took us longer to get them, and we bought them at higher prices, so it will take us longer to pay them off.[7] Our starting salaries were hindered by the Great Recession in a way Gen Z doesn't seem to understand. They entered the job market during a historic boom; we entered when one in five young people was unemployed. The data is more than simply numerical. Just as interest in our generation starts to pass its peak, as Gen Z grabs the limelight, an awful, clichéd story about us persists. We are often accused of being failures to launch, of rejecting grownup life. Books have been written telling us to get it together, despite the economic, cultural, and political conditions that pushed back the age at which it was generally possible to reach adult milestones. There are self-help articles now with titles like, "How Can I Update My Millennial Style?" and "How to Tell You're a Geriatric Millennial."[8] Skinny jeans are passé. Facebook is over twenty years old. So is Gmail. Mark Zuckerberg has passed 40. AIM is dead.

I find these developments unsettling. I know that many other Millennials do, too. If there's one theme I pick up on in almost every interview I do with a Millennial, it's of a certain sense of failure. I think it comes from the fact that from the beginning, our expectations were set impossibly high. During most of our childhoods, the economy was flying. Our helicopter parents told us to fly higher. Our future living standards were supposed to be better, easier, and just more fun than those of the generations that came before. Politicians were supposed to take us forward. By and large, those expectations have not been met. The world has failed us in this regard, and I will cover those failures later in this book. But a deeper fear, one I hear more often now seeping into my interviews, is the one that comes from the uncomfortable realization that maybe, in some ways, over the past twenty-five years, we have failed ourselves.

When people feel this way, it makes them behave in strange ways, sometimes ways easily caricatured by the outside world. There are the aging jokes about Millennials who can't afford houses because we spend all our money eating expensive avocado toast. There are *SNL* skits about how we are so obsessed with real estate that Zillow is our porn now. Theories abound for why we're allegedly so addicted to our phones, why we switched jobs so often, why we all want to be remote-working digital nomads, why we still pine for gold stars and trophies for everything, even if they're now emojis affixed to our Slack messages at work. There's some truth to these theories, but none of them paint the whole picture.

In 1962, a sociologist named James Davies popularized the theory of the "J-curve" in an article published in the *American Sociological Review*. He wanted to explain why populations descend into revolutionary unrest. What he found: Rebellions follow quick downturns in economic progress that happen after long periods of prosperity. Expectations continue on an upward trajectory, but the actual satisfaction of needs veers downward, in the shape of an upside-down "J."[9] There develops a big gap between what people want or expect and what they actually get. Related theories about relative deprivation, about *disappointment*—that gap in perception between expected outcomes and reality—have been used to explain everything from the persistence of racism to the ratcheting up of the culture wars to the return of Donald Trump to the White House.

I am writing this book because Millennials are reaching an important crossroads—midlife—with this tension between hope and reality unresolved. Rather than looking for blame or fault, wondering if others failed us or what we ourselves did wrong, I want to understand how it all happened. What have we actually done? What are the choices we made, and how are they shaping who we have become? A quarter century into a "new" millennium, we've been told we've lived through an enormous amount of change. Measuring the extent of it will give us the power to shape our story on our own terms as we enter the second half of life. And our story, which I think is a good one, is our best defense.

I'll tell this history in two ways. The first will document what was going on around us as we became a generation. It was an evolution. We were first called Millennials in 1991,[10] the reason being that the oldest of us would become adults just as the clock struck Y2K—we're a generation where the oldest of us were born in 1981; the youngest, 1996. (There is some fuzziness on the precise boundaries of our cohort, and I don't think we need to be complete sticklers about it. Generational differences are often about moods and vibes just as much as or more than numbers.) But the term "Millennial" did not catch on, really, until we started entering the workforce en masse and falling under the microscope of those who had come before. The early conclusions were fatalistic. The participation-trophy generation was expected to need endless kudos at work, lest we wilt. Articles appeared speaking of how we were "killing" just about every common noun you could think of: the telephone, the car, the hotel, mayonnaise, meat, marriage, homeownership, capitalism. Books were published, mostly written for our parents and bosses, to help them understand us.

If much of this feels like astrology, it's because it basically is. Harvard professor Louis Menand said it starkly in *The New Yorker* not long ago when he argued that supposed generational traits are "about as meaningful as the difference between a Leo and a Virgo."[11] If anything, there is a strong corporate interest behind talking about generations. Analyzing differences between people born in different decades makes consultants a lot of money. Researchers have found that the consulting industry made $70 million in a year explaining the alleged differences between age groups in places like the office and the supermarket.[12] In an article in *Aeon,* Slate editor Rebecca Onion finds that "the dominant US thinkers on the generational question tend to flatten social distinctions, relying on cherry-picked examples and reifying a vision of a 'society' that's made up mostly of the White and middle-class."[13] Even the Pew Research Center has begun taking a more cautious approach to generational research, noting that "the field has been flooded with content that's often sold as research but is more like clickbait or marketing mythology."[14] Pew, a bastion of explaining how and why Americans think the things they do, will continue to report on generations, but only when they truly can conduct proper analysis.

Still, it's pretty hard to argue that there are no differences between groups of people born during different periods of time. The fairest way to think about the differences between generations, in my opinion, comes from King's College professor Bobby Duffy. In his book, *Generations: Does When You're Born Shape Who You Are?*, he argues that when you are born matters . . . to some extent. But so, too, does the period of life you're in at any given point—your biological age. Add to that the things that are going on around you and affecting everyone else in the world, and you have three lenses—cohort, age, era—that comprise a helpful way to make a history of a group less astrological and more accurate. That's what I'll try to do in this book.

My second strategy to defend us is to tell the story of our generation through the experiences of people who actually lived it. At some points, I'll do this by examining the influence of people who had money, power, and fame. Their experiences often took place in big cities like New York and Washington. But I will also rely heavily on the stories of more every-day people. It's important to remember that there isn't really one "us." Racially, Millennials in America are far more diverse than prior generations. Only about 55 percent of Millennials are White, as compared to 63 percent of Gen Xers and 71 percent of Baby Boomers.[15] About 21 percent of Millennials are Hispanic, versus 16 percent for Gen X and 11 percent for Baby Boomers. Millennials have slightly larger populations of Black and Asian Americans than older cohorts. More identify as working class than prior generations.[16]

Trying to tell the story of a generation is a bold move. It's the sort of thing that an overly confident White man might try to do. And if you look at the jacket of this book, you'll probably come to some not-entirely-inaccurate conclusions about me. (Although I do, like many members of our cohort, have a more complicated story than might meet the eye.)

So I drew on a piece of journalistic advice from Marty Baron, the former editor of the *Washington Post*, who once hung a sign in the newsroom that said, "Go talk to people." To that end, while I used statistics, data and research to understand our generation, much of what I also did was to spend hundreds of hours on the phone and in person following that advice: talking to people.

I have interviewed hundreds of Millennials in my career as a journalist. I picked five in particular to focus on in this book. I chose them because they intimately witnessed important facets of Millennial life that have changed over the past twenty-five years of our adulthoods. This story is told in four parts, and I check in with my subjects at four different turning points over the course of the past two and a half decades.

The people I interviewed agreed to speak with me because they believe in the power of our history and want to preserve and share it. I spoke with them across roughly four years, starting in 2021, asking them to tell me their stories from the beginnings of their lives to the present day, with particular focus on their adulthoods. None of their names have been changed, and our conversations were completely on the record. I did change the names and some details about the people my sources talked about to protect their anonymity. If you read carefully, you'll see how *Buffy the Vampire Slayer* helped me with this. As you'll read below, the introductory contours of these stories may at first sound familiar, but be careful not to presume too much. As the years went by in my reporting for this project, I began to see a common thread. In various ways, each of my interviewees felt trapped by what others thought they knew about them and want to correct the record. It reminded me of the tagline you used to hear at the beginning of that early 2000s MTV show *Diary*. It followed celebrities around. The show used video that looked like it had been filmed on a camcorder and included confessional interviews with its subjects about what was really going on. It sounds fluffy, and it was. But its tagline stuck with me: "You think you know, but you have no idea."

On that note—and to unapologetically draw on the reality-television antics that influenced the culture, history, and most certainly the politics of our generation—let's meet our cast:

Olivia Vilardi-Perez suggested we meet for brunch one Sunday on a part of Long Island that Long Islanders say is the real New York. If I craned my head at the right angle, I could look across the street, and then the bay, and then the Costco parking lot, and then the car dealership asphalt, to downtown Manhattan. Olivia and I had been talking for years, and I had that particularly Millennial sentiment of meeting face-to-face for the first time someone I already knew quite well from the internet. I had time to think about this because she was running late for brunch. *"I'm stuck at the railroad crossing,"* she texted me, and I hoped she was using hands-free. *"I'm sorry!"* When she arrived we got buzzed together on mimosas as the Sunday scaries sank in and we talked about how—if—you can ever get over the hurt of a Great American Tragedy.

Aaron Roach picked up the phone on his lunch break at work. He'd finally gotten the job—*the* job. He'd worked at Burger Hut, Arby's, Circle K, in a factory, in the Army National Guard, and as a welder. But he'd at long last landed a job as a drug and addiction counselor at the local VA near Alliance, the town where he grew up in northeast Ohio. At many points in my conversations with Aaron, he compared himself to a cat. He always managed to land on his feet. But he also often reminded both of us that he doesn't have nine lives. His work as a counselor was starting to provide the sort of stability he'd been searching for, and in a lot of ways couldn't believe he'd found. It brought with it the pain of the past, the memories of friends he lost who still cling to him like ghosts around his small town, memories of an opioid epidemic he made it out of.

I watched Tereza Lee watch kids plunk badly through "Ode to Joy" and "It's a Small World." Their rich, Millennial parents were taking high-def video of them on the latest iPhones in one of the most expensive neighborhoods in Manhattan. Later, she sat down at the keyboard and blew them all out of the water playing a piece by Czech composer Franz Drdla. I knew that Tereza has serious questions about wealth in America. As a child, her mother taught her how to squash the bugs that lived in their basement apartment with her fingernail. They didn't have heating. The piano gave Tereza a way out, but on the way, she became a poster child for someone else's version of the American Dream. The people who put her in that position tried to freeze her as a perfect, useful story. She made it clear to me that she's ready for revolutionary change.

Justin Knapik and I walked the quiet streets of his suburban Charlotte neighborhood. It was a bustling morning downtown in a city that has become known as a "Millennial magnet," drawing young adults from other states in search of jobs and housing. Justin was there, strolling with his daughter as the workday flew by. He is part of a demographic group that has struck researchers with an increasing sense of urgency: White men who dropped out of college and later, the labor force. By all accounts, Justin's life is very good. He and his wife have two cars, two children, and a three-bedroom house. But in large part, they were only able to get these things because Justin stopped serving as a direct financial provider for his family and became a stay-at-home dad. He sees the rewards that came with this choice, but there are moments when it vexes him. He is dreaming of making it all work.

Miju Han watched a storm roll in over the San Francisco Bay as she drifted back to the time before she was such a success. When she moved there, Miju was closeted, stuffing herself into business-casual attire, and so new to the world around her that she couldn't even tell you where Silicon Valley was on a map. In just a few years, she became a tech executive at some of our generation's most influential companies. But in those years, too, she began to rethink her relationships with work, capitalism, monogamy. At the moment in time we spoke, Miju was pregnant with her second child, witnessing the ways in which suburban America, even in its most progressive zip codes, has yet to catch up with today's many modern domestic realities. In Miju's case, it was one with not just two kids and two parents, but maybe sometimes other partners, and a lot of friends around in what has come to be known as her chosen family.

We are the generation of seventy-two million Americans born between the founding of CNN in 1980 and Fox News in 1996. We are the country's largest living cohort. We are Millennials.

This is what happened to us.

PART I
COUNTDOWN

DECEMBER 1, 1999

Looking back, the expectations were too high. There were countdown timers on Angelfire websites. There were talk-show segments and gossip magazine splashes, huge spreads and lots of sexual innuendo. There was much too much said about her virginity and her breasts. More fundamentally, there were the promises made about her future. Her debut album had just sold ten million copies.[1] It was a classic American turnaround tale: Only a year before, her family had filed for bankruptcy.[2] Her story was the apotheosis of the 1990s. Globalization, cable television, and mass consumer capitalism had shaped the world in which we became cognizant beings. They had made her, too. And now Britney Spears, the uber-Millennial, the most extreme example of the highs and the lows of our generation, born at the dawn of our era, was becoming an adult. It was a very big deal.

"You're about to turn 18," Matt Lauer explained to her.

The former face of the *Today* show was still one of America's male sweethearts. An everyday hero figure, a regular guy who had somehow made his way onto national television. He was someone who felt like a just-barely-better-looking version of your dad. (In fact, he told Spears he felt like her father that day, live on air.) It would be eighteen years, the span of an adulthood, before Lauer was fired on allegations of sexual harassment in the wake of #MeToo.[3] But in 1999, all he was doing was wearing a black felt hat, leaning creepily close to Britney Spears as the two of them appeared on primetime television. They were in Manhattan, the center of the post–Cold War, pre–Great Recession world, in Rockefeller Center, lighting its famous Christmas tree for the last time of the old millennium.[4]

The part Spears played for Matt Lauer and the camera was the part America expected of, and wanted for, its new Millennial adults. It wanted innocence and sweetness. It wanted success to match the success of the era, of the rising stock market, of the booming economy, of the triumph of capitalism over communism that had started to fully sink in over the mere eight years since the fall of the Soviet Union. America's newest adults were getting ready to inhabit what talking heads had been calling the "end of history," a commonly articulated belief that Western liberalism was the endpoint of our sociopolitical evolution. It trickled down into a sense that all you had to do was sit back, log on to the internet, and let the good times carry you into the future. On camera, Spears looked and sounded like all of this, like someone who only knew brightness. She wore a brown, chunky-knit sweater-cape over a pink turtleneck. She sang "Silent Night." New York's freezing December air whirled around her as she answered Lauer's between-set questions about her plans to celebrate her birthday, which would begin just a few hours later when the clock struck midnight.

"Three of my girlfriends came up for my birthday party, which we're gonna have tonight," she told him. "You always have to make time to spend with your family and your friends like that so I can be sane and be normal."

A few hours after the Christmas tree show, Spears made her way downtown to a club called Halo. It was a splashy, underground place. One style reporter warned it rejected "all who aren't very good looking or flashing $5,000 shoulder bags."[5] The songstress had transitioned from the pink turtleneck into a snake-skin dress.[6] Spears's mother and her now-estranged father were there at the party. Her boyfriend at the time, Robbie Carrico, was of course at the club, too. He had spiky, blond hair and was a member of a band called Boyz 'N Girlz United, basically a coed version of NSYNC whose lead single was written by JC Chasez. Carrico's friend, Justin Timberlake, was there, too. The NYSNC singer was photographed later that night feeding Spears a cherry.

That night at Halo, there were so many contradictions coming together. Who was grown-up Britney Spears? What was her adult life supposed to be? Was it sweater capes and Christmas carols with squeaky-clean pronouncements about friends and family, or would it be hot clubs and Justin Timberlake? Maybe this sounds like superfluous tabloid banter, and I won't pretend it's not. But celebrities are also revealing subjects to study because our cultural obsessions represent what we value in a given historical moment. Looking both in and outside Halo at that time, it becomes clear a breaking point had arrived.

In the world at large, the stock market and economy were steaming forward, so much so that policymakers worried about it all going too fast. And those stellar, historic, once-in-a-century, tech-fueled markets were indeed about to crash in what the *Economist* would a few years later term "the biggest and fastest rise and fall in business history."[7] But that's me getting ahead of myself. Back then in 1999, a consensus had emerged that globalization was good, that international trade might mean an end to international conflict. China had begun negotiations to enter the World Trade Organization.

The same night as Spears was turning 18, searing questions about these developments were arising on the other side of the country. Tens of thousands of people had gathered at what has come to be known as the "Battle of Seattle," a multi-day protest of the WTO conference gathered there. The conference was supposed to showcase America's leadership on free trade. Instead, the city was placed under curfew, the authorities called in the National Guard, and clouds of tear gas hung heavy in the air.

"My throat hurts," a young music store clerk who came to protest that week told a reporter on the scene.[8] "My lungs still hurt."

The Seattle protests don't always feature in the minds of Millennials as a turning point in American life, especially since all but the oldest of us were still relatively young children at the time. But looking back, they serve as a foreshadowing for battles ahead. Sociologist Zeynep Tufekci points out that the protests in Seattle "were among the earliest manifestations of an emerging, networked global movement" organized using the internet and geared at extracting greater accountability from large, opaque, transnational corporations and institutions.[9] They were some of the first mass protests to be organized using the emerging consumer internet, with its communication tools like email, forums, and AIM.

The fact that activist internet users could effectively shut down parts of a major American city and stymie negotiations of the world's largest international economic organization stunned the mainstream. Even Bill Clinton, who flew to Seattle amidst the protests, seemed surprised. In a speech the same day Spears was singing "Silent Night," Clinton chided the WTO for its opacity, saying he sided with the people protesting.[10] "What they are telling us in the streets is that this is an issue we've been silent on," he said. "And we won't be silent anymore." But it didn't matter. He'd been impeached. He was a lame duck. The race to succeed him was on. That same day in Iowa, George W. Bush was campaigning for president, talking about $483 billion in tax cuts as a way to "take down the tollgate on the road to the middle class."[11]

"Never look back," Britney Spears sang that day in Rockefeller Plaza. "How was I to know I'd miss you so?"

Part of the reason asking Millennials about their AIM screennames can be so revealing is that it tends to tap into a deep sense of nostalgia we feel about the 1990s. Millennials often look back on the period with a glow seemingly so strong that it has become an entire business strategy for brands to bring back products from the era like Crystal Pepsi or Dunkaroos. Our nostalgic tendencies often prompt journalists to write articles such as, "Millennial Nostalgia Sells. Just Ask These Influencers Making Their Livings Off It," "Why Are Millennials the Most Nostalgic Generation Ever," and "Why Millennials Are Afflicted with 'Early-Onset Nostalgia.'"[12]

Those are great headlines. But they're also wrong. Millennials aren't the "most nostalgic generation ever." If you look at the internet lately, it seems Gen Z is taking our place. They're certainly dressing like it's the 1990s, a decade few of them were even alive for. Baby Boomers had a nostalgic phase in the 1970s, with movies like *American Graffiti* and *Grease* meditating on how life had been when they were teenagers. In fact, an expanding body of research on nostalgia has found that it tends to surface at life transitions.[13] In some senses, every generation is the most nostalgic generation as it comes into adulthood and leaves its childhood behind. What is unique about Millennials is that our massive movement into the workplace took place at a time when social media–friendly news articles were exploding. We aren't some sad, mournful group of people; we were coping with a transition as any other generation might, it's just that the internet made it more visible.

Nostalgia is a messy emotion. Scientists once thought it was a form of melancholic depression and even called it "mentally repressive compulsive disorder." In a way, this makes sense. It's hard to live in the present if you're constantly thinking about the past. But researchers are now finding that nostalgia can be a good thing, too. It can literally make us feel warmer, motivate us, and make us feel less lonely. It is, in a word, complicated.

That's the sense I got the first time I met Olivia. Our first conversation was on Zoom in 2021, which I suppose is the modern version of meeting in a chatroom. She took my call during a break in her workday as a science teacher on Long Island, sitting among stacks of papers with an old green chalkboard behind her. I immediately liked her. But I could feel her anxiety through the screen, too. Back then, she was just 30, and she was finding that even though she'd done everything she was told to do, it somehow wasn't enough. She'd gotten a solid job and felt respected at work. She was pretty and smart and quick with words, funny and good at the internet. And yet, in quieter moments, I could feel a certain sadness, a frustration of expectations unmet, perhaps never to be in her acquaintance at all. It's a heavy feeling, she said, that carried her to her shrink's couch at 2 p.m. on the dot—"every damn Tuesday."

In the 1990s, Olivia online was CoolBlue91. And that's cute, but what comes up when she tells me about it is deeper than the simple fact of her username. It's that she used to use it to talk to her dad, Anthony.

Anthony and Olivia's mother never married, and that put Olivia in the crosshairs of a new, national trend that would shape life for many Millennials. The day after she was born in 1991, in fact, the *Washington Post* ran a big headline: "NONMARITAL BIRTHS: AS RATES SOAR, THEORIES ABOUND."[14] "In the summer of 1965, one of the most explosive government reports ever written disclosed that one-quarter of all Black children were born out of wedlock," the article read rather breathlessly, referring to research conducted by Daniel Patrick Moynihan, something of a political maverick who would go on to become one of New York's most famous senators. The article continued on to its point: "Twenty-five years later, there is a new statistic: More than one-quarter of all children born in America are born out of wedlock."

Olivia was one of them. Also around the same time she was born, a woman named Janet Yellen—long before she became Joe Biden's secretary of the Treasury—was an academic helping write a paper outlining theories about why this monumental change was occurring not just in America's Black communities but in all communities.[15] A quarter of America's babies were born to unwed mothers! Conservatives, she documented, attributed this surge to welfare benefits. Liberals liked to think that the lack of good jobs had made men less marriageable. Yellen landed on a different answer: Changing attitudes toward sex, marriage, and abortion meant the end of shotgun weddings.

Regardless of the broader cultural factors at play, what this all meant for Olivia was that her dad wasn't always around, and she could often feel alone. Olivia lived in Nesconset, a town on Long Island that feels as if it were designed specifically to be boring and safe, a predictably repetitive place of lawns, SUVs in driveways, schools, and supermarkets—the antithesis of New York City, fifty miles down the Long Island Rail Road tracks. Anthony lived closer to Manhattan in a town called Locust Valley, with a woman he'd married who wasn't her mother and the children he'd had with her.

Olivia's line out of Nesconset arrived one day when Anthony came over to set AOL up on her mother's computer. He did it using one of those compact discs they mailed just about everyone in the country. At one point in the 1990s, more than 50 percent of all CDs produced worldwide had the letters "AOL" printed on them.[16] Anthony's screenname was NYAvenger. "NY" because New York, "Avenger" like The Avengers, the Marvel characters. Olivia thought this was the coolest. She couldn't drive to Anthony's house yet, and she definitely couldn't walk there. But whenever the digital stars aligned, that creaky AOL opening door sounded, meaning that he was online as well, and they could talk about anything.

We tend to be especially nostalgic about things from the past that were limited, either in quantity or time. And so it would seem that some of the particulars of Millennial nostalgia may stem from the fact that the time many of us had with our parents was more limited than it was for the likes of our Boomer parents. More children born out of wedlock, more divorces, more blended families. In many ways and many circumstances, these less conventional family structures had positive outcomes. Unhappy families do not get happier by staying together. But they also often had the unintended consequence of creating a sense of scarcity of parental time. If your parents lived apart, by default there was a whole world going on elsewhere that you knew you weren't a part of, at least not always. If your parents lived apart and then married and had children with their new spouses—as happened with Olivia's family—parental time could feel even scarcer.

That's why CoolBlue91 gets so nostalgic about certain memories she created with NYAvenger. Her favorite involves a bridge. The bridge leads to Babylon. Not the one in the Bible; the one on Long Island, the one that leads from the mainland to the islands in the bay. It's called the Great South Bay Bridge, and it's a long and majestic sight, stretching over 2 miles shore to shore and soaring some 60 feet into the air. Olivia anchors herself to a memory there, one day in the late 1990s when she wasn't chatting with her dad on AIM, she was actually in the car beside him. He was so handsome with his olive skin, perfect jawline, hair so dark you could lose your fingers just ruffling through it. He loved *Star Wars* and computers and sold cars and even worked at Cablevision before he got a fancy job downtown. He was driving and looked over at her. She wasn't even 10.

"Do you want to see how fast we can go?" he said.

"Yes," she said.

So then Anthony floored it, and they flew 118 miles an hour over that miracle of New York State infrastructure. It felt like they were flying.

Anthony's fancy new job downtown was with Cantor Fitzgerald, a big financial firm near Wall Street dating back to 1945. Thanks in part to the Dot-Com boom, the American economy was booming in the 1990s, too. The economy grew by an average of 4 percent per year between 1992 and 1999.[17] It added 18 million jobs. Median household income grew by 10 percent. (In the years that followed, it vacillated and ultimately shrank, making Americans feel poorer and less certain about their wealth than they had been in the 1990s.[18]) Stocks in that decade quadrupled their value, and the Dow Jones Industrial Average increased 309 percent. Much of this had to do with the maturation of the computer. In the 1990s, American workers simply became more productive, and a lot of it was because, when they weren't AIMing, they had figured out how to incorporate computers into work in ways that saved time and made money.[19]

This is what Anthony did. He worked for a very Dot-Com-era part of his company called eSpeed, founded in 1996, which gave Cantor its own electronic bond trading platform. Anthony had an opportune job because at the time, new technology and market exuberance were encouraging more people than ever to jump into the markets in which Cantor Fitzgerald traded. It was especially perfect for him because he loved video games and high speeds and new things, including all that tech wizardry.

He wanted to share it with Olivia, and he did. Olivia remembers the time he gave her her own private "Take Your Child to Work Day." Before the official one became yet another banal day on a calendar filled with endless awareness days, it was part of a more specific, more strategic campaign spearheaded by Gloria Steinem and the Ms. Foundation for Women. They called it "Take Our Daughters to Work Day," and the first was held on April 28, 1993. Newspapers across the country covered the launch, in which as many as a million girls were estimated to have gone with their parents to work.[20] The goal was to combat new findings that showed girls' confidence declined after puberty, thereby leading to fewer of them taking part in the workforce in the same way boys did.

But Anthony picked a different day. "We're gonna lie," he said. The new millennium had already come by then, and Olivia stood outside his office down at the bottom of Manhattan. They craned their heads up and looked at the massive building Anthony had just started working in. It was a sight to behold, a behemoth: almost 10 million square feet of rentable office space, the size of three Disneylands. More than 430 businesses from nearly 30 countries. There were 15 miles of elevator shafts and enough concrete used in the whole thing to build a sidewalk from New York to Washington, D.C. It had its own zip code.

Olivia and Anthony walked in the front doors. That day was her first time in an office ever. Her mother was a nurse, and where she worked looked and functioned nothing like this. Anthony warned her as they shot up the elevator that her ears were going to pop. They changed midway onto a different elevator and made their way up to the 103rd floor.

Anthony's office was a different world. Floating above Earth were a thousand staffers across five floors. Olivia remembers an open seating plan, low dividers between desks, a lot of friendly nerds at yellowing computers with papers everywhere, chunky calculators, the Wall Street style from the turn of the millennium in which suits hadn't completely vanished but baggy, pleated trousers and wan, white shirts ruled the day. The sort of clothes Chandler Bing used to wear.

Olivia walked to the windows. She could see the Statue of Liberty from one side of the building, Manhattan on another. And the place she knew best: Long Island's south shore. She walked to her father's desk, and there were pictures of her and her half-siblings there.

"Someone get this girl a T-shirt!" a worker called out.

Anthony's colleagues liked him and were fun and helpful and loved having a 10-year-old in the building. They gave her a T-shirt that was way too big and said "eSpeed" across the front; at that time, it looked like a dress on Olivia. But she wore it proudly to lunch, proudly when Anthony's boss showed up and she told him that prepared lie: "My mommy had an emergency, and no one was able to watch me." The boss was a nice guy and caught the drift. Anthony made a few phone calls, and his boss let him go home early. Olivia didn't want the day to end. Alone, together with her father. The scarcity of him.

"Call me to tell me what your new school is like," he said after he dropped her off at her mother's house. She was about to start sixth grade.

Olivia lights up when she tells me these stories. She's told them before, and she has their rhythms down to a beat. But there is a sadness to the way she tells them so well. It comes from the fact that she has a limited inventory of memories of Anthony to share with me. If only she could get those unscripted moments back.

* * *

In the economy of the 1990s, the myth of the "job for life" had become a zombie. It was a vestige of America's post–WWII boom, in which companies hired twentysomethings and kept them on for decades, investing in their labor and reaping the benefits of a trained-up, loyal, and predictable workforce. That began to change in the 1980s, the beginning of the Millennial era, when the American economy entered what University of Chicago historian Jonathan Levy calls "the Age of Chaos." It was a shift away from a time in which capital was invested back into workers and factories with an eye toward long-term success, toward a new age in which investors were constantly scouring the globe for bigger, quicker returns. The benefits for such investors were clear. If you acted faster and took more risks, you could potentially get bigger rewards. But this change created less certainty for everyday workers, whose jobs were often terminated when investors decided that their companies, even if profitable, weren't profitable *enough* to justify backing with their funds.

But culture moves more slowly than capital. And even as the Age of Chaos came to be, there was a lingering belief in the idea of the job for life—that after school and maybe college, just like your parents, you'd just "become" some profession and stay that way until retirement. In many ways, it lingers on, despite the fact that the median number of years Americans stay on the job is now down to just over four.[21]

It could feel like the job for life was still a thing in Alliance, Ohio, in the 1990s. Alliance sits in the heart of steel country. The industry had been bled thin of jobs in prior decades by painful layoffs. The American steel sector is one of the country's most famous and most important, but it has also always been one in flux.[22] Changes in demand and technology have affected its fortunes, as has competition from abroad. By the 1990s, although in the popular imagination the steel industry was all but gone, it had actually reached a period of "uneasy stability," with demand increasing across the growing economy.[23] In steel towns, this was a welcome stasis, part of the reason that myth of the cradle-to-grave job persisted.

This fact gives Aaron Roach's early life an almost unbelievably nostalgic varnish. The way Aaron describes his childhood is an extreme example of a theme I picked up on often in my reporting for this project: how slowly time seemed to move for us in childhood, yet how quickly it zips by in adulthood. Most of my sources said they felt as if technology has sped up their perceptions of time, with information coming into their lives faster and faster and in greater and greater volume as they grew up and got online, got BlackBerrys, got smartphones. There is scientific basis for our sense of time speeding up as we age. The rate at which we process what we sense slows, so we effectively end up with fewer "images" of the world in our brains as we get older. Because there are fewer images, our minds skip between them faster, making it feel as if time has gone by more quickly.[24]

For Aaron, these differences are even starker than usual. That's because when we started talking, Aaron was coming down from one of the worst phases of his life. He spoke to me with the brutal honesty of a recent convert to sobriety. Not to sound like a D.A.R.E. ad, but Aaron says his memory is different now. It's one of his biggest regrets from his years using. He makes clear that one of the reasons he wants to talk is to get his story out there where it can help others. But parts of it are hard, because there are full years where time zoomed by, where it's hard to remember things straight.

So I ask Aaron to take me to the memories that feel longest. To take me with him to Alliance. I want to know more about the life he thought he would have—and how it was taken from him as he grew.

In the 1990s, the Walmart had not yet come to town. Downtown Alliance was tranquil, with gas lamps and Victorian-era buildings that stretched along Main Street to the railway station. A few blocks up, Aaron spent countless hours in the Rodman Public Library, tearing through books. He was that kid in elementary school who maybe even read too much. Before class, you could catch him with a book in his hand. After the teacher finished talking and the assignments were collected, he'd crack open his desk and take out a novel. After school, before dinner, before bed. It was *Super Fudge, Beezus and Ramona, Little House on the Prairie.* It was the serious ones, like *A Child Called It.* Even eventually grown-up books like the Stephen King ones. And there was anything and everything by Walter Dean Myers.

The Rodman Public Library was a sanctuary for big readers. It was adorned by low-set, mid-century modern tables there not for stylistic purposes but because they literally had been there since the middle of the century. Back then in the early evenings, Aaron's father could walk over from the factory where he had been working for some twenty-five years to pick Aaron up after a long day of reading. Aaron's father had one of those jobs that everyone expected to last forever. It was at American Steel Foundries, just ten minutes away off Main Street. What they made at the factory were mostly railcar couplings, the metal things on either side of a carriage that link them together into a train.

Aaron's mother was a descendant of Great Migration immigrants who had come North from Mississippi looking for freer lives. They had ended up in Alliance, and it was there that Aaron's mother met Aaron's father, who was working at a car wash. Not long after, Aaron's maternal grandfather helped his father get a union job at American Steel. He worked his way up to being a foreman, and the job paid for the comforts of a middle-class life. They took family trips to Six Flags and hung out with their cousins in the summer, drinking Clearly Canadian soda and eating Dunkaroos.

Aaron remembers spending Friday nights with his family watching television marathons (mostly TGIF), ABC's primetime lineup (including shows like *Family Matters*, the series that introduced America to Jaleel White as Steve Urkel), and the 1993 movie *The Meteor Man*. In the movie, Robert Townsend plays a meek Washington, D.C. substitute teacher who transforms into a superhero after being struck by a meteorite. His powers include the ability to fly and to read and remember any book he touches for thirty seconds. His nemeses are the Golden Lords, a group of drug-dealing thugs.

Aaron's childhood memories line up with a major development that took place around that time. Mainstream film and television studios started producing and promoting entertainment with Black stars more frequently, marketing not just to Black audiences but to crossover ones as well.

"I'm from a town where it's mixed company," Aaron said. Alliance is about an hour from the border with rural Pennsylvania, along Route 62, a junction of sorts of many little Ohio roads that lead to small towns with main streets decked with gas lamps that all look almost exactly the same. Norman Rockwell landscapes with small fields and well-kept farmhouses with red barns and red tractors outside. The town's Black population was, and is, just about 10 percent. (Ohio's as a whole is around 15 percent, which is roughly in line with America's.)

When shows like *Family Matters* became crossover hits, that success came with an unintended consequence: a certain type of suburban White person could watch programs and films about successful Black families and be lulled into thinking everything was fine with race in America. A quarter of the entire American population once watched *The Cosby Show*.[25] Steve Urkel became such a phenomenon that tabloid reporters camped out on the streets in front of Jaleel White's house in the 1990s to try to get photos and interviews with the then 14-year-old.[26] Meanwhile, in real life, legal changes at the federal level were making life harder for many Black communities across the country. A law passed in 1994 and commonly known as "The Crime Bill" amplified the effects of prior legislation that disproportionately led to mass incarceration in Black communities.[27] You didn't see that on *The Cosby Show*.

Aaron recalls older family members passing down the sense that he had to be extremely careful, that actions he took from a place of benevolence could be read negatively. Aaron's family was careful. They also kept a hermetically tight social circle, although that was largely due to the fact that they were Jehovah's Witnesses. Aaron's paternal great-grandmother was devout, and she brought Aaron's father into the fold when his parents died young. The Witnesses are one of the strictest and perhaps most secretive evangelical sects of Christianity in America, and in Alliance, their church is a small, cinderblock-and-tan building that looks like it could be a physical therapist's office. Jehovah's Witnesses often do not celebrate holidays, vote, or take part in the military or politics. Before everything fell apart, Aaron as a child found himself in a suit and tie in that Kingdom Hall, three times a week, hanging out with old people and talking about Jesus.

There is something else notable about the early part of Aaron's childhood, something that hit me when Aaron shared a fact about his parents: They bowled in a league when he was young. That might sound like a minor detail. But it links to an idea that informs how America finds itself in such an angry and contested place today. In 2000, a Harvard professor named Robert Putnam documented the breakdown of American civic engagement—voting, volunteering, protesting, signing petitions, the sort of activities that are crucial for a healthy democracy—in a book called *Bowling Alone*. He attributed this breakdown to the fact that Americans had, over the years, stopped taking part in civic organizations such as labor unions, volunteer groups, religious orders and bowling leagues. These groups had long given Americans not just a sense of belonging, mitigating feelings of loneliness, but also practice at managing conflict and disagreement in the peaceful ways required of democracy. When you're a member of an intimate, in-person group, that group won't function well if you just decide to cancel people with opinions you don't like or to say that someone with views that diverge from yours are a side-effect of them having some kind of "woke mind virus." You have to hear each other out and then compromise. Although Jehovah's Witnesses don't vote, that group, coupled with the bowling league, gave Aaron and his family that thing so many of our peers were losing over time: community.

In the 1990s, Aaron's life was stable. He had the distinct sense that as long as he kept doing more or less what was asked of him, things would work out. There was a feeling of security and even an underlying assumption that getting into a little harmless trouble could be sort of funny. One of Aaron's earliest memories took place on an Alliance playground at school. He and a friend were holding each other's hands, spinning each other around, laughing hysterically. Suddenly Aaron's friend let go and scraped his hands on the concrete. They got into trouble for horseplay, but it was the kind of horseplay that teachers sort of liked. It gives you a personality. Later, Aaron and that same friend had to be separated because they'd cut each other's hair. One had a mullet, the other a rat tail.

*   *   *

It might be hard to believe now, but at the turn of the new millennium, America's primary economic concern was what to do about extreme financial excess. In 1998, for the first time in almost thirty years, the United States had racked up a budget surplus, one that would go on to become the largest ever.[28] By the year 2000, it would reach a high of $236 billion, and experts on both the left and the right thought it would simply keep on growing. The Brookings Institute saw the rise of the surplus as the end of an era. "Projections suggest that the surplus will rise significantly over the next decade," they wrote in a policy brief a few months after Britney Spears's eighteenth birthday. "Just as perennial budget deficits dominated policy discussions in the 1980s and early 1990s, choices regarding how to use the surplus play a central role in the current presidential election campaign and will shape fiscal debates for years to come."[29] The *Economist* noted something similar: "Resisting temptation is not one of Bill Clinton's more obvious skills," the publication noted. "Yet, so far as his plans go for spending the federal government budget surplus—now forecast to total $4.5 trillion over the next 15 years—the president has shown remarkable self-denial, virtue even. Most of his proposals are economically prudent."[30]

In other words, there were going to be trillions of extra dollars for Americans to spend from 2000 until at least 2015 and maybe even beyond. The great question was what to do about it. How to keep the good times rolling.

George W. Bush had an idea. By late 1999, he was the frontrunner in the Republican primary campaign. The same day as Britney's big birthday bash, Bush Jr. had unveiled his economic blueprint in Des Moines, Iowa.[31] He'd released it earlier than was typical, ahead of his first debate in New Hampshire, and his big idea was to use the extra money America had accumulated to cut taxes. The plan would cost $1.3 trillion in the first decade and was criticized by executives and economists as risky and unnecessary. Bush defended his plan bluntly that day, though. "Sometimes economists are wrong," he said. He called his plan "insurance against economic recession," the logic being that if Americans paid less in taxes, they'd continue spending, helping businesses grow and the surplus expand.

It's easy, in the aftermath of two recessions and the War on Terror, to forget how much the election of President Bush represented a culmination of the ideas, aspirations, and optimism of Americans in the late 1990s. Presidencies and their campaigns always tend to embody the national mood at a particular moment, and Bush's team sought to capitalize on a particular strain of magical thinking popular in 1999: the idea that we could have a lot of contradictory things at once. Bush promised to fuse free-market capitalism with a more socially conscious side, with "the notion that caring for the disadvantaged could be a hallmark of the political right as well as the political left."[32] It was a rebranding not unlike the famous 1993 "softer side of Sears" advertisement, in which the retailer tried to convince Americans it sold more than just barbecues and power tools. Bush's Republicans wanted to show they wouldn't simply cut taxes, they'd also take care of the poor. They called the idea at the center of their rebranding "compassionate conservatism."

"There is a problem with heart in America," Bush said in his first debate.[33] "One of the great frustrations just being a governor is I wish I knew the law that would make people love one another, because I'd sign it."

In his early months in office, Bush's administration pursued policies that now sound as if they could have come from the left flank of the Democratic Party. Nowhere was this more visible than in their early maneuvering on immigration. In his presidential victory speech, Bush said that together, the nation would "create an America that is open, so every citizen has access to the American Dream."[34]

His goal was to make the most significant changes to America's immigration laws since Ronald Reagan had in 1986. That was when Reagan signed the Immigration Reform and Control Act, outlawing the employment of undocumented—"illegal"—immigrants and punished employers with criminal penalties for repeated noncompliance. The act was the first ever in American history to require people to show papers in order to get a job.

Alongside its punitive measures, the Immigration Reform and Control Act had one silver lining: It granted amnesty to any undocumented person who had entered the United States before January 1, 1982, so long as they had lived in the country continuously and had not committed serious crimes or "taken part in political, religious, or racial persecution." Such people would be offered the status of permanent resident, be legally allowed to work, and after five years, have the ability to apply to become American citizens. The act followed a decade of debate about what to do about undocumented immigration, and it was the sort of hard-yet-soft policy that fit like a glove into the compassionate conservativism brand. Bush wanted a repeat.

"We must show that our welcoming society values the ideals and contributions of immigrants," Bush said in the summer of 2001, six or so months into his presidency. By that point, his administration had already overseen the sort of recession he had hoped to prevent with tax cuts and was leaning even harder into the "softer side" of conservatism, trying to appeal more to women and immigrants. In a move that now seems surreal, a task force led by Colin Powell and John Ashcroft recommended the Republican administration allow some of the three million undocumented Mexican citizens in America to apply for permanent US residency.[35] Days later, the president suggested the plan could expand to undocumented citizens from other countries as well. President Vicente Fox of Mexico went to Washington in early September for the first state visit of Bush's term and called for the granting of legal rights to Mexican immigrants in a joint meeting of Congress.

It was in this context that Tereza Lee, who had just turned 18, took a big chance. It was part of a plan to get her out of a dangerous situation, one that had followed her and her family ever since they landed in America sixteen years before.

Have you ever been watching the news on television and seen the program cut to some senator on the floor of Congress, telling someone else's very personal story in front of a big poster, maybe even with a huge picture of that person's face on it? When she was young, Tereza became one of those people. At that age, a person would be forgiven for thinking that lending her story to strangers in Washington would be something quick, done once and then moved on from. But instead, it has become a part of Tereza's life story, a sometimes-uncomfortable part that comes with a lingering feeling she was used as a political prop.[36] But back then, it was hard not to believe the things politicians were saying about what her story could do—about change, about values, about the American way.

In the first year of her adulthood, Tereza became the inspiration for a piece of legislation that would follow her—us—through twenty-five years to the present, still part of the conversation but still not made law, unmoved, unsolved, representative of a more optimistic time. Tereza at 18 became the inspiration for the DREAM Act.

"I rise today to introduce legislation aimed at benefiting a very special group of persons—illegal alien children who are long-term residents of the United States," said Senator Orrin Hatch, a lifelong Mormon, a cofounder of the Federalist Society, and staunch Republican, standing on the floor of the Senate in the summer of 2001.[37] "This legislation, known as the 'DREAM Act,' would allow children who have been brought to the United States through no volition of their own the opportunity to fulfill their dreams, to secure a college degree and legal status."

When she was young, Tereza thought her family was the only undocumented one in America. Her parents had originally fled what was then an authoritarian regime in South Korea for Brazil, following a path that both governments had been encouraging for decades. Tereza's name is spelled the Portuguese way, the only real trace she has of having been born there. In São Paulo, her family started a small clothing business. But in that tightly knit group of immigrants starting over, a wayward relative stole her father's checkbook, forging his signature and depleting all of his savings.[38] The Lees, strangers in a foreign country, didn't see much of a point to sticking around somewhere they'd been swindled. But they'd sold their land in Korea; there wasn't anything for them to go back to there. So Tereza's mother sold some jewelry and her wedding ring, and the family bought plane tickets to the United States. They had tourist visas. They settled in a Chicago suburb that by the mid-1980s had become a Koreatown, Albany Park.

The Lees moved into a basement apartment on Drake Avenue that didn't have heating or hot water.[39] It didn't have furniture, either, and Tereza slept in a hammock, wearing a winter coat to bed when it was freezing. Mice and bugs crawled around a lot. There were days when the Lees didn't have food. The goal was for Tereza's father to become a minister. His hope was that he would start his own church and switch onto a religious worker's visa. He did get ordained as a Presbyterian, but he couldn't get enough congregants and so was denied the papers. His status—and the family's status as legal residents—disintegrated.[40] They became undocumented.

"You can't tell this secret to anyone outside the family," Tereza's father told her and her brother one day.

At the time, Tereza didn't understand what "undocumented" meant. She wasn't familiar with the particulars of the 1986 law, knew nothing about the arbitrary line that separated people who had arrived before or after a certain date. What her parents made clear, though, were the consequences. If anybody found out they were undocumented, they would be separated. Tereza's younger brother, who had been born in America, would be sent into foster care in Chicago. Tereza would be sent back to Brazil. Her parents would be deported to South Korea.

It's a lot for a child to carry a secret that could destroy a family. That obligation manifested for Tereza in the form of dreams. They were nightmares that would take on slightly different forms with slightly different characters, but the theme was always the same. Sometimes it was a paramilitary-style raid on her apartment. Sometimes it was an ordinary police pickup. The antagonists were always figures in positions of authority, occasionally even teachers. The conclusion was always that Tereza and her family were found out and then separated.

Tereza's family's secret bound them together, but it also isolated them. It could feel like the outside world was behind a panel of soundproof glass. The risk of slipping up mid-conversation and letting their status be known made having normal conversations dangerous. By and large, they went mute. They weren't allowed to pick up the phone when it rang. They were instructed to stay quiet when they saw the police, to sit up straight. Friends were to be kept at a distance.

The "A" in "DREAM Act" stands for the word "alien." It is a woefully out-of-date and dehumanizing way to classify a person born in a different place. But the second meaning of the word, the literal, extraterrestrial one, describes the way Tereza was made to feel in those years. It was as if she were growing up with a space helmet on. She could see the warped visions of people moving around the other side of the glass, she could hear them, come close to them, but she couldn't speak back, not really. There was always the risk that her air supply would be cut for some arbitrary reason, that she'd be released from the gravity that kept the others grounded but that would send her shooting far into a distant, black space.

Release came in the form of an upright piano. A rich congregant from Tereza's church visited their house one day and noticed the lack of furniture. She donated a desk, a bed, a table, and that piano. Tereza's father forced her to practice for hours a day. The lesson plan was simple: Start with church hymns, and learn a hymn a week.[41] Eventually, she'd memorized hundreds of them. She started playing for her church, and then for her school, and the hours of practicing became of her own accord. As a teenager, she played as a soloist for the Chicago Symphony Orchestra.

Tereza still had to hide most of herself away from law and authority. Yet even while hiding, she could go public downtown in front of a crowd of hundreds of people and be as loud and emotional, as mocking and as antiauthoritarian as she wanted, as long as it was through music. At 17, she discovered Sergei Prokofiev, a Russian composer, with a savage, sardonic sense of composition. Tereza loved his Sonata No. 2, particularly the second movement, written in 1912. In the middle part, there is a moment that sounds like rich, bourgeois people dancing around. It could be mistaken for maudlin schmaltz but is really a joke; he's poking fun at the vanities of the rich, maybe even suggesting the need for a revolution.

So she loved it. And she was good at it. But without a Social Security number, Tereza couldn't legally work. She figured she'd graduate high school and just freelance, earning cash playing gigs around Chicago. It would never be very much, but it was all she figured she could do.

"That's ridiculous," one of her teachers at the Merit School of Music, Ann Monaco, said when she heard of Tereza's plans.[42] Ann was an elegant but down-to-earth woman in her fifties, sort of an iron fist in a velvet glove, who had been working at Merit since 1982. She was the school's artistic director and ran the tuition-free conservatory for gifted students that Tereza attended. "Everybody goes to college." She printed out ten applications for music programs around the country and told Tereza to fill them out.

Tereza filled out the applications and returned them to Ann. But Ann noticed Tereza's Social Security number was missing. "Why don't you bring this back to your parents. They'll know your Social Security number," she said. Of course they didn't, because of course Tereza didn't have one. And of course Tereza's parents didn't want her spilling the secret they carried with them to some lady with an apparent White-savior complex downtown.

Tereza went back to Ann with the Social Security box still empty. And though she knew her status wasn't something she was supposed to speak about at all, it was so much to keep in on the verge of an entire adulthood about to unfold. This wasn't something she could contain in a painful piano movement, doloroso. Her family couldn't keep living trapped behind glass.

So there in front of Ann, in the year 2000, Tereza started to cry.

"Please don't report me to the police," she said to Ann. "I can't be responsible for separating my family."

The idea of the American Dream has been in conflict with reality since the phrase was popularized in 1931. Its author, the historian James Truslow Adams, called the American Dream one "of a land in which life should be better and richer and fuller for every man, with opportunity for each according to his ability or achievement."[43] But even as he articulated that term during the Great Depression, he feared for its longevity, writing that a growing obsession with money and materialism threatened its ideals. Economic changes risked limiting the intellectual and spiritual rise of everyday Americans.

Yet at the dawn of the new millennium, in the sparkle of the surplus, it was easy to believe in a story of unlimited potential. Ann did. After Tereza told her about being undocumented, she called up the offices of Dick Durbin, an Illinois senator whose mother was born in Lithuania. Ann asked if there was anything Durbin's office could do to help Tereza get documentation to get to college.

Initially, Durbin's office declined to help. "Even if she had the cure for cancer, she'd be deported back to Brazil," they told her. But Ann, who was something of a local power broker, started soliciting letters from teachers at Merit and donors to the school. She knew that a lot of those patrons were also donors to Durbin, which ratcheted up the pressure on the senator.

There is no federal law requiring students to prove their immigration status in order to attend college. Each university is free to come up with its own set of rules on how it's going to handle undocumented students. Many welcome them. (Although some state restrictions do exist: South Carolina, for example, does not allow undocumented students to attend public colleges.) Broadly, though, what makes attending college diffi-cult for undocumented people is the cost. Undocumented students are unable to receive federal financial aid, which can make the expenses prohibitive.

A relatively unknown way around that exists, however. Senators have the power to create private bills that can grant individuals other-wise unable to get a visa some form of residency or even citizenship. Private bills, which are intended to benefit individuals who have exhausted all other administrative and legal avenues to get something they need, have a history of passing. That seemed like Tereza's best way forward.

But word got out. Other undocumented people kept coming up to Durbin, telling him that they'd heard about the upcoming personal bill. They'd tell him they wanted to know if there was anything he could do for them, too. These clandestine approaches made the senator realize he needed to write a broader piece of legislation. It came to be known as S.1291, the Development, Relief, and Education for Alien Minors Act. Or as it is known more popularly: The DREAM Act.

At the time, it looked as if its passage was all but guaranteed. Durbin, a Democrat, introduced the act in the Senate in August 2001 with Senator Hatch, a Republican. Hatch used the rhetoric of the early Bush admin-istration, talking about wanting to leave no child left behind. He later said he looked forward to working with members of the Senate to "ensure that the American Dream is extended to these children."

It began to look like a slam dunk. Bipartisan legislation: A liberal Democrat and conservative Republican coming together to help children who had done nothing but be born across a border. Wasn't that great? Later, Tereza, her fellow DREAMers, and their allies would come to question the simplicity of that story, the effects of portray-ing one group of undocumented immigrants in a shining, innocent, "deserving" light while effectively painting the rest as criminals. But in 2001, the broader conversation hadn't gotten there yet. Tereza's job as a talented student, a prodigy, a perhaps unexpected immigrant, was to be a face of the bill.

There is a point in any performance when you know you've got it in the bag. You're rounding out the fourth lap of the mile. You have three questions left on an exam and you know all the ones you answered before were a cinch. The audience is rapt and you're two bars from the finish, certain it will be all sweetness until the very end, which you can see so clearly. That fall, Tereza started at the Manhattan School of Music, a private conservatory near the Hudson River in New York City where she went on scholarship despite her lack of documentation. The DREAM Act was set up to pass, and she had made plans to fly down to DC to testify in its favor. It felt as if everything was settled.

Tereza had just left history class and was about to get into a cab for the airport. The testimony was slated for the next day. Durbin and Hatch had sixty-two votes lined up. It was supposed to be a victory lap. That was the morning of September 11.

*   *   *

One of the most influential books on Millennials at the turn of the century was called *Millennials Rising*. It theorized that the children and teenagers of the day were likely to become an optimistic, community-centric "hero generation" not dissimilar to Tom Brokaw's World War II veteran "Greatest Generation."[44] The idea was that we would react to the individualism of the 1990s by becoming more trusting, positive, team-oriented, scientific, and honorable. In order for this to happen, the book encouraged our parents to set our expectations sky high.

"For the sake of Millennials—and, through them, the future of America—the most urgent adult task is to elevate their expectations. Rather than dwell on all the negatives, on problems such as youth violence or substance abuse that are clearly ebbing, America should set goals big enough to engage the imagination of this generation of achievers."[45]

Much of *Millennials Rising* focused on the cultural landscape of the time period. In his 2000 review of the book, columnist David Brooks noted that "the pop culture that works with teenagers these days is not the alienated grunge rock of a few years ago, or even ironic and subversive stuff like the *Mad* magazine young Boomers consumed. Instead, it is wholesome, uncynical, let's-be-happy-together culture—Buffy and Britney."

With the benefit of hindsight, *Millennials Rising* feels far too rosy. It was based on only a few years of our generational data. But near the end of the book, the authors did issue an apt warning.

"Should a crisis arise, with Millennial lives at stake, history could mete out good, middling, bad, or truly horrible outcomes. While no one can predict how a crisis would climax, and what a new postcrisis era would be like, it would probably include a redefinition of government's relationship to the economy and society, a redefinition of man's relationship to technology, and a redefinition of America's relationship to the world. Millennials could play an epic role, crafting new myths of lore, doing deeds only dimly imaginable today. The consequences, for good or ill, would be enormous—not just for America, but indeed for the entire world."[46]

* * *

In the late summer of 2001, that same summer Olivia had gone to work with Anthony to see his office downtown, the big fear in Nesconset in early September was of West Nile Virus. In 1999, crows across New York had begun mysteriously dying in large numbers. Scientists were initially confused over what was causing it, later discovering that it was West Nile. The virus is transmitted by mosquitoes, can be fatal, and had never been seen before in the Western Hemisphere. By 2001, it was spreading fast through the country. That summer, a Nesconset case hit the headlines, perhaps the biggest news the town had made in years. "A 49-year-old Suffolk County woman has tested positive for the West Nile virus after suffering fever, stiff neck, headache and a rash," the story read. "Nesconset, where the woman lives, was sprayed for West Nile on Aug. 9 before she fell ill and after dead birds and mosquitoes were found with the virus."

That was the news in the air as Olivia began middle school. No offense to the Great Hollow Bulls, but the place looks like a prison. Yellow busses turn up a hill and then right to face a long, low, Brutalist drudgery dating back to 1964. The building is two stories, gray/yellow concrete with crimson trimmings, and little middle-school-sized sports fields out back. To enter the front door is to come into what looks like a stock-standard set from a public-service film about the difficulties of dating, puberty, and drugs. That was where Olivia found herself on a Tuesday, five or so days into the new school year. That day she was sitting second chair violin in her music class. Everything was normal until it wasn't.

Out of nowhere, kids started getting pulled from the classroom. It didn't take long for the rumors to start flowing. "Terrorists are putting sharks in peoples' pools," someone said. That's why parents were showing up to take their children home. Each story was more insane than the last; after all, they were middle schoolers, and they were just back from summer break. But there was a chill that had overtaken the school, too, and it was like nothing they had ever felt. Time passed slowly. Olivia and her peers were stuck in orchestra. Kid after kid kept getting pulled from the room. Finally, the ones left couldn't take it anymore.

"Please," one of Olivia's classmates begged the teacher. "Why are all these kids leaving?"

The teacher hesitated. She wasn't supposed to say anything.

The next period was lunch. By then, Olivia already knew Anthony was dead. Nobody had told her directly, but based on what her teacher had said about the World Trade Center, she just knew. It was well past commuting hours already. Anthony would have been at work bright and early. He was always very punctual, never late to anything. He would've been there at his desk with the pictures of her, with the windows and the view of the Statue of Liberty and the colleague who said, "Get this girl a T-shirt!"

Olivia wept silently as the teachers moved them from orchestra to the lunchroom. Again, the place looked like a film set. The American flag hanging in the corner, metal buffets with counters built for pushing trays along, tables on wheels with benches built in so that you can never adjust the position of your seat. A lunch aide walked over to her and asked if she was doing alright.

Mydadisdeadmydadisdeadmydadisdeadmydadisdeadmydadisdead

It's hard to remember if she was saying that or just thinking it over and over again. The lunch aide stood staring at her until Olivia blew up. "My dad just died!" She ran up a staircase at one end of the cafeteria toward her Social Studies teacher's room and sat there. She sat there until she was walked down to Guidance. She sat in Guidance until the end of the day. And at the end of the day, she got on the bus, and the bus dropped her off at her usual stop.

That day, Angel, a neighbor friend two grades younger who usually got home well after Olivia, was already there. Unusually, Olivia's mother and stepfather were also at her bus stop.

"Please," Olivia said. "Please, can I go play with Angel."

She didn't want to go home. Home would mean confirmation of the thing that until then had merely been a new sixth-grader's speculation based on rumors and silence. But Olivia's mother said no. She could not play with Angel that day. Once home, Olivia sat down on her princess bed, and that's when she saw her mother cry for the first time.

"I don't think you're going to see your father again," she said.

That night on television, President Bush said that "terrorist attacks can shake the foundations of our biggest buildings, but they cannot touch the foundation of America." In his address, he used the word "evil" four times. He read from Psalm 23:4, the one people often read at funerals. It goes like this:

> Yea, though I walk through the valley of the shadow of death,
> I will fear no evil;
> For you are with me;
> Your rod and your staff, they comfort me

They had a funeral for Anthony.

"Anthony was an amazing friend to me. We worked together for almost three years, and he was the brother I never had," one mourner eulogized.

"He was the first boy I ever kissed," said another.[47] "He was a sweet little boy who grew up to be a great guy."

"We spoke mostly on IM from time to time," a former Cablevision colleague remembered. "I valued his intelligence, his humor, his insanity, his loyalty, and his devotion to his children."

Olivia hid in the basement of the funeral parlor, curled up and crying. She didn't know how to lose somebody like this. Adulthood had hit before puberty arrived. That childhood feeling of safety amidst Long Island's samey-same houses and lawns and air-bagged SUVs evaporated. Olivia felt as if she aged decades in mere days. The outpourings of grief continued long after the funeral, growing so trite she became inured to them. Great Hollow Middle School had 263 sixth graders. Each month, it singled out one with something called the MVP award, for the most valuable "player." One month not long after September 11, the students unanimously picked Olivia as their MVP. In her English class, they made her read out the reasons she had been chosen. Each one said some version of, "Because her dad died on 9/11 and she has a lot of strength."

That's who she became, from then on and for years later: "9/11 Girl." She became one of those people in one of those families that has a bench with a bronze plaque on it honoring someone who died young. *You have gone home to heaven and our risen Lord you shall see.* That's what it says on Anthony's bench, which is on the boardwalk in Long Beach, New York. It faces out to the open ocean. It's not too many blocks from the house in Island Park, a neighborhood just up Long Beach Boulevard, where he grew up.

"Have hope," a well-wisher at school said to Olivia in the aftermath. "They'll find your dad in the rubble still."

Childhood optimism no longer sheltered her. It hurt her instead. Anger replaced naïveté. Olivia learned to hide it. She put a metaphorical mask over her own distress when she sensed her mom was tired, when her stepfather had a lot on his plate. She absorbed the shocks, grew quiet, felt as if between school and family and the overwhelming heaviness of loss, there was never time to process what was happening. The landscape of her life became as repetitive as the suburban landscape of Long Island. She woke up, brushed her teeth, put on her clothes, went to school, did her homework, ate dinner, showered, went to bed, repeated. Everything became a blur.

* * *

Nearly a quarter century after it happened, it is tempting to look back at September 11 and talk about it in big, vague, clichéd terms. The date is often preceded with the phrase "the tragic events of." It was the "moment everything changed." It was "the day our childhoods ended." It became every AP US history teacher's least imaginative essay prompt, asking ambitious students to "explain the effects of September 11 on America." It turned into the topic of cheap keynote speakers' introductory addresses for decades, which it unfortunately sometimes still is.

But you can't understand Millennials without understanding the way September 11 really did change everything for us. We had been living in a decade of post–Cold War victory. No one—at least, no one except the nerdy kids who played *Risk* on CD-ROM—had ever imagined an attack on American soil. Despite the fact that Osama bin Laden had declared holy war on the United States in 1996, the year the youngest Millennials were born, few had ever even heard of him before September 11. Those who had would be forgiven for thinking he wasn't a threat. In September 1998, the *New York Times* ran a story about bin Laden not on the front page but in the Arts & Ideas section, between one feature about pink lawn flamingos and another reviewing an opera. "In some ways, Osama bin Laden is a thoroughly modern terrorist," the author noted with dismissive amusement. "He announces his intentions on CNN, directs his worldwide financial network by satellite telephone and sends messages to his supporters in Saudi Arabia via cassette tapes. Asked last year by a Western reporter what operations were planned next in his jihad, or holy war, against the United States, Mr. bin Laden replied: 'You'll see or hear about them in the media, God willing.'"[48]

Old-fashioned media was how most Millennials found out about September 11. One study shows that 90 percent of Americans got their news about the attacks by television that day.[49] Aaron was one. He was in class at B. F. Stanton Junior High when someone rushed in and said, "Hey, turn on the TV." Kids started crying, and then going home. Even though he was a Jehovah's Witness and, by the strict rules of his religion, not supposed to get involved in politics or the military, not even supposed to stand up for the Pledge of Allegiance, the attacks weighed heavily on Aaron. They cracked his sense of safety and innocence. He'd only read about war in books and never felt it could come to the US. But the day got him thinking that maybe he wasn't entirely safe in his small corner of northeast Ohio. World events had never felt personal before.

The word "trauma" gets thrown around a lot in daily life. But it is a clinical term, one that refers to "any disturbing experience that results in significant fear, helplessness, dissociation, confusion, or other disruptive feelings intense enough to have a long-lasting negative effect on a person's attitudes, behavior, and other aspects of functioning."[50] Nobody would doubt that for Olivia, September 11 was a cause of severe trauma. Going to sixth grade one day, playing the violin, and then finding out your father has been killed in a televised national tragedy by Islamic jihadists was emotionally overwhelming and did alter the trajectory of her life.

To get past a trauma, we have to mourn. But for most people, mourning is difficult. It requires looking back at the truth and confronting what actually happened: who enabled it, who failed to stop it. Victims often resist this. This challenge relates to what scholar Judith Herman calls the central dialectic of psychological trauma: "the conflict between the will to deny horrible events and the will to proclaim them aloud."[51] A frequent coping mechanism used by trauma victims as a resistance to mourning is the process of creating "a fantasy of magical resolution through revenge, forgiveness, or compensation."[52] That happened on an individual level with Olivia. In the depths of her sadness, she'd imagine Anthony had just run off to Mexico and really, everything was fine. She imagined him on a beach drinking a Heineken, his favorite beer, having faked his own death.

This desire for magical resolution can happen on a societal level as well. Collective trauma occurs when an entire society witnesses a horrific event that shatters its sense of meaning. It enters into the group's collective memory and can persist not just among the people who were directly affected, but also in people whose daily lives did not fundamentally change.[53] Take Aaron. He was not—and most Millennials were not—directly connected to September 11. But witnessing mass violence in a shocking, unexpected way upends basic assumptions about how the world works and creates a sense of long-term fear that is characteristic of a trauma. "Entire communities can display symptoms of PTSD, trapped in alternating cycles of numbing and intrusion, silence and reenactment," notes Herman.[54] September 11 was not the Holocaust. It was not Darfur. It was not Rwanda. But it still meets the definition of a collective trauma, and it helps explain what happened to us not just in the immediate aftermath of the event but what is still happening to our generation today.

As our country struggled to make sense of 9/11, we collectively did what individual victims of traumas do: We rushed for quick fixes that provided a sense of fantastical resolution through revenge. We did not deal with the deeper questions. Was the United States growing weaker? Was democracy, was capitalism, was the current world order something that could just carry on as though it had, in trouncing Communism, claimed an ultimate victory? Why had we failed so spectacularly to prevent the attacks when blaring warnings were there, on CNN, in the *New York Times* between the features on flamingos and opera? Few wanted to ask these questions, even fewer wanted to hear their answers. It was comforting instead to throw our trust behind the government and its eventual war as if that would bring us back to a more peaceful, optimistic place.

A month after the attacks, Bush's approval ratings rocketed to 92 percent. A president who entered office with solidly average public standing was suddenly the commander-in-chief with the highest approval ever recorded, surpassing peaks which themselves had been untouched since the administration of Franklin Delano Roosevelt.[55] Nearly two thirds of Americans expressed trust in the federal government itself, something that hadn't happened in the preceding three decades.[56] They gave news organizations, previously and later again some of the favorite punching bags in the country, top ratings for their professionalism.[57] American flags popped up in the background of *Friends* episodes. The Harvard Institute of Politics polled 1,200 college students, including some of the oldest Millennials, in the month after September 11. The polling found that 75 percent of undergraduates trusted the military to "do the right thing" all or most of the time.[58] A full 92 percent said they considered themselves patriotic, 68 percent said they supported the use of ground troops in Afghanistan, and nearly 80 percent said they favored the use of air strikes there. Those air strikes began on October 7, 2001.

Washington iced over. An administration that had days before been talking warmly about amnesty for undocumented immigrants was now turning foreigners into an easy scapegoat. "Let the terrorists among us be warned: If you overstay your visa—even by one day—we will arrest you," Attorney General John Ashcroft said at a conference for US mayors later that October.[59] Remember: Mere weeks before, he had been arguing in favor of legalizing undocumented immigrants. Tereza's testimony was cancelled. She didn't fly down to Washington. The DREAM Act fell off the legislative agenda. In days, it was replaced with bills that had similarly threadbare acronyms but very different meanings. The Uniting and Strengthening America by Providing Appropriate Tools Required to Intercept and Obstruct Terrorism Act of 2001 passed the House on October 24, 357 to 66. It passed the Senate 98 to 1.

Better known as the PATRIOT Act, it gave the government new powers to detain foreign nationals suspected of terrorism, in some cases indefinitely and without trial. One of the characteristics of Washington in the days following September 11 that most Millennials, especially younger ones, might not remember is how rapidly things moved. Bills were rushed through Congress so fast that some members complained, saying that few in the capital had taken the time to debate or really read the legislation. A report by the Justice Department would find in 2003 that "even in the chaotic aftermath of the September 11 attacks, we believe the FBI should have taken more care to distinguish between aliens who it actually suspected of having a connection to terrorism from those aliens who, while possibly guilty of violating federal immigration law, had no connection to terrorism."[60] The PATRIOT Act was intended to help the government detain suspected foreign terrorists, but it became tantalizingly easy to use it to detain anyone who was an immigrant.

The creation of the Department of Homeland Security in 2002 set into motion a force to be reckoned with, sopping up responsibilities from other agencies such as the Treasury, Justice, Agriculture, Energy, Defense, and Transportation Departments. It brought along with it two new agencies: the Customs and Border Protection agency and the one known as U.S. Immigration and Customs Enforcement, or simply ICE.

* * *

For Tereza, it felt as if life were moving in a backward direction. For the DREAM Act, of course, but for more than that. Not long after the DREAM Act failed, Ann Monaco went for a run and never came back. Tereza had been staying at her big home in Oak Park when it happened. She was hit from behind by a van. At the scene, police arrested a late-twentysomething man in the vehicle who would later be charged with reckless homicide and aggravated drunken driving. They said the alcohol levels in his blood were three times the legal limit. For Tereza, it felt like the death of a parent. It felt like the whole city of Chicago was in mourning. It was as if the lights guiding her had gone dark.

The piano was supposed to save her. The hours sitting on that bench alone, pounding into the keys with that big hope, that relentless pursuit of perfection. Now it was falling apart. She was in New York doing the thing she and Ann had fought for. She'd gone public, risking her family. But Bush had gone from big, lovey-dovey softie to steely enforcer. Ann was dead. Congress had forgotten about her. Even if she made it through college, what next? Colleges may have been able to admit undocumented students, but there was no way she'd be able to get a real job after. What was the point? The alien space helmet was back on. She wanted to just pull the plug. There were heavy days when she felt suicidal. There were gentler days when she figured she would deport herself to Brazil. She spent $5 on a book, a guide to teaching herself Brazilian Portuguese.

It is hard to watch optimism fade. At the end of the old millennium, there had been such an abundance of positivity that idealism about continued peace and democracy came from even the more conservative, more stoic corners of the intellectual world. Two ideas in particular stick out.

The first was the so-called McDonald's Peace Theory. I remember hearing about this in my seventh-grade social studies class, the year before September 11. It was first published by newspaper columnist Thomas Friedman in 1996, and it postulated that "no two countries that both have a McDonald's have ever fought a war against each other." Friedman allowed when he published the theory in 1996 that it was tongue-in-cheek but still held that it was apt. His idea was that by the time countries reached the level of economic development at which their populations could dine at McDonald's, they'd be more interested in waiting in line for hamburgers than in waging war. It's admittedly a goofy notion but is also startlingly grounded in actual socioeconomics: When citizens see themselves as part of a globalized supply chain, with beef patties from the United States combining with grain buns from Canada combining with ketchup produced in Spain, they have fewer incentives to destroy such linkages and much more incentive to preserve them.

The second idea sounded more serious, but was perhaps even more outlandishly optimistic. I've mentioned it before: the "end of history." The idea has long roots that date back to theorists Karl Marx and Friedrich Hegel, but it was political scientist Francis Fukuyama who articulated its contemporary iteration. In a 1992 book called *The End of History and the Last Man*, Fukuyama wrote that the world was witnessing "the universalization of Western liberal democracy as the final form of human government." Fukuyama wasn't saying that nothing would ever happen again in history. But he was arguing that at least politically, we had reached the end of our evolution. Communism was dead. Democracy had won. That was that.

Except it wasn't. The attacks on the Twin Towers and the ensuing wars that followed forced a quick reckoning in the intelligentsia with both ideas about peace and government. What did it matter if countries with intertwined economies avoided war if the wars that did happen were waged not against countries at all but instead against terrorist networks that paid little attention to modern borders? And it was hard to imagine that democracy could have reached a static endpoint as we tried with limited success to export it abroad. There are many post-9/11 think pieces headlined, "The End of the End of History."

Not everybody reads *Foreign Policy* or the *New Republic* or watches geopolitical debates on C-SPAN, and fewer young people still. Millennials were at the time, after all, quite young. But ideas from those places trickle into everyday conversation, often with great speed. In the early months of the new millennium, you could already hear hints of a change in tone in our lunchroom banter, in passing remarks down hallways, in AIM chats. Maybe the future wasn't going to be as radiant as the one we had been promised.

PART II
13/F/VA/BI

Jon Stewart was in the green room waiting. The plan was to go on CNN to promote his new book, *America*. It's one that many Millennials may remember browsing in Barnes & Noble stores in the early aughts. It was a book that captured a mood of increasing frustration, political angst, and incredulousness as that autumn's presidential election approached. For months, Bush had been backing away from his administration's guarantee that the United States would eventually find weapons of mass destruction in Iraq.[1] Such a find would have linked the regime there to September 11 and justified the 2003 invasion as part of the battle against global terrorism. Problematically for the president, though, a few weeks before, the chief U.S. arms inspector had released a damning nine-hundred-page report, the conclusion of a fifteen-month investigation, which found no evidence that Saddam Hussein had chemical, biological, or nuclear weapons when the invasion of Iraq began.[2] Most of the country's illegal weapons had been destroyed after the 1991 Gulf War.[3]

The Daily Show host was nervous entering the studio CNN used at George Washington University in DC.[4] The show Stewart was about to go on was called *Crossfire*, and, at the time, it seemed like the bigger, more culturally relevant phenomenon than his. *Crossfire* was billed as a debate program. A widely aired commercial for the show presented it as a boxing match, pitting the hosts—one liberal "long-horn leftie" against a conservative "bow-tie brawler"—against each other.[5] The liberal was Paul Begala, a former adviser to President Clinton. The conservative was an improbably fresh-faced Tucker Carlson, then 35 years old, not yet aged by the weight of hawking conspiracy theories or interviewing Vladimir Putin, but coming off the back of a recent sit-down with Britney Spears, in which he asked her how much Pepsi she drank in a day.[6]

Crossfire epitomized the mid-Bush era, the time when his second term was just on the horizon. It was a time of stiffening polarization. The phrases "red state" and "blue state" had only just been canonized by the media as meaning Republican- and Democratic-leaning, respectively. As recently as 1996, some news outlets had used red to indicate Democratic victories and blue to indicate Republican ones on their election maps. And it wasn't just the language but the voting patterns that were hardening. In the 1992 election, twenty-two states swung from one party to the other. In 2000, half as many did.[7] By the 2004 election, which was still several weeks out, only three would ultimately switch parties. The number of counties where one party won by a landslide victory was increasing. The share of people who voted split ticket, giving one party a vote for president but another for Congress, was decreasing. The elections in which Millennials were first old enough to vote were increasingly tribal affairs.

It was all turbo-charged by cable news. It's true that in the years since our childhoods, social media has altered the news—but before that, cable changed it first. It was the precursor to social media as an always-on, globally connected stream of stories. Although relatively few Millennials now actually sit down nightly to watch the news, the creation of CNN in 1980, the year before the birth of the first Millennials, reshaped how politicians pitch themselves to Americans and how Americans understand politics. It's hard to overstate the importance of that platform to the messy, angry, partisan, choose-your-own-reality environment we now find ourselves in. Much has been written about how Donald Trump managed to co-opt the cable news ecosystem to turn himself from a long-shot reality-television candidate to America's forty-fifth and then forty-seventh president. Less has been written about the fact that the system Trump manipulated was one made by a man with striking overlap to him. Billionaire Ted Turner was a brash media mogul who first pitched CNN "on the side of the common people against the northeastern television establishment," i.e. ABC, CBS, and NBC.[8] He gave interviews to *Playboy*. A *TIME* magazine cover story from 1982 called him "famous above all for being famous. He is not so much renowned for his achievements as his achievements are renowned for being his."[9]

Before CNN, the three major networks each ran only one news program per day. That's thirty minutes of news, just twenty-two when you take into account commercial breaks.[10] On CNN, there was an entire day to fill. The twists and turns of Washington helped fill the void. Elections became an almost perpetual event, not just something people paid attention to in the few months leading up to them. In America, there had been a long understanding that "all politics is local," a sense that to get and stay in power, politicians needed to focus on winning in their communities first. It connected to the idea that at the end of the day, what voters really cared about were the people and policies in their hometowns, the events that happened in their backyards. But cable news made it very easy to track what was going on in backyards thousands of miles away, to get enraged about things that might not even directly affect your own life. It amplified the culture wars by creating an entire theater—nay, a Colosseum—in which we could watch, debate, and debase things that would never, really, have any bearing on our own lives at all.

As cable news evolved, it also gave low-profile backbenchers in Congress a mouthpiece that reached across state lines. Take, for instance, Georgia's 14th congressional district. It's a rural corner of the state, encompassing the small cities of Rome and Dalton, bordering Alabama and Tennessee. Ordinarily, there would be no reason for most people to feel vested in the Congressional representative of the region had she, Marjorie Taylor Greene, not had the opportunity to spew strange, headline-grabbing, far-right conspiracies all across cable.

More than just serving to fill air time, though, politics became the cable channels' biggest asset in their pitched battle for audience. In 1996, the year the youngest Millennials were born, Rupert Murdoch and Roger Ailes launched Fox News in Manhattan in an old Sam Goody store. Before he was known for his #MeToo-era sexual harassment legal troubles, Ailes had a reputation as a shrewd political consultant who understood the potential of television. He worked for Richard Nixon's successful 1968 presidential campaign, convincing the candidate of the power of the new medium. Ailes pushed the idea that TV would eventually replace the political party.[11] And in some ways it has. In our time, parties have lost much of their power to select presidential candidates. Until 1968, the candidates were effectively selected by parties themselves at conventions, with primary elections acting more like polls than actual selection tools. That system was still evolving even as we were growing up—"Super Tuesday" took its current form in 1988—and gradually, pandering to audiences on television grew more important than impressing party leadership.[12]

After the Nixon campaign, Ailes worked for CNBC, turning the business-oriented channel into a chattier, more entertaining destination. When he joined Murdoch to create Fox, few thought it would be a success. Its first day was filled with glitches.[13] Halfway through an important interview, the feed dropped.[14] The channel wasn't even viewable in New York City due to a legal battle with Time Warner, CNN's parent company. That first day, Fox was stacked with figures who would come to define many cultural and political battles of Millennials' more recent years. There was an interview with Israeli prime minister Benjamin Netanyahu and shows featuring Bill O'Reilly and Sean Hannity. Despite the network's rocky start, however, Murdoch and Ailes struck television gold. They did so by selling conservative audiences the stories they wanted to hear.[15] Their strategy got a boost two years later, thanks to President Clinton's affair with Monica Lewinsky. The network moved O'Reilly to the prime 8 p.m. hour so he could cover it at length.[16] Fox got a further bump from the tight, contested election between Al Gore and Bush two years after that. These events helped the network identify core viewers and hone how they wanted to be talked to. Journalist Gabriel Sherman charted in a 2010 article for *New York Magazine* how at Fox, stories morphed into two general archetypes: one of viewers as victims of some overreaching, socialist government, the other of viewers as rebels "coming to take the government back."[17] They are familiar stories in Washington today.

Fox became the most-watched cable network in January 2002, beating CNN for the first time. Other networks realized they would fall further behind if they didn't understand their audiences and cater to them in at least some of the same ways. MSNBC, which launched the same year as Fox, first pitched itself to busy, urban professionals on the coasts. It eventually tilted left as something of an antidote to Fox, a political shift that began before the Iraq war. Rather than reaching for the median American news consumer as networks had done for decades, cable channels were increasingly planting themselves on either side of a partisan divide.

This political cleaving of the media helps explain why America, and by extension Millennials, now seem almost impossibly divided. Media matters because it influences who we think we are. An influential book called *Imagined Communities* by the political scientist Benedict Anderson, first published in 1983 and reissued in 1991 and 2006, argues that mass media is so powerful that it helped create the modern conception of the nation in the eighteenth and nineteenth centuries. Anderson argues that nations are "imagined communities," a bunch of people living within a border who—and this is key—think of themselves as the same group. The creation of the modern printing press combined with the rise in literacy rates led to a "mass ceremony" in which readers across a country knew that millions of other people—their fellow citizens—were doing the same thing, learning the same things, even though they had no idea who those fellow readers were and would likely never meet them. This was part of what led to the rise of the modern nation. That imagined togetherness was an extremely powerful force, based on the idea of community that came from that mass ceremony of reading (and later, watching) the same things. Anderson argued this ceremony—this media consumption—was so potent, it could motivate people who didn't know each other to do things as difficult as joining armies to defend each other in war.

It is hard to understate how much the defining war of the early aughts, the War on Terror, influenced the cable news industry. It provided ample television fodder, dramatic storylines that could be spun depending on the views of the audience. And audiences tuned in for those updates. CNN's popularity had already risen in the early 1990s because of its nonstop coverage of the Gulf War.[18] The war in Iraq sent all of this into hyperdrive, with hundreds more reporters than ever telling differing versions of the same story across more channels than ever. It was at this time when the "whooshing" sound that comes before headlines took hold across the networks, when they started overusing flashes like "Breaking News" and "News Alert" to capture people channel-flipping between news networks to find out what was happening in Baghdad.[19] The "news crawl," that steady, hard-to-look-away-from stream of text at the bottom of screens that is now ubiquitous, also originated around this time—in fact, its first use was on Fox twenty minutes after the first plane hit the North Tower on 9/11.[20] "This deluge is creating a classic paradox of the information age," wrote the *Wall Street Journal* in the early days of the Iraq conflict. "We know more than we ever did before, yet we may not be any closer to the real truth."[21]

Jon Stewart walked onto the *Crossfire* set that Friday in 2004 in the context of this new information haze. It was increasingly partisan, increasingly rapid-fire. The ostensible goal of him being on CNN was just to promote his book. To do what celebrities do when they go on talk shows, what Stewart himself had been doing on other shows in recent weeks: be cute and try to get people to like their stuff. But there was an inkling in his mind that maybe he should use this appearance to do something bigger. The writers at *The Daily Show* had a particular dislike for *Crossfire*.[22] They saw it as a missed opportunity for actual debate and conversation. Looking back at that moment, it's hard not to be struck by the fact that as recently as 2004, people as cynical and smart as *The Daily Show* staff weren't writing off a cable news program as a partisan exercise. It shows that 2004 was still a moment of transition for television.

Jon Stewart sat down on set.

"Our show is about all left vs. right, black vs. white, paper vs. plastic, Red Sox against the Yankees," Paul Begala began.[23] "That's why every day, we have two guests with their own unique perspective on the news. But today, *Crossfire* is very different. We have just one guest. He's either the funniest smart guy on TV or the smartest funnyman."

That day, *Crossfire* was indeed going to be very different. But maybe not in the way the hosts had expected. The show that day was set up to feature Stewart in a softball segment for some light banter, to talk about his latest project and then go.

But seconds later, it became clear that Stewart had decided to go rogue.

He looked down at the desk in front of him. He'd forgone the suit and tie of the hosts, which he also often wore on the *The Daily Show*, and wore a plain black sweater. He paused slightly, giving off the grief of a disappointed doctor about to deliver some bad news.

"Why do we have to fight?" he said.

The hosts looked stunned.

"Why do you argue, the two of you?"

The hosts nervously chimed in, with snarky, surface-level asides about Bush and John Kerry, running that year to unseat the president. Stewart didn't take their bait. He stayed on message, and that message was clear.

"I made a special effort to come on the show today because I have privately, amongst my friends and also in occasional newspapers and television shows, mentioned this show as being bad. I felt that that wasn't fair, and I should come here and tell you that I don't—it's not so much that it's bad, as it's hurting America."

Nervous laughter erupted in the studio in the sort of way that only happens when a live audience knows something is veering off course. The softball segment goes hard. The audience picks up on the nervous energy of the hosts, the obviously unscripted words of the guest, a comedian getting serious.

"We need your help," Stewart said. "Right now, you're helping the politicians and the corporations."

His point was that rather than hosting a serious debate that would hold powerful people accountable—with hard questions, fact-checking, follow-ups—the hosts of *Crossfire* were helping politicians and corporations by simply letting either side come on air and spew spin, basically unchecked. It was a prescient warning. What Stewart was criticizing would only become more prevalent in successive years: a system that allowed people with political agendas but no real facts the space and time on air to influence enormous audiences. Even if those facts were untrue, they could catch on.

Take the political group Swift Boat Veterans for Truth, which that same year tried to cast doubt on Kerry's military record. The candidate's Navy career had been a big selling point in his campaign, which targeted Bush's War on Terror. Kerry had earned three Purple Hearts in Vietnam, as well as Bronze and Silver Stars; his criticisms of the conflict were credentialed. But the Swift Boat Veterans pumped out advertisements questioning whether Kerry really deserved those accolades, basically asking if he had been injured enough or brave enough to deserve them. Fox's Sean Hannity debuted the first ad on his show in early August of 2004, billing it as his "top story".[24] The group's claims were rebutted by those who had served with Kerry, but the topic nonetheless became fodder for prime-time features on Fox. Then, because it had become part of the national conversation, it also wound up on CNN and MSNBC. A day after Hannity featured the group's commercial on his show, *Crossfire* invited Kellyanne Conway on air to defend it. "Why are they dishonorable liars and why is John Kerry credible?" she asked, already indicating a prowess for spinning "alternative facts" that she would become known for during Trump's first presidency.[25] In such a way, shows like *Crossfire* were like huge fields covered in dry grass. Someone without ethics, ready to spout untruths, who liked attention and wanted power, could come through with a match and easily light a wildfire.

That's part of what Jon Stewart was trying to point out that day in October 2004. After that, his segment quickly descended into the name-calling, bickering, false equivalences and "whataboutism" that is common today on cable, on the internet, on social media. Tucker Carlson, in addition to calling Stewart a "butt boy," tried to claim that the comedian wasn't a serious enough inquisitor of the powerful, and maybe as such wasn't entitled to criticize CNN. Yet that played into Stewart's whole critique.

"I didn't realize—and maybe this explains quite a bit—that the news organizations look to Comedy Central for their cues on integrity," Stewart said. "You are on CNN. The show that leads into me is puppets making crank phone calls."

The show went to commercial break. It was cancelled several months later. But the system carried on, twenty-four hours a day, seven days a week, year after year. Cable news positions itself as something unimpeachable. The hosts wear suits and power dresses. On promotional billboards, they cross their arms and glare at the camera. But really, cable news was and still is an easily manipulable space, with so much airtime to fill, so little capacity to check facts, and so much hunger for bombastic headlines and audience. It was almost begging for some audacious, attention-hungry politician to come along and co-opt the system. That year, Donald Trump was still busy acting like a successful businessman on air. *The Apprentice* had debuted its first season. The day before Stewart went on CNN, Trump was shown giving a speech to his contestants, who in that particular episode were designing clothes. His speech was about the importance of knowing your market.

Stewart's appearance on *Crossfire* was an early indicator of something else changing in the new media landscape. It was the fact that many Millennials saw the incident not as it was unfolding live on cable but instead later, online, out of context, in one of the earliest viral political moments of the internet age.

"The online transcript and video clips of the program immediately became an overnight sensation among Web surfers, bloggers and pundits alike," the tech website CNET reported.[26] "The volume of downloads outpaced CNN's recent ratings numbers for the actual show."

Hundreds of thousands of people viewed the interview on a website called iFilm. YouTube hadn't been founded yet, but the transcript made its way to blogging sites like Xanga and Myspace and LiveJournal.

It was the beginning of our current moment, in which we read and watch things in echo chambers, in polarized news feeds that give us fundamentally different realities. Thinking about *Imagined Communities*, I guess the question for the future of our generation is: What happens to the nation now that our mass ceremony of reading together has ended?

*   *   *

Consuming media in our reconfigured digital era was exhilarating at first. If you knew the right places to click, you could find free news, music, and movies, as well as the sorts of information you'd previously only find in pamphlets on college-campus billboards—all from the safety of your parents' chunky desktop. You could talk to people about it all, too. This new media world could be especially liberating for anyone who was a little different, trapped in any place that could feel constricting.

It was for Miju Han. For her, a curious and precocious teenager from the conservative Richmond, Virginia, suburbs, the internet was a place of unparalleled exploration. Offline, she was a teenager whose biggest musical credentials included playing in the jazz band at school. On the internet, though, she could be a niche expert on alt rock, punk rock, ska, NOFX, AFI, Less Than Jake, everything she downloaded on Napster and then KaZaA. She'd post her thoughts—so many thoughts—on forums. Forums were a place where someone smarter than her years could, for a little while, *be* older than her years, and nobody would know she was just 13.

Miju means "America" in Korean. But as it does for many Millennials, Miju's name only tells part of her story. I connected with her because we are opposites in some regards. Despite my name, which basically means "White boy" to anybody reading, my mother was born in Korea and immigrated to the US as a teenager. Despite her name, Miju grew up in a very Jewish household in a very Jewish community in a very not Jewish part of America. Although Miju's father's family came from Korea, her mother's family emigrated from Eastern Europe, settling in

Chicago. Eventually, her grandmother moved to Virginia to marry her grandfather, who was serving there in the Air Force.

Anybody who grew up a political outsider in a place with rigid politics knows how exciting it is to first find people who think like you. Before the internet, those connections came most often from books. Miju would browse the bookshelves at Barnes & Noble for ideas that stimulated her. Her mother thought it was great she was reading but didn't always pay much attention to what; in retrospect, Miju thinks her parents probably would have had some questions about the age-appropriateness of what she had picked up. Miju felt like Jon Stewart *got* her. She campaigned for John Kerry. She wrote an op-ed supporting the local Democratic candidate for lieutenant governor. She hung out in a part of Richmond called Carytown where there were independent bookshops and galleries, and it all just gave her a sense that maybe there was something bigger out in the world waiting for her. She just had to get old enough to access it for herself.

Two hours north up I-95 from Richmond in Washington, D.C., on the same day Jon Stewart was on *Crossfire*, a group of conservative Christians were marching to show their opposition to same-sex marriage. Tens of thousands of people had assembled on the Mall, the largest of many such rallies across the country that year geared at energizing voters opposed to gay marriage. Their participants were concerned by what trends in voter registration could mean for their politics. "If you watch MTV today, you will see they are registering those kids who have been filled with propaganda," James C. Dobson, the founder of an evangelical group called Focus on the Family, said at the march.[27] At the rally, he said he would get down on his knees to beg attendees to vote in November. That year, Massachusetts had become the only state in the nation to allow same-sex marriage. It was only the year before that the Supreme Court had struck down anti-sodomy laws, which had still existed in fourteen states.

That was the environment in which Miju would log on to AIM and type two words to strangers: "I'm bi."

More directly, she'd just go: 13/f/va/bi. The internet had helped her figure out she was different. There was a way on AOL of looking up member profiles by screenname. But you could also search by location, gender, marital status, computer type, or even just "bi." Miju chatted to strangers whom she approached or who approached her under any of the new screennames she created, sifting through possibilities and trying on sexualities as if they were pieces of clothing. She knew she couldn't tell anyone in her real life that she wasn't straight. Yet she also came to understand how right that short label felt on her. *Bi*. In this rare heavenly space of juvenile freedom, she could be whatever she wanted. She could be a music expert, she could be bi, she could just explore *being* in ways she couldn't yet in life offline.

That was how Willow found her.

When you're a 13-year-old girl telling people on the internet that you're bi and it's the new millennium, things aren't always going to go perfectly. Mostly it's going to be weird guys with small boners, and they are going to ask you if later you might go and make out with a girl, because that'd be hot. But sometimes, it does go perfectly. That's the sense I get when Miju tells me about the stranger who contacted her one day out of the digital nowhere. It was a girl around her age who was also bi. They talked a lot, connected in this intimate way she couldn't with anyone else around her. Maybe they had never met, maybe they would never meet, but at the keyboard, it was thrilling to know that there was someone in her own state who was also attracted to women, trying to figure out what that was going to mean for the rest of her life.

They did meet. It turned out that the woman from the internet was Willow, Miju's best friend's sister. Miju wasn't even out to her best friend. But one day at her best friend's house, Willow revealed that she was the Willow from AOL. Cue mind blown, palms sweaty. It was this pivotal moment in Millennial puberty that I don't think really even happens now because everyone is always online. But back then, when it was a landline thing, when we logged on and off, there was this moment when something from your internet life took real form, suddenly and unexpectedly. It didn't have to be sexuality. It could be the ramifications of something you typed to someone else, it could be the intimacy you felt online with a friend at school you didn't really know too well in the real world. It could have even been you, acting like a different person on the internet, then coming off of it and having to reconcile with who you really were. Whatever it was, in that moment, it crashed like a meteor from the zeroes and the ones and through the stratosphere you kept between who you said you were online and who you actually were in real life. And that is how Miju—barely a teenager, living life in a place she felt was so homophobic—got a girlfriend.

The way Miju remembers it, Willow pursued Miju more than Miju pursued her—which was exactly what Miju felt she needed at that early stage. She needed a guide, and Willow, who was a little older, was it. She liked the rush of connecting with Willow in a way that was clearly not friendship. That's something she'll never forget. Even today, she carries that memory of feeling so good about something she knew everyone around her would have thought was wrong. But that also became a source of tension within her. Miju was a good kid. She usually did the right thing. She had four brothers and got along with them. She did the activities her parents wanted her to, and she got good grades. But now she had this secret, and she lived in fear anyone would find out.

The relationship was intense but short-lived. As Miju tells me her story, she makes clear that while she wants to share it, she wants to protect Willow's privacy, too. So she doesn't reveal every detail of their time together. But what she does say is that over the course of their relationship, Miju could tell there were some issues going on at Willow's house that were difficult to deal with. More importantly—and they never discussed it as a couple—one day, Willow decided she needed to come out to her family. They were conservative and, in response, kicked both her and, for some reason, her sister out of the house. Miju found out when they both showed up at her door with nowhere else to sleep that night.

Cue sweating palms, cue a racing heart. Cue another crash-landing from the internet world. Up until that point, Miju's parents had only known her as the good girl. Now there was her best friend and her girlfriend standing at her door because, at least in part, Miju was bi.

"You think you're bi," Miju's mother told her later. "But you're not."

That was confusing because Miju's mother was not only an active Democrat but a big LGBT ally. One of her best friends was gay and lived in San Francisco. Looking back, Miju is still a little confused about what happened. She feels as if maybe her mother wanted to protect her; maybe she thought being out would make life harder for Miju and she didn't want that. Either way, Miju's mom called Willow's house and persuaded her parents to let the girls go home.

The relationship ended. Willow and Miju were so young that separating them was easy, not because they didn't care about each other, but because as minors they had little agency in the face of their parents. They had no path forward. The AIM chat fire of their friendship extinguished. And Miju was so used to doing what other people said was right that she went along with it. She believed her mother; maybe she wasn't bi. It was confusing, and she was looking for some certainty. Dating Willow had felt like that, but when it was torn away, going back in the other direction felt convenient and, more than that, safe.

After it ended, I get the sense that Miju was lonely. But she was too young to name the hollowness, couldn't mourn what had happened. So she distracted herself. She threw herself into the activities of the gifted child. There was jazz band, music, Model UN, learning French and Italian, sports. All the while the issue of gay marriage—specifically, banning it—became an increasingly frequent political talking point and then campaign platform promise. Bush, wavering in the polls, in early 2004 announced his support for a constitutional ban on same-sex marriage.[28]

"Some activist judges and local officials have made an aggressive attempt to redefine marriage," Bush said at the time. "The union of a man and woman is the most enduring human institution, honored and encouraged in all cultures and by every religious faith."

It was enough to make a queer teenager want to crank up an emo song and never turn it off. It made Miju feel like she just had to wait it out, get to college. She knew, as she says now, that she had to "get the heck out of the South."

* * *

Hating on gays was a convenient rallying cry as Bush sought to avoid the one-term fate of his father. His vow to protect the "sanctity of marriage" fit in with a broader pattern. Despite the president's infamous difficulties with grammar and sentence construction, his team evinced a mastery of language. They offered comforting catchphrases as solutions to enormously complicated problems: "No Child Left Behind," "Compassionate Conservatism," "Homeland Security," and of course, that thing about sanctity.

You might even say such terms marked battles in the ugly culture war Americans are still waging. It has been another hallmark of our generation. In 1991, a sociologist at the University of Virginia named James Davison Hunter reintroduced the country to the phrase "culture war" to describe the conflicts we were (and still are) having over gender, sexuality, race, education, the workplace, and religion. English speakers had used the term sporadically before. It came to our language through the German *Kulturkampf*, which translates directly to "culture struggle" and emerged in the context of Otto von Bismarck's attempts to bring the

Catholic Church in line with German law in the nineteenth century. At the end of the Cold War in America, Hunter applied it to a clash between progressive and orthodox Americans, duking it out to define what our nation truly meant.

Once those battles started, they only ramped up. We no longer had to worry about the spread of Communism; all we had to fear were our neighbors. Media organizations, as we know, began aligning with either the progressive or the conservative camp. Identity came to dominate both media and politics, with the story you told about yourself—and the one other people told about you—determining what you felt you could and should do. With each passing year, the importance of our individual stories took on ever greater import.

Those stories could distract from larger, more real problems. One of the enormously complicated problems facing Bush at that time was the economy. Months after he first took office, it tanked. It wasn't entirely his fault. It was the Dot-Com bubble bursting. It turned out that companies like Pets.com, which had raised tens of millions of dollars going public on the stock market promising to revolutionize how people bought things like dog food, didn't quite have their business models down yet. The irrational exuberance of the burgeoning internet industry nosedived. Companies folded. The economy entered a recession that was only exacerbated by September 11. The uncertainty that came from the attacks temporarily affected the markets, and business and consumer confidence alongside them. For a while, people stopped buying things, stopped going to big events, stopped traveling. That made things worse.

The recession technically ended in November of 2001, aided by a resumption of economic activity spurred by emergency reductions in interest rates by the Federal Reserve. But the end of a recession does not mean the economy has fully recovered, and the aftereffects dragged. This was capitalism's Age of Chaos, after all. The job for life was wheezing out its final breaths, investors were hunting for fast returns on their money and wanted them quickly; they'd move on if they didn't materialize fast enough. All of this contributed to a system in which the economy could recover quickly from a recession, but fast job growth wouldn't follow. The economy lost 1.6 million jobs during the millennium's first recession; 2001 was the first year-over-year decline in employment since Bush's father was in office.[29] [30] Even after the recession ended, however, the jobs kept vanishing. An additional 1 million were lost in the year and a half of post-recession recovery, with the unemployment rate ultimately hitting a peak in June of 2003.[31] These losses were overwhelmingly concentrated in manufacturing, where the declines were precipitous, falling more than 17 percent between the middle of 2000 and early 2004.[32] They would never return to the levels seen before that recession.

Ohio turned into an epicenter of this employment crunch. The state lost more than one hundred and sixty thousand manufacturing jobs between Bush's first day in office and Jon Stewart's appearance on *Crossfire* in 2004. One of those jobs—a supposed job for life—belonged to Aaron's father.

It happened one Friday in February. The management team at American Steel, where Aaron's dad had worked for twenty-five years, was called into a meeting at 1 p.m.[33] A decision had been made by the higher-ups at headquarters in Granite City, Illinois. The plant in Alliance was shutting down. At 2 p.m., union employees were notified. Jon, the plant manager, gave one of those talks that anyone who's ever been laid off in a big cull can recite verbatim: *It's not you, it's the industry.* American Steel had cut costs over the past three years, but it wasn't enough. They just weren't getting railcar orders like they used to. The memorandum was posted for all employees working at the plant to read. In compliance with the Warn Act, which requires sixty days' notice before mass layoffs, most staff found out they would be let go indefinitely effective April 12. A small section of the factory would remain open for a little while at a reduced level, the part that handled the last stage of the production process: cleaning and finishing railcar couplings. Those workers would stay. Everyone else had to go.

The news hit city hall at 4:30 p.m., just as municipal employees were about to head out for the weekend.[34] Mayor Toni Middleton, a retired fire chief who'd been on the job two years at that point, compared the closure to the death of a relative who'd been sick for a long time.

"You hold out hope for recovery while preparing yourself for what appears to be inevitable," he said the day the news broke. "But it still comes as a blow."

Bush had flipped Ohio in his race against Al Gore in 2000. He'd also pulled Kentucky, Missouri, Tennessee, and West Virginia from the Democrats. He knew any hopes for reelection would run through these states, too. He'd tried to lift the local steel industry with 30 percent tariffs on foreign products, but they were ultimately ruled illegal by the World Trade Organization, and Bush had to drop them. Tariffs or no, the broader steel industry, crucial to that swath of the country, was in crisis. Around the same time Aaron's father was learning about his lack of a future at American Steel, *thirty-one* companies in the industry were in bankruptcy proceedings. Others were running enormous losses. As with any meltdown, the factors responsible varied. Foreign imports hurt business. The recession dampened demand. Factories couldn't operate as efficiently as investors wanted. Maybe they could get profitable, but not profitable enough to justify those investors keeping their capital around. (What's the point of earning 2 percent on your money from a steel plant when you can quickly shift out of that investment and get 20 percent in some other investment?) Firms faced huge costs from their pension obligations to employees who had retired decades before but were living longer than ever. No matter the reason, it was too late for Aaron's father. His job was gone.

I've been writing about how the economy affects real people's lives for over a decade. One of the things I've learned in that time is that peoples' eyes tend to glaze over when you use too many numbers in a paragraph. People see "1.6 million jobs lost" and feel they've got the point, even though 1.6 million is a tough number to conceptualize. (It's a number as large as the population of Philadelphia, if that helps.) They'll see "17 percent drop in manufacturing employment" and think, "That's a pretty big amount, I guess," but not always humanize it by realizing that this is a loss of nearly two out of every ten jobs in the sector. It's numbers from people's individual stories that hit home harder.

Here's one: In Aaron's 2004 freshman yearbook at Alliance High School, he was pictured four times.[35] One photo shows Aaron and a friend as they "kill time before the bell rang." In that picture, Aaron is a bespectacled kid in a polo shirt holding a book he'd been reading. In the second photo, he's wearing a basketball jersey, looking a little nervous for his school picture. In the third, he's pictured at a powderpuff football game. And the fourth photo represents one of the best memories of Aaron's life. It's a photo of Aaron in jersey number 34 under the headline "Freshmen Win Championship." It was the culmination of a phenomenal basketball season that made Aaron feel like a star.

Sports in Alliance are a huge deal—to win is to be a part of the town's psyche. Alliance is home to the University of Mount Union's Purple Raiders, the team that put Alliance back on the map under the leadership of Larry Kehres, one of the winningest coaches in college football history.

The day of the championship game, Aaron, in that same uniform from the yearbook photo, had an anti-skip CD player with *Get Rich or Die Tryin'* by 50 Cent playing to pump him up. It's the album with "In Da Club" and "P.I.M.P." The team arrived at Poland High School, an hour away, just shy of the Pennsylvania border. Warmup started. Layups, dribbling, quick passes. The vibe of the team was confidence. When the game started, Alliance broke ahead early. Aaron was shooting guard most of the game. By halftime, they were ahead something like 28-22.

"Don't let this slip through your fingers now," Coach McGeehan warned them.

They went back fired up. Although Poland broke through their defense in the minutes before the buzzer, the Alliance Aviators maintained their lead and won that championship game 54-44. Aaron even scored four points. The season ended with medals and a title: league champions. Their record was 16-2. As their school bus drove back to Alliance in the cold of that January night, Aaron got that high school feeling of greatness. The buzzer sound and all eyes on the shooting guard. The court lights were so bright. Couldn't he keep the feeling of standing in them forever?

But Aaron's father had lost his job. And the changes were slowly bleeding into the economic realities of his home life. Sometimes, these changes take years to show up, so long that you forget what caused them in the first place. They did in Aaron's life. Sophomore year, Aaron only showed up once in his yearbook—for his official portrait, the one everyone gets if they show up for picture day. He wasn't on the basketball team. It was the same junior year. Senior year, Aaron wasn't pictured at all. He skipped picture day.

A big part of all of this was because Aaron was just around less. After American Steel shut down, Aaron's father started working at Circle K, the gas station. Money in Aaron's home after the foundry shuttered "just wasn't the same," Aaron says. So he started working, too.

The place where Aaron got a job, Burger Hut, was on the north side of town, a mile up from Rodman Public Library, situated on the railroad tracks where freight trains rumble north toward Cleveland and passenger trains shuttle people between Chicago and Washington. Until very recently, two eggs, toast, and coffee there would set you back just $2.50. The Monday special cost a mere $4.75 and included pancakes, sausage, bacon, and eggs. Fridays, you could get all the fish you wanted to eat for

$6.95. A white, pink, red, and yellow sign outside reminded customers: "We do ice cream too!" But the good prices and cheery signage couldn't distract from the fact that it was a pretty depressing place for a teenager to work. One of Aaron's colleagues smelled like cat piss. His manager was a douchebag. Eventually, Aaron switched to working at Arby's, right near the University of Mount Union. After that, he started working in the kitchens of Mount Union itself.

One of the realest songs on 50 Cent's debut studio album—the one Aaron was listening to on that bus ride to his championship night freshman year—is called "21 Questions." In it, you'll likely remember the rapper asking a series of questions to his girlfriend, how she'd feel about him in various situations, if she'd be ashamed of him or still love him. One of those hypotheticals: How would she feel about him if instead of rapping, he flipped burgers at Burger King instead?

*   *   *

The year 2004 was peak auto-tune. It was peak the Neptunes producing tracks for Britney and Justin. It was peak trucker hats and lieutenant caps. It was peak Kelly Clarkson black-and-white skunk-streaked, heat-straightened hair. It was the year the sleek Motorola Razr cell phone debuted. For Olivia's part, she wanted nothing to do with all this.

She calls those years of middle and early high school her "blur phase." It's hard for her to access memories from that time. When I ask her about them, she can't recall much. Which makes me sad, because it's supposed to be fun being a teenager—at least in the lore. When you're smart and sassy and spend a lot of time on the internet, it's a little harder. It's even more difficult when you're 9/11 Girl. You have a hard time getting excited about Homecoming and who won the big game and who made cheerleading and who's in and who's out with the rich kids from Sunnydale, a town north of Nesconset from which the bougie kids hail. You feel trapped by the lugubriousness. Everyone seemed like a bitch, or insane. Take Riley, one of the rich Sunnydale kids. He once got in a fight and slammed someone's head against a microwave. Olivia didn't need that.

When Olivia thinks about the blur phase, she can remember sixth grade turning into seventh grade turning into eighth. A dance, Usher and Lil Jon playing in the background of that same cafeteria where she'd yelled at the lunch aide. High school arrived, and she had people telling her "you should really put yourself out there more," mechanical as she still felt. She tried out for the freshman softball team. But that same day, she got a stomachache, went to the bathroom, and realized she was getting her period for the first time.

"I'm not doing this," she said in the stall.

Thankfully she'd read *The Care and Keeping of You*, the book published by the American Girl doll company about growing up. From it she remembered a tip: If and when you have your first period and you're caught out without a pad or a tampon, wrap your underwear in toilet paper and voilà. That night at home, her mother said Olivia had turned into a woman. But Olivia had felt like a woman for a long time

Key symptoms of trauma survivors are detachment from emotional life, indifference, and profound passivity. In her 1992 book *Trauma and Recovery*, Judith Herman finds that victims of traumas can live as if in a "hypnotic trance," disconnected from friends and family. This is because traumatic events "shatter the construction of the self that is formed and sustained in relation to others. They undermine the belief systems that give meaning to human experience. They violate the victim's faith in a natural or divine order and cast the victim into a state of existential crisis."[36]

Still, in the back of her mind, Olivia held out hope. There was the fantasy about Anthony living in Mexico. But there was another one, and it involved her AIM Buddy List. Dial-up shifted to broadband, desktops to laptops, but Olivia kept adding his screenname, NYAvenger, to her Buddy List, just in case. One night, she heard that creaking door sound open. She saw NYAvenger online. She nearly threw up.

Was he back? Was the fantasy true? That he was in Mexico drinking beers, waiting out the end of his faked death, and he'd logged onto America Online? They still, after all that time, had not found his remains.

But it was just her uncle, Anthony's brother, logging on to Anthony's AIM account, shutting it down.

Over time, Olivia's hope turned into a plan, almost a mission. The first part of that mission involved traditions. She decided she wanted to go to college at Syracuse University, where Anthony's brother had gone. Olivia felt she'd missed out on the sense of continuity that other families had. In a way, Syracuse would be a way to get that.

The school's anthropology department was its other draw. Olivia's plan was to study there, become a forensic scientist, and help people take the remains of the dead, analyze their DNA, and help identify who they were for their families. Hearing this, I couldn't help but think that even if she knew it was unlikely, even if she knew in her head that it defied logic, deep down, what Olivia wanted was to find her father.

* * *

Bush won the election in 2004. His second win wasn't a landslide, and it left people like Miju in Richmond worried about the direction of the country. "America has spoken," Bush said the night he was reelected. "I'm humbled by the trust and the confidence of my fellow citizens. With that trust comes a duty to serve all Americans."[37] But words like that were starting to ring hollow. In that cable-news, us-versus-them, one-or-the-other type of way, Bush had been increasingly casting himself and his followers in the "us" camp and broadening out the definition of the very bad "other." "Either you are with us, or you are with the terrorists," he'd declared soon after September 11.[38] After a while, it wasn't just terrorists who were "them," but anyone who didn't like his definition of "freedom," as it pertained to laissez-faire economics and cultural conservativism sprinkled with evangelical Christianity. "The enemies of freedom are not idle, and neither are we," he liked to say.[39] That kind of line could leave people wondering who, exactly, the enemies of freedom were.

The Iraq War will endure as Bush's biggest legacy. But his second term shaped domestic American life, too. It had lasting outcomes. One of the most consequential, one sometimes forgotten but that continues to influence our lived experience to this day, involves real estate.

"See, I believe when you own something, your life is more secure, you have more dignity, and you have independence," he'd said at a rally in Moosic, Pennsylvania in 2004. "There's nothing better in America than somebody opening their door saying, 'Welcome to my home.'"

It was the most tangible plank of the president's big, second-term push to create an "ownership society." Encouraging homeownership served as a helpful distraction. The wars in Afghanistan and Iraq had been going on a long time by then—three years for the former, over a year for the latter. Bush's "Mission Accomplished" photo op, declaring the supposed end of major combat in Iraq, had taken place some eighteen months before. The wars were not going well, and Bush knew this was a vulnerability. In his campaign, he had leaned heavily into domestic policy, touting homeownership at rally after rally, including in his marquee speech at the Republican National Convention in New York City. Sometimes, he connected homeownership to domestic security. In a big logical stretch in a speech at a Black church in Atlanta several years before, he'd even linked terrorism to personal finance.[40] "As we work on our security from possible attacks by terrorists, we also work on economic security. The two securities go hand in hand," he said, adding, importantly, that "part of being a secure America is to encourage homeownership."[41]

By 2022, over half of Millennials had become homeowners.[42] Some part of me is still surprised it happened, given that the narrative for so long was that we would never be able to afford property. (Take the headline of one Business Insider story from that very year: "Sorry, millennials, you're never getting a good home.") Although a majority of us are now lucky enough to own property, it's taken us longer to get it than it took our parents, and the typical age of the first-time buyer is now around 38 years old, up from the late 20s in the 1980s.[43] There is an emotional side to all of this. A Bank of America survey in 2023 found that 60 percent of Millennial respondents think homeownership is more important than it was during our parents' generation.[44] Research from Zillow itself found that 61 percent of Millennial home buyers found the ordeal so stressful, they cried at least once during the process.[45] Millennials have indicated they view real estate more favorably as an investment than any other generation, and they are less likely to invest in stocks than real estate.[46]

There are many reasons for this property obsession. Sometimes, we become obsessed with things we think we'll never be able to get. The Great Recession, which began in 2007 and was triggered by a real estate meltdown, would shape Millennial views of risk, debt, markets, and property for years after it ended in 2009, largely by making the generation more risk-averse. One survey found that Millennials feared certain types of debt more than dying or the threat of war.[47] A drop in construction rates after the Great Recession also meant that as we inched toward prime home-buying age, housing came in shorter supply. Meanwhile, social media turned keeping up with the Joneses into a whole new level of competition. By the time the pandemic rolled around in 2020, low interest rates and the rise of investing apps finally pushed Millennials into a speculative mindset, leading to our *SNL*-parodied Zillow hobby—only to be followed by interest rates soaring to their highest point in more than twenty years, lowering housing supply further as existing homeowners declined to sell, digging in to wait for lower mortgages.[48] Recent research has also shown that on top of all of this, even adjusting for inflation, Millennials had it harder than Gen Z does in getting homes because our incomes lagged for so long early in our careers. Many Gen Z workers found themselves in the fortunate position of entering the labor market during the "war for talent" between late 2020 and 2024, when the unemployment rate plummeted to historic lows and salaries surged, making it easier to save for down payments.[49]

When Bush started pushing his "ownership society," there were plenty of understandable reasons. Homeownership can bring financial stability: the chance to build equity, mortgage costs that are more predictable than rent, tax benefits, the potential for rental income, and maybe appreciation in value. But there was also a political reason for Bush to push property ownership, aside from distracting from the War on Terror. It goes back to a strategy pioneered by Britain's former conservative prime minister Margaret Thatcher.[50] One of the problems long faced by conservative parties has been that people tend to vote in favor of their economic interests. While this leads to support for conservative policies among the smaller, richer portion of the population, it's generally in the interest of a much larger portion of society to vote for politicians who will redistribute wealth from the rich to everyone else. The solution conservative parties found to get around this—in a sense to get poorer people to vote against their own immediate economic interests—was to push the idea of ownership. People who own things are less likely to vote in favor of redistribution. The biggest things most people ever own are their homes. If you get more people onto the housing ladder, even if their homes are worth only $100,000 compared to party grandees' portfolios worth, say, $100 million or more, and even if those $100,000 homes are mostly mortgaged, the masses will theoretically start thinking—and voting—like owners. The strategy started to work, with new owners switching their votes to conservative parties.[51]

By 2004, American homeownership rates had rocketed to nearly 70 percent—their highest levels in history.[52] But that goal of an "ownership society" didn't stop with housing. Bush talked a big talk about people owning their retirement plans and health plans, too. On retirement, he pushed for the "partial privatization" of Social Security, which would have allowed young people to divert some of their payroll tax into individual investment accounts, directed by themselves, rather than the public pension system. On health, he pushed "Health Savings Accounts" that were supposed to let Americans create tax-free savings accounts for their medical needs so they could decide how and where they wanted to spend on services. "You own your own account," he'd said in a debate against John Kerry.[53] (The criticism of such accounts, and why they have yet to be adopted at scale: Workers, justifiably, feared they would never earn enough money to put into such accounts to cover big medical expenses if they arose.)

Despite some of these less popular ideas, there was a sense at the time that the solutions Bush offered for the economy were working. The feeling buoyed him into a second term: a fantasy of magical resolution. Housing became a positive distraction for a nation waging war abroad. Property values accelerated. "Housing prices keep rising faster than almost anything else," the *Wall Street Journal* reported in May of 2005.[54] Home values rose an average of 50 percent between 2000 and that year, adding some $5.5 trillion to the market value of residential real estate.[55] Contractors began building more, too, with a nearly 60 percent increase in home construction between 2000 and 2005. Debt balances ticked upward. To get the money to buy the consumeristic must-haves of the era—Hummers that could go for nearly $100,000 in today's dollars, Von Dutch hats, expensive low-rise jeans—people started using their more valuable homes as credit cards, borrowing against them with home-equity lines of credit to get the cash.

This had a dark side. In effect, it involved the government allowing lenders to run far too fast and loose with debt. Financial firms gave home loans to people who would never be able to afford to pay them back. These were people with bad credit scores, "subprime borrowers," as they were known. Subprime mortgages had been used in the 1980s and 1990s mostly for refinancing, not new purchases.[56] In some ways, that sounds like a bad thing. Shouldn't more people have access to financing to buy homes? "Yes," answered the market, along with some very tricky financial engineering. By 2005, subprime mortgage originations had ballooned to $625 billion. A fifth of mortgages given out that year were subprime. Banks wanted these people as customers so they could get more business, and policymakers were happy to see them get mortgages so they could live in the "ownership society." But doing so pushed people to buy homes they couldn't afford, which ended up hurting them and, in turn, all of us.

Before it crashed, it felt so comfortable. I remember driving around McMansion neighborhoods with my friends playing *The O.C.* soundtrack, feeling like "Mr. Brightside" encapsulated all of our teenage angst. I didn't like Bush. But I liked how good it felt to be with my friends in our American Eagle and Abercrombie finest. My best friend—we'd grown close on AIM—was the queen of the "going out top," that economic indicator of Millennial culture in the moment. Going out tops were a sign that a shopper had spent so much on her tight, boot-legged, stylized-back-pocket jeans that she had to economize on a top, and would usually do so with a reasonably priced but showy, brightly colored, flowy, blousey thing.[57] It was so that era: spending too much and covering up the difference.

*   *   *

Even in the brashness, there could be beauty. I'm reminded of that when I call Justin and ask him to tell me about life in Southern California in the early 2000s. Tall, blond, handsome, and masculine, Justin was the kind of guy for whom the band Sublime meant a lot in high school. I grew up in California, too, and I knew guys like Justin. I was the gay drama nerd who did things because I prayed they'd look good on a college application. Justin, meanwhile, did things because he liked them. He was the boy in the neighborhood who'd spend all the long, light hours outside, only heading back home at dusk when the sky was the color of lilac bushes and fire, skin dusted with sunburnt sand and smelling like the chaparral—sage, liquorish, eucalyptus—a rough but comforting cologne people from the California coast know well.

I wanted to talk to Justin because he was part of the population of young, non-college-educated White men that journalists started examining with greater curiosity and occasionally concern as the Trump era began. Justin is a Democrat, and the group is diverse. Yet somehow, it feels as if we have lost our understanding of them. We have still yet to understand them completely. Historically the dominant force across work, life, and politics—literally the patriarchy—White men are, on average, behaving more and more like a uniform bloc. This has been a long time coming: There has been a gender gap between men and women in presidential elections, with women preferring Democrats, since 1980, and since 2000, so-called educational polarization has pushed non-college-educated Whites toward the Republican party.[58] What it adds up to, though, is the fact that in 2024, nearly two thirds of White men without college degrees backed Trump.[59]

A lot of writing on this topic tends to attribute that trend to men's diminished outcomes in education and the workforce, which some conclude gives way to anxiety about them losing their cultural power. A 2023 book showed that in high schools, on average, the top 10 percent of each class is two-thirds women, and the bottom 10 percent is two-thirds men.[60] (Even though standardized test scores are about the same.)

When it comes to college degrees, the gender gap is now even wider than it was in 1970, but with the proportions reversed: Men are in the same position women were before Title IX took effect.[61] Of course, men still famously hog seats in the C suite, and there is a big gap in average pay between men and women. But although wages for college-educated men have continued to grow astronomically, weekly earnings for working-class American men have been declining since the beginning of the Millennial era in the 1980s. In 1979, weekly wages for men with just high school degrees were $1,017 in today's currency. Today, those wages have dropped to $881.[62] That's a decline of 14 percent. Meanwhile, wages for working-class women are up 10 percent for the same time period.[63] There is no doubt that wage growth for women is an excellent thing, but we have to acknowledge that men are facing relative challenges, and those challenges are having consequences. One consequence of lower wage growth is that one out of every three men without a college degree is no longer in the labor force. That's five million men.

Justin is one of those men. His pathway out of the labor force was, as is the case for many of his peers, complex, and I'll return to that later. But for now, I will start by saying that he is a great example of how we could stand to talk about the American White guy with greater nuance. It's so easy (and lazy) to fall into the left-right tropes when talking about men: Either men are the enemy, sucking up power and resources that rightfully belong to others, or they are emasculated by the rise of women and need to have their rightful power restored. Justin doesn't have a college degree. He doesn't take part in the labor force, at least as currently measured by the Bureau of Labor Statistics. But he has a happy life. He is a proud father and devoted husband. And, true to Millennial form, in some ways, the life he is living revolves around a house. Getting it took hard work, sacrifices, the uprooting of an entire family, and, actually, a love story.

It started with a letter.

Hey Tara,
Sorry I didn't make it to your party.
Have fun in Florida.
You seemed cool in high school.
Hope everything's great. Maybe I'll see you around sometime.

Justin

He hand-wrote it in the summer of 2005, when he and Tara had just graduated from James Madison High School in San Diego's northern Clairemont neighborhood. That year, house prices were up 345 percent from when he was born in 1987. Tara was having a going-away party and, surprisingly, Justin was invited. It wasn't that they didn't like each other, it was more that they had really only exchanged about a dozen words to each other in the years since 1998, when they became classmates at Sequoia Elementary.

Possibly rude: Justin accepted Tara's invitation, but he didn't end up going to the party. Tara lived kitty-corner to him, which perhaps took the urgency out of attending. He'd see her again, just like he'd seen her many times before. Less often, since she was soon off to college in Florida, where she had a great-aunt, but she'd still come home sometimes. College in Florida was her reward for all the AP classes she took and varsity tennis games she'd played. Justin wasn't going to Florida for college. He actually wasn't going anywhere for the foreseeable future. His post-high-school plan was to stay home, maybe take some classes at community college to figure out what he wanted to do, and work at White Dragon, the martial arts academy where he spent a lot of his time. What Justin wanted in the short term was to have fun. Regardless, in his nonchalance, he missed the party. But because he was well raised by small-town polite parents, and because back then text messages cost

10 cents each, he scribbled down that note, dropped it in Tara's mailbox, and sort of forgot about it.

What's interesting about Justin's real estate journey is that although he grew up in a suburban Clairemont world of cul-de-sacs and strip malls where owning was the dream, he came from a family that rented. His mother and a father had met after high school at the Thirty-Second Street Naval Base in San Diego and lived in the same house for decades. (Tara's family owned theirs.) Justin and his friends spent the summer after high school carelessly roaming the neighborhood with its low-set ranch homes. Clairemont was once the largest and most innovative suburban development of its kind in the city, made up of five hundred homes with twenty different floor plans designed by two very enterprising developers. Its wide, postwar roads were built to accommodate automobiles as they cruised up and down the mesas and canyons. Clairemont was named after one of the wives of its developers, Claire.

Unexpectedly, in late summer, Tara came back to Clairemont. Justin and a friend were in the Genesee Plaza shopping center, its asphalt and concrete hot in the California August. Amidst the staples of American big box retailers—Target, The Home Depot, Marshalls, Party City, PetSmart, Walgreens, GNC, Fantastic Sam's, Starbucks—there was Tara, basically out of nowhere, roaming too, with a friend.

"Florida sucked," she said. She was moving back home.

That day, it all felt like a happy coincidence. Tara being back, them bumping into each other. So the four of them—Justin and his friend, Tara and hers—decided they should take advantage of the summer already slipping away from them and go to the beach the next day.

It quickly became a habit. The four friends would hang out at the beach during the day, maybe get some Mexican food when they got hungry, then head back to someone's house in the evening to watch a movie. Tara loved the John Hughes classics: *The Breakfast Club, Ferris*

Bueller's Day Off, Sixteen Candles, Pretty in Pink. Soon Justin and Tara had a scene like one of those to call their own.

It was early evening, and Tara was driving Justin home from one of their days out. The light lingers past the day's warmth in California, a chill slides up from the Pacific in the 8 o'clock hour. Their moment took place in that witching time between hot day and cool night, and the radio in the car was playing—it's hard to remember what, exactly. But the feeling, Justin remembers: relaxing and exhilarating. All they were doing was hanging out. It was calming and yet shocking how quickly he was falling into this comfortable pattern with her.

Justin was 18. He felt a sense of urgency, like he needed to do something to keep all this going. Was it sustainable, this new adult life? Would it work, getting so close to someone so quickly and so young? There was something Justin had been thinking about doing, that he wanted to do. He hesitated. Yet he could wait no longer. Justin kissed Tara in the summer of 2005 and then left her there in her car as he walked into his parents' rented house, the one kitty-corner to hers.

Researchers are starting to get a better picture of why men are underperforming in secondary schools. While boys' high school grade distributions are less impressive than girls', their standardized test scores are essentially equal. "It's not that girls are smarter than boys, or of course, the other way around. It's that [in high school,] girls have just got their act together a bit more," notes Reeves.[64] Part of this has to do with male brain development, which generally finishes two years later in boys than it does in girls, with the part that controls decision-making and thought processing lagging behind.[65] Those two years are crucial in high school. They fall precisely at the point where turning in homework on time and getting organized for activities and exams can determine who gets into college and if they do go, where. All of this presents a relatively new challenge for men. After all, the educational system has favored them legally and culturally for centuries. It wasn't until the 1970s when large numbers of women were encouraged (or even allowed) to continue on from high school to college. And at that time, college was less of a necessity, with many men earning middle-class wages without it. It's in recent years that, as the race to college has gotten more competitive, it also become more important, leaving a lot of men in a more difficult position than previous generations found themselves in.

Looking back, school was never something Justin knocked out of the park. There was a semester sophomore year of high school when his grades got so bad, he wasn't eligible to take part in drama. He turned things around, but even so, neither of his parents went to college, and he never felt pressure to go. He did things because he enjoyed them. In the classroom, Justin often got an overarching sense from teachers that when he messed up, it was because he was lazy and unmotivated or just plain not good enough. Really, it was that he didn't yet have the organizational skills others had. He understood the assignments and could do them when he hadn't lost them. He got A's on tests. He just never felt like school was his thing. So he focused elsewhere.

School was Tara's thing, though. And Justin knew he wanted to be around her. So they enrolled in community college together. They went to a school called Mesa College, San Diego's largest such educational institution. It was the opposite of Madison High. Where Madison's thousand-strong student body of choir nerds and tennis punks and jocks and geeks and stoners was contained within familiar cinder block and stucco, Mesa's twenty-one thousand students were free to roam around expansive grounds with cold, sterile-feeling buildings that look a bit like space shuttles. One building looked like the Death Star, another like The Enterprise. It was all a little overwhelming.

They got jobs. Justin started in the instructor training program at White Dragon. Tara found a role at a jazzed-up RV campsite called Campland on the Bay. Their days followed the lovely, relaxing, predictable pattern they'd had in the summer, just with a few more adult responsibilities thrown in. Some days, Tara might have school when he didn't. Those mornings, he'd go over to his friend's house and play video games. He'd wait for her hey-do-you-wanna-hang-out text. She'd come over and watch them play. They'd talk and laugh and eventually watch a movie. Some days, he'd go visit her while she worked at Campland. Early in their relationship, they went to a Foo Fighters concert when the band played with Weezer on a Tuesday night in late September. Before long, they were introducing themselves as "boyfriend" and "girlfriend." They said "I love you" in Tara's mom's backyard a few months later. But where they were heading, what their future was or was not supposed to be, Justin didn't really think about. It was all just fun.

*   *   *

The War on Terror simmered in the background of the aughts like a bad medical diagnosis. In the average Millennial consciousness—only sort of understanding the news, hearing parents and teachers talk about it, seeing "Support Our Troops" signs everywhere—at first it sounded like something scary but winnable. Authority figures made it sound as if there would be a clear beginning, middle and end. In Afghanistan, Kabul fell as early as November 2001. People rallied around an invasion of Iraq like well-wishers beside a hospital bed. Just before the invasion, 72 percent of Americans said they supported going to war in Iraq.[66] Much of this support was based on falsehoods spread by an administration "obsessed with Iraqi dictator Saddam Hussein."[67] That year, 57 percent of Americans said they believed that Hussein had played a role in the September 11 attacks.[68] (To this day, there is no evidence that he did.[69]) And the Bush administration ardently forwarded the idea that Iraq had "weapons of mass destruction," a phrase I heard so many times uttered by other teenagers during break at high school that it became background noise. Vice President Dick Cheney did not mince words about it, saying in 2002, "Saddam Hussein now has weapons of mass destruction. There is no doubt he is amassing them to use against our friends, against our allies, and against us."[70]

The initial burst of the war, the toppling of the regime, was brief. It lasted only from March through April 2003. Yet the occupation and the bloody insurgency that came next lasted much longer, and that's what lingered in the minds of teenagers and early twentysomethings. It was confusing to be told a war was being waged abroad against an idea, and that it was over, but it was also still going. All the while, American soldiers continued dying. By 2006, over 3,300 had been killed in both Afghanistan and Iraq.

Although support for the war in Afghanistan stayed high, by 2006, a majority of Americans had begun to say they thought using military force in Iraq was the wrong decision.[71] By 2007, overall trust in the government had cratered. Six years before, in the immediate aftermath of 9/11, 54 percent of Americans said they believed the government would "do what is right just about always/most of the time."[72] By 2007, that figure had fallen to just 24 percent. It has never exceeded that figure again.

All of this was, of course, a challenge for Bush to navigate. For months he'd been talking about "staying the course in Iraq." But that wasn't working. A form of democracy had been put in place in the country, but insurgents threatened its survival. "It is clear that we need to change our strategy," he said in a twenty-minute address to the nation in early January 2007. "This will require increasing American force levels. So I've committed more than twenty thousand additional American troops to Iraq."

The new strategy was called "the surge." It came at a time when many branches of the military were struggling to recruit. There had been significant concern the previous year that both the Army and its reserve components would miss their annual recruitment goals.[73] Without enough soldiers, their struggling campaigns overseas would fare even worse. To boost their numbers, the Army had raised the maximum age for recruits from 35 to 42, increased enlistment bonuses from $20,000 to $40,000, and started allowing people with neck and hand tattoos to join. It met its goals, but only barely, and the Army reserves fell short. For fiscal year 2007, they were hoping for seventy thousand new recruits, but nobody was holding their breath.

"There are a number of likely causes for these recruiting difficulties," noted a report to Congress.[74] "One factor that can have a powerful impact on military recruiting is the state of the economy." The post-Dot-Com recession was far in the rearview mirror by then. The housing market was going bananas, the stock market up 102 percent from its turn-of-the-millennium lows. That meant recruiting was harder. What's more, rates of college attendance were climbing, so the military was now in competition with higher education. But something else was contributing to the shortfalls, too. "One factor likely affecting recruiting for the Army, Army Reserve, and Army National Guard is the major role they are playing in the Iraq conflict. Survey research conducted in 2004 indicates that certain segments of the adult population—especially women and African Americans—have become less likely to recommend military service to young people since the war in Iraq began."

The report identified "influencers" as part of the problem. (Although that term is commonplace now, it was nearly unheard of then.) These were people like parents, teachers, and other authority figures who were able to shape the thoughts of the young. What these influencers saw reminded them a lot of the Vietnam War they'd seen in their own teen years, and they didn't like it.

That partially explains the shifting tone of the military's advertisements. In the late nineties, with the Cold War won and widespread cultural optimism, the Army had tried attracting young talent with the phrase, "Be all you can be." But by the new millennium, executives were finding that that phrase sounded to young people like "the voice of their parents telling them what to do."[75] In response, they rolled out a campaign between the years 2001 and 2006 under the headline "An Army of one." There were commercials, print ads. There was even a video game meant to show how exciting the Army of one could be. The idea was to communicate that Millennials' individuality was welcome in a massive, hierarchical institution fighting bloody battles on foreign soil.

Yet with nightly news reports detailing the struggles of the war and running images of coffins coming home, despite attempts by the Pentagon to ban them, the Army began to sense it needed to pivot again. It picked up on the concerns of the helicopter parents who were giving rise to the sheltered Millennial. And so in 2007, it planned to spend an estimated $1.35 billion on a new campaign, developed in part by McCann Worldgroup, the advertising agency that serves as the crosstown rival in *Mad Men*. The new campaign was built around two words: *Army strong*.

"You made them strong," announced the actor Josh Charles, of *The Good Wife* fame. "We'll make them Army strong." The message was partly for the youths, partly for the anxious parents: They had done their part, and they could let the Army do the rest. Despite this change of tack, the Congressional report explained that Army recruiters were still "having difficulty signing up high school seniors, especially those below the age of 18, who require parental consent to enlist."

Aaron needed that consent.

His senior year, the year he vanished from the Alliance High School yearbook, was 2007, the year Bush announced the surge. That year, Aaron felt adrift. He was hardly going to class. His older brother had moved off to college, and Aaron himself had moved out of his house. He'd been partying, and his parents didn't approve. So he went to live with a friend named Spike. Spike's mom had a boyfriend in the next town over and stayed with him, so the boys had free reign over her house. (Woe betide that house.) Spike's mom paid for utilities, so all they had to cover was food, which they could do given their jobs. They felt like grown-ups who were still going to high school. But given the way Aaron had mostly checked out of school, college didn't look like it was in the cards right away. He didn't apply. He figured he might go later, but even with those vague plans in mind, Aaron didn't like where he saw life going. He wanted to be somebody, make something of himself. The summer before, Spike had joined the Army National Guard. He kept telling Aaron it could be their chance to see the world. Aaron had been to Canada before, but never really abroad. He'd never even been to the beach. He was enticed.

So one day, he went to talk to a recruiter, the kind of guy who wears a military uniform and struts the halls of high school campuses, whose goal it was to make up for that anticipated recruitment shortfall for fiscal year 2007. That recruiter, Aaron remembers now, sold him "the biggest dream ever." A career, glory, pride, stability.

But—as the congressional report noted was so frequently the case—it was Aaron's "influencers," in this case his parents, who were holding him up. Even though he didn't live with them any longer, Aaron needed them to sign the paperwork because he wasn't turning eighteen until August 31 of that year, after graduation and after training was slated to begin.

Aaron's father was against the idea. It wasn't just the years of Jehovah's Witness teaching in him, which preached against joining the military. It was also the memories of one of his cousins who'd gone to Vietnam and come back lost, a completely different person. His father didn't want to lose Aaron any more than he already had. But Aaron begged. This was his way out of the burger kitchens, the boredom, the confined feeling he got in that small town. He felt alone with his brother away at college and he needed an anchor. He wanted to show his family that he wasn't the baby anymore, he wasn't just running his mouth. This was the way back to the glory he'd felt as that champion in freshman year.

The recruiter came to his house in February to try to convince his parents.

"If you make me wait, I'm still going to do it," Aaron told his parents. "You know, you might as well let me go now."

His mom caved first.

His dad hesitated, but when he saw that Aaron wouldn't relent, he gave in. They signed the papers on the dining room table. The moment felt like a turning point to Aaron. Something was finally happening, it felt like a big dose of reality hitting home.

"Their youngest son was no longer their baby," he told me.

That year, the Army National Guard recruited 66,652 personnel out of a goal of 70,000. Aaron was one of them.

* * *

In 2006, Miju made it out of the South. Or rather, she rocketed out of it to one of the best colleges in the country. It's called Williams, and for every year since 2004, it has been ranked as the number-one liberal arts school in America by that infamous guide to college decisions, *U.S. News & World Report*. The school sits in the Berkshire Mountains in Western Massachusetts, on 450 wooded acres with about that many students per class year. Williams is known colloquially as "The West Point of Wall Street." That's because despite the fact that students there can spend four years studying Arabic, theater, political economy, and comparative literature, many of them soon find themselves in lower Manhattan, selling bonds, securities, and financial services.

One of the things Miju discovered at Williams was that just because most of the other people there had also voted for John Kerry didn't mean they were also the same type of liberal as she was. Williams was a competitive, buttoned-up place. Despite what conservatives might say, it wasn't some hippie bastion. It was the sort of place where a lot of guys walked around in Barbour coats pretending to be British. Women toted Longchamp bags, wishing they were walking the Champs-Élysées instead of the small streets of rural Massachusetts. As was true for most colleges, the people there gossiped about each other, slept with each other, and dated each other. But in Miju's experience, it wasn't a place she necessarily felt comfortable exploring her bisexuality.

She found a podcast that helped her with that, though. It was called *Savage Love,* and its first episode came out the fall that Miju started at Williams.[76] On it, Dan Savage gave some pretty blunt advice.

"There's really no nice way to tell someone they suck at kissing or suck at giving head or suck at vaginal intercourse or suck at fist fucking or whatever it is that they're sucking at without making it all about you, without making it not about them. It has to be an 'I' statement."

Savage Love was incredibly influential for Miju and for many other Millennials as we tried to figure out how to make sense of our sexualities at a time when it could feel as if societal norms were changing rapidly without a clear map for how that applied to our own lives. What Miju took away from Dan Savage was that as long as there wasn't harm involved, and as long as you were clear and consensual and communicative about what you wanted with the other person, then why not?

Miju did the things ambitious young liberals in college did during the twilight of the Bush era. Growing up, the concept of tikkun olam was important in her household. It's the concept in Judaism that means "fixing the world" and was first recorded in the Mishnah, known as the Oral Torah. In the present era, many interpret tikkun olam as a call to pursue social justice, bettering the world not just for oneself or one's people but for all. Fighting poverty felt to Miju like the way to better the world for the most people in the biggest way. So she spent a winter term in Senegal doing an internship for the World Bank. With bravado, she went to Cameroon her junior fall because she wanted to study development and speak French and be off the beaten path. "Americans are just soft and weak," she thought as she embarked upon her travels. "That's why they don't do these more hardcore things to potentially help people." One of the more hardcore things Miju did that term was almost die of malaria.

She's not entirely sure when she got bitten. She was taking the anti-malarial medications that make your hair fall out a little and should mostly be effective. But at some point, her host family got sick, and so did she. She never developed a fever, one of the common symptoms of malaria and the biggest sign you need to get a test, so she figured she just had a cold. Before she left for Cameroon, she'd been told that malaria is like the flu, except that if you don't catch it in time, you'll die. The illness is caused by a parasite that enters a human's bloodstream through the bite of a mosquito and eventually makes its way into the liver, where it grows and reproduces. Sometimes, the parasite remains dormant in the liver for months or even years. That dormancy seems to be what happened with Miju, because when the malaria reawakened in her a while later while she was still in Cameroon, it was severe.

Somewhere on Facebook there is (or at least there once was) a picture of Miju before she was admitted for malaria treatment. She is smiling, sweating profusely, giving a thumbs up. Looking back, Miju now thinks that her nonchalance was probably a front. The first few drugs they tried her on didn't work. Drug resistance had been confirmed in two of the four human malaria parasite species, and the Centers for Disease Control and Prevention had said that the development of that resistance posed "one of the greatest threats to malaria control," resulting in "increased malaria morbidity and mortality." Normally, cases of malaria detected quickly are straightforward and respond well to treatment. But 15 percent of people in Miju's age range get severe malaria, and the fatality rate for people with severe malaria is 27 percent.[77] At the private clinic, they kept trying new and stronger drugs on Miju. One night, she went to bed and thought she might not wake up, that that would be how her story ended.

It kept going. But in those malaria nights, Miju was alone and far away from home. She missed her parents and her boyfriend. What had seemed like a passing problem was turning into what really felt like the moment she might die, just as she was emerging as an adult, figuring out what she wanted to do with her life. She had felt so invincible and strong. She hadn't really had to reckon with her mortality before. And there she was, hazy and dehydrated, maybe vanishing from a world she hadn't fixed yet.

That's when she had the dream. It felt like a negotiation, but looking back, it was really more her begging. In that delirious state, her negotiation took place with Dumbledore from *Harry Potter*. Speaking with him, Miju had to articulate an idea that only hits a lot of us when we become adults: Life has an end.

"You can't let this happen," she said in the dream.

The figure was calm and reassuring and told Miju that it wasn't her time to go. But he also made her answer a difficult question: "Why do you want to keep on living?"

When Miju thought about it, she knew she was miserable doing development work. Being out in the field was far from satisfying, and she was questioning how much the projects she'd worked on were truly helping others. Miju is a gregarious woman who loves connecting with people. What she realized in Cameroon was that what she wanted was a life that would let her do that in deep, authentic ways. The truth is, it's very hard to connect like that when you're always a foreigner. You can find commonalities, and those are amazing and powerful and beautiful, she felt, but it's different from being fully seen and understood in your own context. I get the sense, too, that there were still silent tensions inside her that she knew needed to be resolved back home, parts of her she might be able to run from abroad but not address unless she faced them head-on in the society in which she was raised. Miju looked into the light in her dream and admitted to herself something that has sometimes been difficult for ambitious people in our generation to stop and recognize: One thing she really wanted in life was to get married and have kids.

She still needed a job, of course. Her timing on that front—as it was for many Millennials—was unavoidably awful. At Williams, the headlines you'd glimpse on MacBooks in lecture halls were ominous.

"Home prices in some parts of the country are falling. Builders are scaling back. Bubble or not, the biggest housing boom in recent U.S. history is coming to an end," wrote the *Wall Street Journal* in August of 2006, before Miju had even gone to Cameroon.[78] "Now here is the big question: How bad will the aftermath be? At this point, most economists expect a 'soft landing,' a gradual decline that won't derail the nation's economic expansion, now in its fifth year. But there is a good chance they are being too optimistic."

They were. The existence of this kind of article busts the popular myth about the financial crisis: that it came out of nowhere, shocking politicians, bankers, and the public. In reality, signs of distress had been popping up years before the crisis began. The above article ran more than two years before Lehman Brothers famously crashed. And it was already able to identify what would be the cause for the crisis and ensuing recession, which wiped billions of dollars from US GDP and trillions from the stock market: Housing prices had reached a ceiling. People who couldn't afford their mortgages stopped being able to pay them back. This meant that the large financial institutions that lent and traded such subprime mortgages didn't have enough cash either, and collapsed. That only created more panic. Governments bailed out banks across the globe, but that in turn rocked confidence in financial institutions, which led to slashed investment and tumbling consumer activity. It all added up to the Great Recession. Each month on average between October 2008 and April 2009, seven hundred thousand people lost their jobs in America.[79]

Everybody experienced the crisis differently. People lost employment, houses, lives. We still feel the effects today. For a huge swath of our generation, what the crisis meant most concretely was that finding a job felt like walking through thick mud. At its height, one out of every ten people in the labor market was out of a job, and new ones were hard to find. By November 2009, there were 6.2 unemployed people per job opening, up from just 1.6 two years before.[80]

At Williams in 2010, Miju's senior year, awareness of the competition for jobs was fierce. Miju felt she needed to get a corporate job, something that could earn her enough to live in a city. It wasn't that Miju wanted to be a wolf of Wall Street. She used to longboard across campus in sun dresses and had contemplated going into the Peace Corps. It's more that she knew she couldn't take going back to Virginia after graduation, and the only way to not do that was to get a big job. For that, she relied on one of the longstanding docents into the corporate American world. It's a book called *Case in Point*. For anyone who has ever wondered why some of America's best and brightest began to forgo the once-desirable entry-level jobs in government, civil service, the military, teaching, and trades, they need look no further. *Case in Point* shows anyone with an above-average SAT score and an ability to read how to (at least in theory) land a six-figure salaried job at big, profitable, morally questionable consulting firm. Think McKinsey, Bain, BCG—"the big three," as they are known on anxious campuses across the country.

It was senior fall when Miju opened the book. "You know the interviewer is going to ask you why you want to be a consultant," says *Case in Point* breathlessly. "Now this is important: not only should your answer be immediate, but you must also look the interviewer right in the eye.

If you look away, it indicates that you are thinking about the question, and that's enough to end the interview right then and there. You should have given this answer a great deal of thought long before you walked into the interview. While I don't want you to memorize your answer, I do want you to memorize bullet points."

Miju can't remember the exact answer she gave. Looking back, she says she felt like part of the honest answer was that her parents would be so proud to say, "Oh, my daughter is a consultant." Miju was good with statistics. She loved microeconomics. She thought then (and somewhat still does even now) that capitalism could be an economic driver bringing more good to more people. She liked solving problems. That was a plus, because to get a job in consulting, you needed to know how to solve problems very quickly in something called the "case interview."

"In essence, a case interview is a role-playing exercise," *Case in Point* says. It explains that after consulting firm interviewers pose the standard "Why do you want this job?" and "What was your biggest failure?" questions, they go on to present candidates with allegedly real-life business problems that a candidate would, if hired, be tasked with solving on the job. The questions are straightforward but challenging, especially since you are supposed to answer them on the spot. "In Q4, the number-three U.S. wireless carrier slipped further behind its rivals in its number of customers, even as profits rose 35 percent. What do you think is going on?"

Not all of these questions have just one right answer. "A large Japanese electronics company wants to enter the high-end headphones market. Is this a good idea?" What they're supposed to do is provide you with an opportunity to show the interviewer how you think. *Case In Point* outlines the Case Commandments, which involve listening to the question, summarizing it verbally to the interviewer, asking clarifying questions, working the numbers, managing your time, and digesting the interviewer's feedback in a way that shows that on the job, you will be "coachable."

Miju was coachable. She did what career coaches always say to do but nobody ever wants to face: She went into a small room and did a mock interview that was recorded. Later, with an expert, she watched it, analyzed it, and realized she needed to splice some words out of her vocabulary and never ever wear such a colorful shirt to an interview again.

She got one out of the thirty jobs she applied to. (She beat me.) It was more rejection than she'd ever experienced in her entire life. But she still got a job, and that meant she wasn't going back to Virginia. The job she got was good because it was in economics consulting, which sounded interesting. Even better—even though maybe she wasn't necessarily ready to admit this to herself, or rather anyone—the job was very, very good because it was based in San Francisco.

* * *

The Bush era ended the November night Aaron was sitting at a bar in Seattle. He was three or so days from shipping out. Barack Obama had just been elected, and the city felt like it was on fire. People were spilling out of bars and restaurants and onto Pike Place, the fish market where all the tourists go.

"This is our moment. This is our time," said the 47-year-old president-to-be, not a gray hair on his head yet, at his victory speech in Chicago, blaring across cable news TV screens in Seattle. "Where we are met with cynicism, and doubt, and those who tell us that we can't, we will respond with that timeless creed that sums up the spirit of a people: Yes, we can."

That day in Baghdad, fifteen people were killed and dozens were wounded. In one incident, a bomb hidden in a fishmonger's stall detonated and killed seven people, wounding eighteen others. Aaron had been assigned to go to Sinai, the peninsula between Egypt and Israel where a treaty mandated that the U.S. military and other forces ensure free navigation in the Straits of Tiran and the Gulf of Aqaba. He'd been a soldier for over a year by that point, broken down the day after his high school graduation and then built back up again in South Carolina at Fort Jackson, the Army's main basic combat training center, where half of all such training takes place. After training, he'd signed up to go to Afghanistan but was reassigned at the last minute.

That night, he thought about the long journey he had ahead of him to the desert. Soon, they'd fly from Seattle to Maine, Maine to Germany, then to Cairo. They'd take a bus from Cairo to Sharm El Sheikh, the city near their camp on the northern coast of the Red Sea. Through that night drinking, Aaron also worried about Barack Obama. The White people around him were elated. So were the celebrities. So were the chattering classes. "My First Post-Racial Column," read one newspaper article on November 6 in the *Philadelphia Daily News*. "America Begins Its Journey Into a Post-Racial Era," "Closing the Door on Victimhood," said others on the same subject. They were treating Obama like a messiah. Of course the man was smart, of course he was inspiring. Of course he was better than Bush. But by then, at 19, Aaron felt like he had developed a pretty good sense of how America works. He put down his drink.

PART III

THE CUPCAKE ECONOMY

When he was 25 years old, a French aristocrat sailed to the United States in an attempt to understand what was happening in our new country. It was the year 1835, and the Revolution was still in living memory. Europeans looked with fascination across the Atlantic as a new nation came together. The year Alexis de Tocqueville landed on our shores, ready to learn about American living standards, culture, and society, a populist president was settling into office. The economy was expanding rapidly. The Transatlantic slave trade had ended but the population of enslaved Americans stood at over two million. The Trail of Tears—the forced relocation west of one hundred thousand Native Americans—was in full swing. On the back of these phenomena, vast and rich cities were growing. Mass culture in the form of novels, newspapers, magazines, and theater was evolving. It was starting to actually mean something to say something was American.

De Tocqueville found at the core of that definition the notion of *change*. In the book he wrote about us, called *Democracy in America*, he commented frequently and curiously on the American tendency to change. "In the United States, a man carefully builds a dwelling in which to pass his declining years, and he sells it while the roof is being laid," he wrote.[1] "He plants a garden and he rents it out just as he was going to taste its fruits; he clears a field and he leaves to others the care of harvesting its crops. He embraces a profession and quits it."

If that 25-year-old aristocrat were roaming the United States of early May 2011, he would have noticed a greater fervor for change amongst a demographic roughly his age. (De Tocqueville's taste for all black attire along with his fluffy dark haircut, wan face, and trust fund would also very likely have made him feel comfortable in the aesthetic environs of some hipster American enclave like Portland or Williamsburg.) By 2011, the oldest Millennials were hitting 30, and most were in their twenties. This is, very roughly, a stage of life that author Satya Doyle Byock calls "quarterlife" in a book with that same title.

According to Byock, quarterlife is an often-misunderstood period between childhood and "real adulthood." In this period, young adults face a confusing tension between finding stability—jobs, partners, homes—and meaning. Some initially tend more toward seeking stability. They begin adulthood trying to lock down the comforts of home, an income, a partnership. Others look more for meaning early on, searching for connections with others, to figure out who they are, what their pasts mean, how they fit into the world. Regardless of where they begin, at some point in quarterlife, the other of these two needs arises. Stability types begin to feel they lack meaning. Meaning types realize they need some stability. Uncomfortable questions pop up. Those who sought stability might start asking: *Is being a dentist really all there is to life?* Those who sought meaning may wonder: *Sure, smoking pot every day is fun, but why am I still an unpaid intern?* We are often fascinated by people in the other camp. In *Quarterlife*, Byock gives an example of how this plays out: Michelle Obama was a stability type who found meaning. Barack Obama was a meaning type who found stability.[2]

Every contemporary American generation has faced this life stage. And, as de Tocqueville pointed out, Americans have been characterized by a drive for change for a long time. What was unique about the Millennial tour through quarterlife, however, was the sheer amplification of the idea of extraordinary change, the amplified articulation of it. Change had swept America before. But in our time, change became, to use the parlance of the era, a brand.

Barack Obama promised it. We hung posters promoting it on dorm-room cinderblock and first-apartment studio walls. In May of 2011, the recession that came after the financial crisis had been over for two years, but over half of Americans still (incorrectly) thought the economy was either in a recession or, worse, a depression.[3] Culturally, the idea that followed was that to get things back on track, everything would have to change. People made changes to their careers. Startup evangelists turned the word "disruption," an even stronger notion of change, into a business model. Their executive overlords talked about the way "creative destruction" was changing our interactions with the newly arrived "sharing economy." Emerging apps served up a seemingly limitless array of choice in almost any domain—from Airbnb rentals to Ubers to Tinder—allowing us to change houses, places, partners with a mere tap on a screen.

But what change actually means varies. It is a vague term. That's why it's useful, but also why it's dangerous. It can set high expectations higher, making them ever harder to meet. Conceptions of what it actually means for people to change themselves change very quickly. Change can fail. This can all get very theoretical, but if you want to look for one concrete object that helps elucidate not just how fickle change is but also how we lived, felt, and understood a particular manifestation of it in the early 2010s—technological, economic, political, cultural change—there is nothing better to consider than the humble but now nearly extinct BlackBerry.

Like some Millennials, the device traces its roots to the mid-1980s. By the mid-1990s, it was going by the awkwardly pubescent name of "Inter@ctive Pager." Some heavy brand consulting by the same people who came up with the words "Swiffer" and "Dasani" led to a rechristening as the BlackBerry. (An early candidate had been the StrawBerry, but the team felt that word took too long to say for a product that was supposed to evoke the idea of instantaneous communication.[4]) The

BlackBerry got a boost in the wake of September 11, when families who were trying to reach each other found it impossible to connect via standard cell phone calls but could get through on these new devices.[5]

Soon, it was cool. It was the new way to work, the new way to be online without being behind a computer, the new way to instant message—but this time, with an exclusive group of people who had BBM pins. Lindsay Lohan had a BlackBerry. So did Victoria Beckham, Kim Kardashian, and Eva Longoria. Barack Obama clung to his in the months after his victory. "They're going to pry it out of my hands," he joked to a reporter.[6] He fought to keep it, often affixed to his belt, and at least for a while, won. "For a High-Tech President, a Hard-Fought E-Victory," one newspaper wrote. BlackBerry sales were reaching their highest point ever by 2011.[7] That year, Hillary Clinton was photographed on a military plane in sunglasses reading emails, staring at her BlackBerry.

* * *

On the first day of May that year, the top-right red light on Olivia's BlackBerry started blinking like crazy.

She was a junior at Syracuse. Like many Millennials, she found herself a part of the peak in college matriculation in American history, enrolled when that figure hit eighteen million students in 2010, a population nearly the size of Greece and Switzerland combined.[8] She was on one of those college-era dates that are a vague yet hopeful combination of a home-cooked dinner in someone's apartment, studying, and some flirting. By then, she had reached a place where she felt she could get close to people again, her blur phase fading. People close to her knew that Anthony had died in 9/11, but she no longer felt like 9/11 Girl. When people found out and said the inevitable "I'm so sorry" to her, she felt confident enough to exert control over the urge to paint her as a victim.

"Don't be sorry," she got comfortable enough to say, "I'm exactly who I am today because of 9/11."

Olivia decided to cast off the loneliness of high school and make college about friends and about the traditions she was searching for, that she felt like she hadn't had as a child. In large part, she did that through technology. If AIM had brought Olivia close to Anthony, it was her BlackBerry that felt like a torch out of her blur period and toward the sorts of relationships she'd always wanted with her peers. She used it in the way many Millennials (specifically those who could afford the extra $30 per month data charge) did to connect with each other in a time when it felt like everything from computers to politics to the economy to social media was different, untested, and constantly shifting.

Olivia provides a particularly elucidating lens on the way those early days of the mobile-social web changed the way we interacted because she was focusing on making friends just as "friends" had also become a Facebook thing. Her college nights followed a rhythm that many of ours did in the 2010s. It would go like this: She'd pull on skinny jeans and a going-out top. Maybe something from American Apparel. She'd get her Nikon digital camera with obligatory wrist strap for later, for after the pregame when she and her friends would somehow find themselves taking photos in a bathroom mirror sticking their tongues out because that was funny, but also because it made their faces look more angular. They'd get to some party, dance on a table, take out the Nikon or maybe even the BlackBerry with its flash for a quick picture and a Facebook "mupload," the slang of the moment for "mobile upload." (Back when all pictures weren't mobile uploads.) Before she'd leave for the night, Olivia would get BBM pins from the new friends she'd met.

Just as she was refocusing on friendship at the height of the Obama era, Olivia was also figuring out adult dating. Here, change came from the introduction of mobile phones into the mix. Dating apps were arriving, with the internet presenting the illusion of an infinite number of possible partners. "Give me your pin" became a pickup line, and staying in constant touch a staple of dating life. You dated not just in person, but also on your smartphone. The joy you'd feel seeing that plastic piece of tech light up with a text from your boyfriend could almost feel better than sniffing his pheromones. Olivia felt too depressed to date in high school, and as she entered the hot morass of college relationships, she joined her many peers in navigating how to get close to people—and how not to—in a digital age.

Giles was part of Olivia's hunt for tradition and stability. He was a glimpse at what she wanted. When Olivia talked to me about Giles, I was reminded of so many of my own ambiguous but meaningful, short but foundational relationships that I wanted to make work but didn't know how to. Giles represented what Olivia was seeking in an adult partner, but that for reasons of timing and emotional development, technology and sex, she couldn't have. Having a smartphone made having a relationship between them easier, but in some ways, it would also be their undoing. And when Olivia tells me about Giles, I can't help but think of some combination of a Taylor Swift song and words a mourner wrote about Anthony. Anthony, that friend wrote, "had a terrific sense of the ridiculous and a beautiful sense of humor."[9]

So did Giles. What captivated Olivia when she met him was his ability to banter, to keep up with her sass, dish it back. Giles was quick and funny. They'd met on a sort of accidental double date. She'd never intended to call him again. But then the thing that high school Olivia, the girl who never dated, could only have dreamed of happened: Giles called *her*. He was quirky and romantic and willing to open up completely to her. True, real, actual, adult, movie-like romance was what she felt for the first time in her life one night when they strolled the entire campus. Syracuse is so many acres. It began to rain, so they stopped on the stairs of a chapel and paused to look at one another.

It wasn't her own lonely, grieving reflection looking back in a Long Island girl's bedroom mirror. It wasn't someone who pitied her. It wasn't someone she was someone else around. It was Giles looking back at her, seeing this new version of her. She felt at that moment, on the cusp of 19, Obama the president, BlackBerry in her pocket, a sense of change all around her, that she could and she should keep moving along this new path.

They fell into something that felt like dating. They did boyfriend-and-girlfriend things. They rushed fraternities and sororities and got in. They drank and made out in the old party houses of Syracuse. But despite it being the height of the "Facebook Official" age, Olivia and Giles never made it such. They did not have the talk that *defines the relationship*, solidifies it in stone—the 2010s equivalent of wearing someone's letterman jacket. In my haunts, we called that chat the "DTR."

Millennial dating involved a level of ambiguity that outdated fairy-tales didn't prepare us for. Our expectations were off. As constricting as it could be, the short, sharp pathway from courtship to young marriage of our parents' generation once provided a predictable point in quarterlife when Americans broke away from their childhoods and redefined their relationships with themselves, their partners, and their parents. This break is called "differentiation," and it is a crucial step on the way to adulthood. The conditions around people that once basically forced them to differentiate have fallen away. In the past, you had to disconnect from your role as a child because you quickly moved into a home with your husband or wife and had a child yourself. People who don't differentiate can feel overwhelmed. Failing to differentiate can create a sense that it's just "too much" to balance your old life and your new, adult one. It is particularly difficult, Byock explains in *Quarterlife*, for children whose parents died early to differentiate.[10] How do you renegotiate an adult relationship with someone who is no longer around?

I think about this when Olivia talks to me about college and tells me that sometimes she'd walk through a cemetery near her dorm. It had rolling knolls that looked like the English countryside. There were bishops, generals, and judges buried there. Anthony wasn't buried in any cemetery. All she had of him by then were photos that already in 2011 looked like the nineties throwbacks that they were: Anthony in a bright pink T-shirt and checkered shorts. Anthony, thin and angular, in a ridiculously fat, patterned tie. Anthony in high-tops and thick, white tube socks. That conspicuous absence could only have weighed on someone trying to figure out who she was going to be, her relationship with her past, how she would become an adult.

Part of having an adult relationship is telling the other person how you feel. That's one of Olivia's biggest regrets from Syracuse. She never told Giles about how he'd shifted in her mind from being just some guy to someone for whom she had fallen "madly, crazy, head-over-heels" in love. She learned her silence had been a mistake one night at a party at his frat. The frat was cool, exclusive. That spring the songs they played at parties were uplifting in an ironic kind of way: "Party in the U.S.A.," "OMG," "Your Love Is My Drug," "Nothin' on You." Inside, she danced to them with her friends. She was a little tipsy, triumphant, and sweaty. She wasn't from the coolest sorority and felt lucky to be invited to Giles's, lucky to have an in with him. She danced in that sort of self-aware way where you know people are watching you, might be coming up to you, might be taking pictures of you to be posted to social media. More importantly, you know there's someone around in the massive crowd of dancing 20-year-olds you know you'll eventually bump into but who you want to have already seen you before you see them, to impress them by being nonchalantly fun and pretty and popular.

Olivia broke out of this warmth for one minute. She turned around.

And there was Giles.

But Giles was making out with someone else.

That someone else was *Kennedy*.

Kennedy lived on Giles's floor. Kennedy was pretty. She was cool. And seeing her kiss Giles made Olivia's heart freeze. In moments like this, one wonders how that Robyn song about dancing on your own can be so real. *I should have known,* the internal monologue beat as the happy 2010s music blared around her. *I'm not pretty enough. I'm not special enough. Of course he wouldn't choose me. Like, of course he wouldn't choose me. I'm in Gamma Phi Beta. Nobody wants to date us.* She left the party, alone into the warm night.

A problem with many of our Millennial relationships was, like wars not formally declared, they never officially started and so ended horribly. How we communicate influences what we become, and how we began to communicate then was in infinite, scrolling mobile conversations that never really had a definitive start or end. It was easy to keep the drama going; it was also hard to stop it. You see this in Olivia's own response to that night, which should have ended when she walked away but instead continued on the internet on her phone.

They started BBMing.

"You were kissing Kennedy."

"?"

"I get that she lives on your floor. I get that she's pretty. But like. What the fuck?"

(. . .)

Those three dots—indicating "Giles is typing"—can be some of the most stressful symbols in the orthographic world.

"We're not exclusive," Giles wrote. "We're not exclusive. We never said we were exclusive."

If they weren't exclusive, what did the strolls mean? The long chats? The nights in his room. How did he have so much time for both her and for someone—who knows how many someones—else? She felt so stupid, stung, rejected.

"Alright," she wrote to Giles. "Whatever."

But she was feeling so much worse than "alright, whatever."

Tight dress, high heels, she walked home, went to sleep, waited for summer to come and then be over.

It was around this time that the second part of Olivia's plan to fix her life started to falter. It turns out, the field of forensic anthropology is very depressing, particularly as it relates to September 11. Even now, some 40 percent of the people who were killed in the World Trade Center have never been identified. Their families are certain they died, but they still have no definitive proof, nothing to bury properly. That's after decades of excavation and recovery, after an entirely new skyscraper has been built on the site.

Even today, a team at the New York City medical examiner's office continues its morbid task of taking samples of unidentified human remains from the destruction, mostly bone, often the size of Tic Tacs, crushing them up into powder, and trying to extract what DNA they can. This is then compared against items families gave to the team. It's been so long that many families have forgotten whether it was a toothbrush or a T-shirt or some other object that they'd handed over, that was last touched by the dead nearly twenty-five years ago. As the medical examiner's office continues its work, a harsh reality is settling in, too: some people were simply incinerated, turned to dust beyond recognition. Before, it used to be that hundreds of victims were identified each year. These days, the average is less than one.

I think about Olivia learning these facts at Syracuse around this time. I see her grasping the reality. The more she learns about forensic anthropology, the more she realizes it's probably going to be impossible to find a trace of her father again.

When Olivia is being very hard on herself, she meditates on a theory she has about why she sometimes has difficulties with relationships.

It's like what happens to celebrities who freeze developmentally at the time they get famous. Parts of Olivia's emotional development seemed to pause on that day in sixth grade orchestra. Giles defrosted her love response, she says, and it manifested as it would not for Olivia the college student, but as it would for that girl sitting second chair in orchestra, before the kids started getting pulled out of class. That girl didn't tell boys how she felt. That girl feared if she said what she thought, the guy would go run and tell his friends and all of them would taunt her.

After Giles, Olivia says she grew *loose with her heart*. There were a lot of guys. She started looking for a future; I think this may be when her twin plans to fix her life morphed into just one. She wanted a husband, a family, a white picket fence. And she felt she needed to search for it fast.

Even so, there are memories she keeps of times that year walking through the night, late, maybe even dangerously so, back to Giles's place. Even after the kiss with Kennedy. It was messy. The relationship never began officially, and it also never ended. Giles got a girlfriend, and Olivia thinks she was studying abroad. Olivia would go over. They'd sit on the couch and watch *Runaway*, that 30-minute short film by Kanye West a certain type of Obama-voting White guy once thought was the most sophisticated piece of art ever to hit YouTube. Olivia would just sit with him. Platonic, in the most forgiving definition of the term. She would sit there and trace with her finger the tattoo on his collarbone. It said "courage."

And then it was 2011.

Giles stayed in the back of her mind as a vision of what she wanted, even as she went on dates with other guys. That's where she was on the first of May, on a date with some other guy, trying to make a fantasy of her future happen. But there would also be these jolts back to the old her. The reminders that as hard as she wanted to change, she still had her past to reckon with. A jolt came that night, blinking on her phone.

"Liv," one of the messages said. "You must be so happy."

"We fucking got him!"

"They did it."

She heard explosions outside, what sounded like rioting in the streets. All the while, her BlackBerry flashed again and again. The explosions Olivia heard were fireworks. Students around Syracuse—and across the entire country—were spilling out into the streets, singing, dancing, and drinking in the late spring night. Barack Obama had just announced they'd killed Osama bin Laden.

A story about Millennials is that our childhoods ended on September 11. I don't know if that's true for everybody. What seems truer by both demographics and lived experience is that a shot of adulthood bolted through our veins the night we found out Osama bin Laden was killed. A key adult experience is being able to grapple with contradictions, moving beyond storybook dichotomies of the world in which we always feel either good or bad, right or wrong. Finding out about the death of the mastermind of the September 11 attacks was one of the first mass experiences Millennials had of holding such a contradiction: feeling the joy of an enemy defeated combined with the uncomfortable truth that those around us (and maybe even we) were celebrating another human being's death.

It felt like a sign of change. It had been a decade since the attacks, and finally there was a trophy. Obama had made clear since 2002 that even if he opposed the Iraq war—he'd called it "dumb" and "rash"—he wanted to get bin Laden.[11] Obama's prospects for a second term were looking shaky in 2011, but that night they solidified. That was perhaps clearest on social media, which then felt like the bearer of a hopeful future, where a serious matter of geopolitical import could spread swiftly beyond the control of traditional gatekeepers.

"It just ripped across Facebook," one 20-year-old in Washington, D.C., told the *New York Times*.[12] This marked a change to the old ways of getting news only after the press briefing was over, on cable or in print. Now, you could watch it unfold in real time. Analysts noted a Twitter explosion when the news broke, with the highest rate of sustained posts ever. In just a few hours, a Facebook page called "Osama bin Laden is Dead" garnered over four hundred thousand fans. It was only an after-thought at the time what else this type of user-generated activity could mean, that any information, true or false, could spread so quickly and affect people's behavior. That same 20-year-old told the *Times* that for the first time ever, his newsfeed, rather than just informing him, "spurred me into action." He grabbed an American flag and headed out into the streets of D.C., where streams of people were heading toward the White House. They were heading to bars, parties, lawns, and squares across the rest of the country, too. They were, in large part, Millennials.

"It feels as though that arc in American history has come to a close," another 20-year-old told a news reporter in Los Angeles, comparing bin Laden's killing to the final installment of the *Harry Potter* film series, set to come out a few weeks later.[13] "It marks the end of our childhood."

It's hard to find a more uncomfortably Millennial quote than one that compares the ending of the *Harry Potter* franchise to the death of Osama bin Laden. And yet this quote is also incredibly revealing about the degree to which bin Laden and, more broadly, Islamic terrorism, had been cast in the story Millennials were telling about themselves. There was an evil force out there, and the villain behind it had been vanquished. While nobody was so naïve as to believe that terrorism ended with the death of bin Laden, it raised hopes of a new stability. That failed to materialize.

Ironically, the stability of our heroes has failed to persist as well. Even J. K. Rowling, who many Millennials once idolized, has become a pariah—less a Dumbledore, more a Voldemort. That's because she has grown oddly obsessed with using her platform to focus on our tiny—half a percent of adults in Britain and the US—population of people who identify as transgender, who are really just trying to live their own private lives. This, in itself, has had fallout. I remember conservative Christians at my school saying their parents didn't want them reading *Harry Potter*. Now for their children, my liberal friends say the same thing. Across the board, little has gone the way we expected.

* * *

In the weeks ahead of the bin Laden killing, the percentage of Americans who disapproved of the job Obama was doing as president had ticked above those who approved of it.[14] Even after getting a big bump from the raid, a majority of Americans still disapproved of his handling of the economy.[15] That did not bode well for his prospects for a second term, already beclouded by chants from members of the far-right Tea Party about the "death panels" that would supposedly arise out of the Affordable Care Act and about Obama's birth certificate. Said document would allegedly prove he was not an American citizen and therefore not entitled to his position. (Obama was born on US soil.) American presidents face an odd paradox. A near-majority of Americans think "improving the economy is something that the president can do a lot about,"[16] despite the fact that an *overwhelming* majority also approve of having a free-market economy—a system where, by design, politicians hold little direct power to change tax law and interest rates, let alone prices or the unemployment rate.

And that rate was dire. At the time, many Millennials were entering the workforce with the labor market in its worst place since the first of us were born in the early 1980s.[17] While 2009 graduates were sending out cover letters and resumes into the Monster.com abyss, the overall unemployment rate was at a peak of 10 percent. In 2011, it was still sitting at 9 percent. But it was worse for young people, at one point between those years hitting nearly 20 percent. Even when job growth did start to improve, albeit at a glacial place, a lot of the roles were just temp positions or their cousin, "gig" jobs, that promised flexibility on one hand but precarity on every other limb. That type of economic struggle early in our adult years had lasting financial and psychological effects.

The first time Aaron thought about the recession, he was working at a skid factory. Skids are like pallets but cheaper because while they have the same slatted, planked tops, they have no bottoms. Making them was an awful job. All Aaron—big reader, fast talker, smart guy—did all day was put pieces of wood together. He'd see other job openings, but they'd either go to people who had college degrees or to people who had years of experience. At that point, he had neither. It led to that feeling many Millennials will remember from the aftermath of the recession, when it felt like realizing your professional goals was the same as knocking on doors trying to sell magazine subscriptions nobody wanted to buy. You'd apply to a job and nobody would ever get back to you. Job sites felt like desolate echo chambers. Everyone in our cohort was competing for the same too-few jobs, the largest generation in history in the worst economy since the Great Depression.

Making skids was the last thing Aaron thought he'd do after his years in the Army National Guard. He'd wanted a full-time Army job. When he returned from Egypt, he started working part-time helping the Guard run courses in Ohio for soldiers before they shipped out. He taught them how to use huge machine guns and how to check vehicles for improvised explosive devices, homemade bombs insurgents in Iraq were using to kill coalition forces. But Aaron kept bucking up against an institutional problem he hadn't foreseen when he enlisted: The Army and the Army National Guard have different hierarchies and hiring needs. It is very difficult to turn a part-time career in the Army National Guard into a full-time, highly paid, prestigious career in the active-duty branch of the Army as most people understand it.

The journey is one that winds through meeting active-duty recruiters; completing a DD Form 368, which requests a conditional release from the National Guard; getting permission from your superiors; submitting a new oath of enlistment as well as the entirety of your military record; and then waiting for your command's decision. Much of that decision is based on what skills the Army needs and where. But it's also political: No branch wants to surrender staff to another and drop numbers unless there is a very good reason.

At the time Aaron had first enlisted, there might have been a very good reason. When the recruiter was making that house call to his parents in the final years of the Bush presidency, unemployment rates were low, America's youth had many options outside of fighting in foreign wars, and the Army was hungry for recruits. But after the recession, it was the opposite. Young people couldn't get jobs and were rushing to join the military. Suddenly the National Guard was exceeding its recruiting goals, and the Army was hitting records. Demand for Aaron was low.

So he continued on in the National Guard part-time, waiting to see if he might get the call to let him move into more stable, full-time work in the Army. Meanwhile, he kept up the cadence of his Guard obligations: a drill weekend a month and a two-week training in the summer, year after year. And he kept building those skids. Skid after skid after skid.

There was a way to beat the repetitive boredom of the Great Recession. It was at a duplex house on the north side of town, on a side street not far from the Burger Hut where Aaron had worked in high school. The house was a deep brownish red, with white trim and three floors, a porch typical of those in that part of the Midwest. It was built in 1916 and sold in 2005 for $60,000, a price still typical of the region that will undoubtedly shock anybody who has hoped to buy a house on either American coast over the past five decades. By 2011, the duplex was looking pretty run down. As far as Aaron and his friends were concerned, this was almost better because it gave the impression that aside from causing a fire or an explosion, they could pretty much get away with anything else inside without worrying about getting into too much trouble.

Aaron and his friends used it as a party house. The rich kids who quadrennially parachuted into Alliance by way of Mt. Union—where tuition, room, and board fees for their years of soft and pleasant study could buy one of those duplex houses three times over—had their quaint fraternities. The buildings gleamed with perfectly manicured lawns on the frat row facing the college on South Union Avenue. Meanwhile, Aaron and his friends had the duplex. It became their sacred space, their *Cheers* bar, their *Friends* apartment. They met there most nights, weathering the storms of working-class labor that grew ever more isolating as they clocked in and out and in and out in the second decade of the new millennium.

They called themselves "The Circle." There were eight or so of them, and they came to think of themselves as a makeshift family. All were in their midtwenties, trying to figure out how to do life and work in the sort of place that out-of-towners would arrogantly classify as "left behind." They were all linked by somebody who grew up with somebody who knew someone else from around the block. There was Brittany, for instance. Aaron originally knew her as this blonde girl who used to run around the playground at Liberty Elementary. Her parents bowled in the same league as his parents. She was a cook and loved trying out recipes for The Circle; her chicken alfredo was legendary. Sometimes, Brittany's sister Dawn would come to the duplex, too. But she was a goody-goody. There was Ethan, Aaron's best friend at the time, with whom he went all the way back to childhood. There was Daniel and there was Owen, who sometimes came around with his kids; they called Aaron "Uncle Dave" for some reason. Aaron went along with it.

Most importantly for the purposes of the duplex, there was Ronnie. A proprietor of the property, his parents lived next door but let them have the run of the place. Ronnie was lighthearted and carefree. He'd do anything for anybody. He was this big, fluffy White guy who liked pot and decorated his room with Bob Marley posters. When dumb shit in The Circle would happen, he'd look at Aaron and go, "Fuckin' White people." But not in the smarmy way people who said they were "post-racial" would say things like that. Ronnie called out bullshit. He got how things worked.

The members of the Circle had jobs like Aaron's. Ronnie worked at a factory for Quikrete, the largest manufacturer of packaged concrete in the United States. Ronnie packed the concrete into bags, the kind you might buy at a hardware store. He distracted himself from the work with his Mustang and his bowling. He also had a dog, Lunchbox.

Nearly every evening in the era from 2009 to around 2012, the meat and bones of Obama's first term, The Circle would gather at the duplex. They'd wait until all of their friends had clocked out from their shitty, repetitive jobs, and then the beer and the liquor would show up from somewhere. That was how they got the night started.

They kept it going with pills.

"Sharing is caring," was their policy. They usually used Percocet. Most of them had their own ways to get pills, connections with people who knew people who knew dealers. But if any one person had too many pills, or another had too few, they'd share. That's what makeshift families did, didn't they?

It felt freeing. The pills were a release from the pressures of the present and past. Aaron thinks of his championship high school basketball game as one of the best memories of his life and had played sports for years. But he also struggled with his weight as a kid. He never felt like he had the self-esteem of a skinny person. When he took pills, that uncomfortable feeling vanished. He became the life of the party. His worries and cares didn't matter. His shyness around new people—not evident, but deeply felt—went away. All of it went away when he got high. People thought he was fun, and he wanted to be. He was.

Some nights, they'd get started in Ronnie's end of the duplex, then walk down the three steps and back up to their parents' end of the house to watch UFC fights. The twins' parents were kind and welcoming, their mom the nicest lady and their dad a great time. They'd watch the fights and then go back to Ronnie's, finishing out the night. On weekends, the parties were bigger, and they acted like the crazy, stupid twentysomethings they were. It was beer pong, keg stands. It was college minus the classes and the assholes.

Occasionally, they'd hit the town. There was a bar called Chives they liked to go to. Ronnie would take them out of town to country bars. He didn't even like country music, but he liked going out to the bars to drink, to meet people, to do random stuff. Sometimes when they were out, Ronnie would start line dancing wildly, talking to anybody who'd open up to him.

America's opioid epidemic arose in the late 1990s, relatively early in the life of the Millennial generation. Between 1990 and 2000, deaths from opioid overdoses rose 2,142 percent.[18] The leading cause of death in Americans between the ages of 1 and 44 is "unintentional injuries," a category which includes motor vehicle crashes, falls, and "unintentional poisonings," the very clinical-sounding term that includes drug overdoses. Before 2011, most accidental deaths came from traffic incidents; overdoses caused no more than a sliver. The relationship flipped that year, and now the leading cause of death in young Americans is overdose by an overwhelming margin.[19] Our country has faced drug epidemics before. What stands out about the current one is how long it has lasted. The heroin and crack epidemics of the 1960s and 1980s loom large in the minds of Americans, likely in part due to their associations with a rise in violent crime.[20] But each of those epidemics peaked and declined in the span of a decade.[21] The opioid crisis has so far dragged on for the entire adult lifespan of our generation.

A team of Harvard researchers connects this long duration to a factor key in Aaron's stories about using opioids: friends. Every time I interviewed him about his drug use, either in person or on the phone, our conversations were always accompanied by stories about friends from The Circle or other parts of his social life. Always. The person who gave him a pill for the first time was his best friend. (Studies show that half of people who have misused opioids first got them from friends or family.) The people Aaron used with were close to him. The people Aaron eventually dealt pills to weren't random people on the street; they were friends.

That selling felt benign. It felt like giving the people he knew something they needed, paying the favor forward. The money was pretty good, and he'd use it mostly to pay for the alcohol he brought to The Circle. A friend would charge him $40 a pill for a supply of Perc 30s. (On the street, the drugs aren't usually actual Percocet, that blend of oxycodone and acetaminophen. They're usually just 30-milligram doses of the painkiller oxycodone.) After paying $40 per pill, Aaron would go on to sell them for $60. He'd usually get deliveries on the first and fifteenth of each month; shortly after is when his phone would ring, with friends asking for "little favors." He'd sell maybe twenty a month. So usually, his bottom line came to about $400. That might seem like small potatoes, particularly if you work a well-paying job and live in an expensive city. But remember that to this day, you can buy a house like the duplex in Alliance for $60,000. Two eggs, toast, and coffee cost just $2.50 at the Burger Hut. Now that Aaron is a drug and addiction counselor, now that he hears peoples' excuses about using in his professional life, he remembers the justifications he made himself. The medical one: "I figured it's a prescription pill." The harmless one: "Nobody's getting hurt, you know?" The self-interested one: "It was just an opportunity for me to make money."

These social connections prolonged the crisis. The Harvard research team found in a 2024 study that the economy for opioid drugs in America evolved into what is called a "thick market." Such markets are so dense with buyers and sellers that they have "spillover effects" that increase demand. These effects include easier access to goods and normalization of use. The researchers found that such spillover is responsible for somewhere between 84 percent and 92 percent of deaths from opioids between 1990 and 2020. What's more, they found a relationship between Facebook connectivity and opioid deaths. Communities with greater connectivity on the social platform saw additional opioid deaths.[22]

This sort of research helps us better understand the opioid crisis not merely as one of supply but also of demand driven by social forces. The Harvard study is part of a broader trend we've seen over our lifetimes of experts and policymakers focusing less on the unhelpful narrative that drug use represents a failing of the individual and more on broader social and structural shortcomings. An idea that was popularized in 2015, during the time that Aaron was using, was that opioid overdoses represented "deaths of despair." The understanding was that economic misery, a weakened labor movement, the empowered corporation, and a greedy health-care industry were all contributing to this new epidemic. Across the country, states in even the most conservative corners began passing "Good Samaritan" laws, protecting people from criminal penalties if they called emergency services to help someone overdosing on opioids.[23] Dramatic newspaper articles splashed stories with photos of young Millennials under a headline popular from local front pages to the national press: "The New Face of Addiction."

Those "new faces of addiction" shown were, almost without exception, White. In an analysis of 100 randomly selected articles about opioids published between 2001 and 2011 in national newspapers, researchers found Black and Latino users tended to be portrayed as criminals in such coverage while White suburban users were portrayed as "victims of over-prescription or people struggling with physical or existential pain."[24] It's part of a cycle in the American drug economy documented by the authors of a book called *Whiteout*. As far back as 1898, when Bayer marketed heroin as a groundbreaking, safe, and effective treatment for pain, pharmaceutical companies have used coded language to market new drugs to rich White consumers. Treatment for their eventual misuse is understanding and gentle, until the patents run out—at which point the once groundbreaking, experimental drugs move into poorer communities, which have historically been communities of color. When the drugs reach there, treatment grows harsher and punishment for use turns criminal.

By and large, liberal White Americans want to get things right when it comes to talking about race. But there is a world of difference between wanting to get it right and doing so, especially when the subject is beyond complicated. And so when I talk to Aaron, I try not to be that White interlocutor who goes, "Right, so. How does this all connect to your views on race? I'm asking because I *get* it." I try to let him lead. What I do know is that Aaron's views on race and drugs are nuanced. Most of his friends in The Circle were White. He has a large family that has been Black in America for a long time. Statistically speaking, in 2011 he was in a minority of Black users of opioids. That would change.

* * *

On bad days after the recession, Justin would look across the street outside the strip mall where he worked as a martial arts instructor. There was a Starbucks on the other side of the six lanes of traffic, just a few hundred yards away from the Jack in the Box he'd walked to the day he met up with Tara the summer after high school. That summer felt like an economic lifetime ago. He was living and working in a tough industry in a tough economy. People in martial arts often note that their business is built on disposable income. As Justin rose up the ranks, he could feel the broader market's squeeze on those last two words. It created a feeling of stasis, wheels spinning in loose dirt.

The lazy hot take in the 2010s was that Millennials were professionally fickle. To this day, if you type in "Millennial job" on Google, one of the most frequent next words the predictive results will suggest for you is "hopping." There was an onslaught of surveys, reports, and research probing why our generation just kept changing jobs, with a common subtext that we were disloyal. The truth is that younger people, no matter their generation, tend to change jobs more often than older workers. Millennials actually did so less than Gen X, in fact.[25] What's more, Millennials didn't have a lot of jobs to choose from. The unemployment rate for young workers had hit that 19 percent figure in the years after the recession. That means about one out of every five young people looking for a job could not find one.

And many of the Millennials who did have jobs were actually *obsessed* with them. We were workaholics. A survey of five thousand full-time employees from the 2010s found that Millennials were more likely than other generations to agree to statements such as "I don't want others to think I am replaceable," "I want to show complete dedication to my company and job," "I feel guilty for using my paid time off."[26] Nearly half of Millennials said they wanted to be seen as "martyrs" by their bosses, compared with 39 percent of Gen Xers and 32 percent of Boomers. It's easy to connect this to how hard it was for us to get our jobs to begin with and how tenuous they felt in the post-recession economy. Beyond that, this obsession was connected with our identities. LinkedIn and Facebook made our jobs even more central to how we thought people saw us, to the stories we told about ourselves. Even today, 48 percent of Millennials report that our jobs say a lot about who we are as people, compared with just 41 percent for Gen Z.[27] And if we were our jobs, we were that much more emotionally affected by a job market with limited growth by the ups and downs of employment writ large.

That contributed to bad workdays for Justin, and for the millions of other Millennials trying to jump-start our careers. The martial arts industry is straightforward, but the business model is harsh. Barriers to entry are low. You need a relatively large space—such as a strip-mall store front—some equipment, liability insurance, and a few instructors. Instructors are the expensive part. It hurt Justin to tell the part-time teachers at White Dragon that he didn't have enough students to give them more hours. Competition is also fierce. Academies are always popping up around the country. There are more than forty-four thousand now.[28] Cash flow is tough in any economy, let alone the one we had in 2011. People are always tempted to quit after a few lessons, so you have to pull out the stops to entice them to stay: package deals, personal training. Justin saw older students quit when their rent went up or their own work hours got cut. Parents ended lessons for younger students and didn't really want to talk about why. It hurts to see someone stop something you know is good for them.

Justin would think about his own career progression. White Dragon is a small empire of seven academies across California's San Diego and Riverside counties. The schools are run by a tight-knit group of guys, and Justin had made it in with them. In one of the proudest moments of his adult life, they'd promoted him to assistant chief instructor. He'd been aiming for the job for a while, a position that meant moving into the upper levels of the organization. It was a promotion the heads of each of the eight schools and the owner, Master Fisher, had to agree to, and they surprised him one winter at their annual banquet at a Chinese restaurant called Jasmine Seafood Restaurant & Express in Kearny Mesa. Dozens of people were there, but only a handful knew about the promotion before they announced it in front of everyone. That was a high.

Justin wasn't blind, though. He knew he'd made a gamble on this life. It was a dream job for the kind of boy who grew up in the 1990s watching *Power Rangers* and playing *Mortal Kombat*, but he wasn't a boy anymore. He'd find himself thinking about what else he could do in life if he weren't working at White Dragon. He'd gradually trailed out of community college to the point where a friend told him he had to stop saying he'd get his degree because he'd been saying it for years yet hadn't. He wanted to be successful; he also saw reality. He was a dude in suburban San Diego without a bachelor's. He'd see that Starbucks across the street and think it was the only other place that might hire him. And Justin didn't want to be a barista.

What he wanted to be was with Tara. They had moved into a neighborhood called Bay Park, gotten their first rental apartment together. If the lighting was just right and you squinted hard enough, you could see down to the water. Their relationship had progressed faster than those of most of their friends. Really early, they got a joint bank account. From that point forward, their salary differential became obvious. Tara moved from Campland to a job at the airport to one at a financial services company. With the exception of just a few weeks when she was between jobs, Justin tells me she's "always made more money than me at every job she's ever worked."

That speaks to a change in our Millennial relationships. In a growing number of heterosexual partnerships, the woman makes more than the man.[29] It's now the case in about 10 percent of straight marriages. This shift challenges notions, outdated but rooted millennia deep, of the man as the provider. It strikes at a unique, daresay aggressive, American vision of masculinity that scholars trace back to the origin story of the nation. It started with the image of the rough-and-tumble American independence fighter breaking away from what was portrayed as the effete British aristocrat.[30] "Will you tell me how to prevent luxury from producing effeminacy, intoxication, extravagance, vice, and folly?"

John Adams once wrote in a letter to Thomas Jefferson.[31] No matter the time period, the fear always tends to be of some other force or people coming and taking control of American masculinity, revealing it to be inadequate. It could be the British, the indoor factory jobs of the Industrial Revolution (as opposed to supposedly more masculine work outside in the fields), the foreign ways of immigrants, the presumed failure of masculinity in gay men. More recently, deeply insecure men have taken things like the rise of feminism or the rejection of the gender binary itself as threats to their masculinity. (Even though they, of course, have no impact on their manhood whatsoever.) This insecurity explains why such men respond in reactionary ways: voting for alt-right politicians. Seeking out "trad wives." Listening to sad, angry podcasters. American men throughout history have been lured into a constant battle to prove their masculinity, for no other reason than culturally it feels like they should.

I get the sense when Justin and I speak that any insecurities he might have had about his salary differential with Tara were compensated for on the martial arts mat, where he spent his days beating the shit out of other men. That was the place Justin—salary differential aside—could eke out an identity as a professional, a partner, a provider, and a man. So it seemed only natural that work was the place he decided to propose.

Justin kept the ring hidden in the bottom of his snowboarding boot for three months. In the meantime, he concocted a plan to surprise Tara.

White Dragon proudly identifies itself as one of the largest and oldest lion dance groups in the county. Lion dances are those performances you'll see at Lunar New Year celebrations, where a giant animal mask and a long stream of a body flutter around colorfully. Lion dancing is good training for kung fu. It's a workout. The front dancer holds the heavy, multicolored face mask. With giant, blinking eyes accented with faux fur, the masks look a bit like a Technicolor version of the face of Falkor, the dragon from *The NeverEnding Story*. The back dancer—called the tail—hunches over, marching in step with the dancer in front, sometimes even carrying that person on their shoulders to emulate a very tall lion standing on its hind legs. Drums and cymbals are the soundtrack.

By May 4, 2011, Justin had done hundreds of lion dance performances. He even coached the team. Around Lunar New Year, they'd do upwards of forty shows in the span of two weeks. Tara had seen many. The idea was that she wouldn't suspect anything all too unusual at the end of the day when Justin invited her inside the Clairemont branch of White Dragon to watch a lion dance routine practice. It was a simple one. Two lions, four instructors, one drummer banging out a rhythm that sounded like heartbeat. One lion was green. The other white. Justin was the tail of the white one.

They danced across the padded red floor of the studio in front of a huge mirror in which Justin could see Tara's reflection. She stood watching politely in a simple, gray, low-slung T-shirt, her pretty brunette hair tied back in a ponytail, bangs swept behind her left ear. It was the day after her birthday; she had just turned 24.

The white lion cantered for a few beats, facing the green lion. Then it turned, swinging first a left leg then a right leg, a left and a right, so that every few beats it moved closer and closer to Tara. The beat of the drum picked up, the lion kicked and then raised its head. The beating accelerated more so that it sounded like galloping footsteps. The head raised one, two, three, four times, eyes blinking in a way that was almost scary. Then with six beats of the drum, the white lion raised its head, inches from Tara's face.

It opened its mouth, and a red scroll tumbled down, sort of like a tongue.

From behind, Justin flung off the costume and leapt forward toward Tara, lunging down on one knee with a box in his hand.

*

They paid for the wedding themselves. It was at the Soledad Club, on a hill in Pacific Beach with a view of Mission Bay in a space owned by the city of San Diego. Justin's mother sewed all the bridesmaid dresses. They got a deal on booze from Jimbo's liquor store, a place down the street in Clairemont that Justin had been going to with his dad since he was a kid. His dad would get a six-pack, he'd get a candy and a soda. For the wedding, Jimbo's sold them some high-quality stuff for as little as $9 a bottle. People they knew pitched in. Justin stayed at his friend's house the night before so he could do that old-fashioned thing of not seeing the bride the morning of the wedding day. He wrote his vows that night—they came easily for him—and then got up in the morning to set up the tables and chairs at the Soledad Club with his groomsmen. Over the course of the day, friends and family stopped by to say hello, the groomsmen got ready, a flask of whiskey may or may not have been passed around.

It was a hot day in San Diego. It was the season when Santa Ana winds from the Mojave Desert push up and then tumble down the mountains of California's coastal ranges, spreading heat across the cities where lots of people live and then outward to the sea.

The ceremony began in the 4 o'clock hour. It took place outside, under a white arbor, amidst trees and succulents. The groom and groomsmen wore black suits with ties and boutonnière roses in different colors. They looked so young, they might have been going to senior prom. Beneath their suits, they wore superhero T-shirts: Batman, Captain America. Justin was Superman. The bridesmaids wore knee-length dresses in gold, red, orange, and maroon.

"What's the next step?" Justin kept thinking as the ceremony started, as he stood there in front of everyone in the hall, as Tara walked down the aisle. "Don't say something weird. Don't look weird. Don't mess up. Make sure she looks great."

She did.

And Justin didn't mess anything up. The ceremony went smoothly. Afterward, the party moved upstairs for the reception. Justin and Tara were the first of their friends to start dating, the first to move in together, the first to get married. Their first dance was to the acoustic version of "Everlong" by the Foo Fighters. They thought about that concert they'd been to on a date in 2005, which already seemed like a long time ago, now that they were married.

* * *

In 2011, Miju started crying in Yoga Tree.

Through a combination of hard work and good luck, she'd established the beginnings of an adult life in San Francisco. But she was going through something that a lot of us dealt with in our quarterlife interludes: the imbalance between the professional sphere of her life and the personal one. Her professional life was finally starting to click into place. She'd made some big changes and was beginning to reap the rewards. But in her personal life, she was still figuring out how to navigate a big shift. It's one that more Millennials have been grappling with in recent years as norms have begun to evolve: whether or not she should be in an open relationship.

After graduating from college, Miju had moved into an apartment in the Castro. She knew what that meant. The movie *Milk* came out not long before. She was living up the hill on 17th Street "in this ugly, ugly apartment building" that she decorated with Ikea furniture. Her rent was $1,100, which felt like a lot, and she shared the place with a college friend's friend from high school and another woman. Still, Miju had her own bathroom and was fond of this place, the first apartment of her real, actual, employed adulthood.

"You're living in the Castro," her mother said. She had come with her to San Francisco to help with the move-in. "This means you're never going to meet a man."

That point was reiterated by the fact that the day Miju moved to San Francisco was the middle of Pride weekend. Same-sex marriage was still banned in the state and across much of the country, but campaigners were working on it, making the point that there really was no difference between a gay relationship and a straight one. That morning, some two hundred people had gathered on the top of Twin Peaks, one of the highest points in the city limits, to put together pink pieces that formed a massive, rose-colored triangle. It was visible for miles around, even through the fog that blanketed the city.

San Francisco is always in some state of metamorphosis. When Miju arrived, that process was happening on steroids. The city was transitioning from a desktop-oriented to a smartphone-oriented tech epicenter. The year 2010 was Uber's first summer in the city—it was still called UberCab then. Employees demonstrated in May what it might look like to use software to order a taxi to an audience of around two hundred people at an "app showcase." Apps still needed showcases then. Most people looked at them then and expected not unicorns—a term coined around the time for companies valued at $1 billion but still not listed on a stock exchange—but gimmicky nothings with about as much utility as might be offered by the "I am T-Pain" app. That one let users transmogrify their voices using the clang of auto-tune.

I know about San Francisco's changing atmosphere then because I was in the city that summer, too. I arrived the same month as Miju. I got a job at a newspaper and was driving around the streets looking for stories in an old, white *San Francisco Chronicle* company car. I wouldn't intersect with Miju yet, but I would, soon, sort of.

If the myth of the job-for-life died for Aaron's family in southeast Ohio in the early 2000s, it fell a decade later for Miju in one of her first few days on the job as a consultant. She was meeting downtown with one of the guys who worked at her firm. She asked him for some career advice.

"This is not a job you stay in," he said.

That wasn't what Miju had been expecting. Consulting had been the plan. She'd left Virginia, gone to college, almost died of malaria, mastered *Case in Point*, expanded her professional wardrobe from two suits to more. Wasn't that how adult working life began, continued, carried on?

A type A person by nature, Miju set that thought aside for the moment. She threw herself into the job. At first, she told herself she was lucky to be paid to think about things like how to mitigate the costs of the damages her clients would have to pay in penance for price fixing. On other days, she would research topics such as the different sorts of plastic resins companies used in televisions. But as she settled in, Miju would sometimes glance around her and see that the youngest and smartest and most interesting people in the city weren't working in consulting. They were working on things that looked like they could change the world, things like Google Docs and Maps and Facebook Search. It didn't take long to notice they were having more fun, doing cooler stuff, most certainly working less, and, in the meantime making a lot more money than she was as a consultant, doing some job she had been told she wasn't supposed to stay in. Miju realized she had to move into tech.

In the aftermath of the Great Recession, the world of technology gained a savior-like sheen. Tech was supposed to do all the things we wanted, but faster, better, and more cheaply. Working in the industry had become a dream for the more corporately minded after working on Wall Street took on the grubby stain of the financial crisis. Yet the climb into that world—which many of us forgot was and is filled with its own fair share of grubby companies—was not glamorous for the Millennials who wanted in. Miju had a lot to learn. Early in her time in San Francisco, her roommate, a tech worker, told her that her job was in Silicon Valley. "Where's that?" Miju asked. She knew she needed to meet people in order to break in, so she went to something called a "Stranger Dinner" where complete strangers got together just to talk, meet, network. There, she met an early employee at what was once the world's most famous microblogging platform. He invited her over to see if she could learn JavaScript in a weekend. Miju ended up being able to make a basic game called *Robots* in that abbreviated time, but knew she needed to be able to do more if she was going to get a job. She'd plop down in coffee shops in the Mission and learn the computer languages everyone around her apparently already knew fluently.

In that time and place, disruption as a force for change was cool, being disrupted was terrible, and everyone wanted to be a disruptor. People believed that meritocracy was real and merit was some pure, measurable thing. Miju came face to face with these 2010s values in job interviews. There was a disastrous interview at the JavaScript guy's microblogging platform, which he helped her get. "We've never interviewed someone like you," someone told her when she showed up, ready and eager. Another guy came in to interview Miju, picked up her resume, took a quick look at it, and then crumpled it up on the table and left it there as he walked out the room. The startup guys Miju did end up talking to were looking to suss out intelligence with brain teasers, which they assumed was the best way to do that in an interview. "Why are manhole covers circular?" That's a famous one from Microsoft. "Why do mirrors reverse right and left but not up and down?" Tech executives used to say they loved asking questions candidates had no possible way of ever answering, just to see how they'd respond.

Eventually, Miju's interviews paid off. In July 2011, a new line appeared on her LinkedIn profile with a new location: Palo Alto. Palo Alto, indubitably the nexus of Silicon Valley. The beating heart of an industry that had become so cool in the Millennial era that executives compared it to rock and roll, the idea being that some of us "young people" followed the twists and turns of new releases in the press as if they were album debuts, went to conventions as if they were concerts, and dreamed of making money and getting rich not on chords but on code. Beneath Palo Alto, Miju added three bullet points written in the type of language that would make the Williams career center enormously proud:

- Developed and presented detailed reports on monetization and retention to executives and product teams
- Designed experiments and interpreted experiment (A/B test) results
- Designed a new system for logging social actions to enable deeper social game mechanics

They were just bullet points. But they represented a victory: Miju had crossed over into technology. She was thrilled. Her job was at a major competitor to *FarmVille*. That was the infamous game—once one of the most popular apps in the world, with sixty million people playing it per month at one point—that popped up incessantly on Facebook around 2011, in which players raised livestock, harvested crops, and generally annoyed other people on social media who were merely there to impress others with their fun photography or witty status updates.

Miju's game wasn't set on a farm but instead in a bustling little digital town in which mystical creatures built habitats. Users could deploy certain foods, including cupcakes, to speed things up. At first, it felt incredible to be part of that world. Not just the fake one of the game but of Silicon Valley, of San Francisco, of California circa 2011. Before, Miju had navigated the internet alone as a child. Now she was making it from the inside.

As fun as it was to work on a game that masses of people were using each time they logged on to social media, and as optimistic as Miju was, she started to have some misgivings. One was the realization of how quickly the winds shift in Silicon Valley. What's sexy and exciting on the internet one month may not be a few months later. That's what happened with social-media games. They were heavily reliant on Facebook for traffic and growth. But Facebook could tell many users were annoyed by them and so stopped promoting them as heavily in its newsfeed, and so they seemed less important, and then became so.

Possibly more disturbing was the way the game made money. That first LinkedIn bullet point from her time working on the game, for instance, reports that Miju "developed and presented detailed reports on monetization and retention to executives and product teams." That means, essentially, that she was looking at how the game was clocking revenue. She was trying to figure out who was playing, how much they were paying, and how to keep them playing over time. It was the freemium business model that blew up in the era: You let people do stuff online without charging them for it, and then *do* ask for money if they want a souped-up experience. That felt fine to Miju, as long as it meant that most players were, here and there, throwing in $10 or a $20 to enhance their experience. She grew uncomfortable as she discovered that wasn't the case. The real money-makers were "whales." Those were big-time users who spent thousands of dollars to do things like dress up their digital houses or give a hell of a lot of cupcakes to other players in the game world. Miju couldn't get them out of her head.

Then out of the blue, someone at the world's largest video-sharing website messaged Miju about a job opening. It felt like a revelation, especially after she'd spent so much time and effort trying to get that first tech job. Miju took it. It solved a lot of problems. It got her away from the cupcakes and the whales. It took her somewhere new and exciting. Work life was falling into place.

Outside of work, San Francisco was a freer place than anywhere Miju had ever lived. It's hard to overstate the position the city occupied in the mind of queer Americans, even ones as comparatively young as we were. I now feel like an old man writing this, but most Millennials will easily remember a time when Pride flags did not fly from coast to coast in the month of June like they do now. Starbucks and J. P. Morgan did not sponsor floats in parades. People did not wear rainbow lanyards to work in suburban office parks. Gay marriage was banned in most places, in California as recently as the year Barack Obama was first elected. It was a time when you had to go somewhere like San Francisco to see visible signs of queer life in the everyday. Miju says that deep down, that was what she wanted. To exist in this freer world, even if she wasn't saying it then, even if she'd shoved her bisexuality into business-casual work attire.

But moving somewhere isn't enough to change your life. And in a way, San Francisco—where Allen Ginsberg wrote poems about men, Harvey Milk became one of the country's first out politicians, and even Kamala Harris started officiating gay weddings over twenty years ago—can sometimes feel almost like the Alamo. It's a site of great battles that now tourists mostly visit for the photo opportunities. The Castro was open and accepting when Miju was living there. But it felt like it was mostly a neighborhood populated by older gay men. There was a women's night at QBar on Castro Street, but that was about it in terms of nightlife oriented toward lesbian or bisexual women. What's more, Miju was back in the closet. It was a place in which she had been firmly planted since she was 14, when her relationship with Willow ended and her mother told her she wasn't bi. There had been the occasional makeout with a female friend in college, but she wasn't part of a queer community then. She had boyfriends. "Identity is tricky," says Miju, who now—again—identifies as bisexual. Back then, even though she had moved to the Castro, and even though somewhere inside she knew what she wanted, Miju thought she was straight.

And suddenly, she met Xander. It was December in San Francisco, with all that that entailed: the Christmas tree in Union Square, the rain, the trolleys dinging, the lights of Market Street, and the people in town from Fresno walking around H&M in Ugg boots as if it were snowing instead of just almost cold. One of Miju's colleagues said she just *had* to introduce her to this guy she'd known from school. Miju needed to meet more people in this new life she was building, so she agreed to it.

The plan was to throw an informal gathering at her place. He'd arrive, and they'd get to know each other. Xander may or may not have even been aware of said plan. But he walked through the door of her apartment, and something in her just knew. Things in her and around her changed. Time skipping beats, going fast-slow—an uneven tempo. He had classical good looks, the vintage kind. It helped that he was the sort of smart you couldn't study to become. Word was that he'd gotten a perfect score on his SAT. He was thriving in tech even though he'd just graduated, working on some elite team at a big firm traveling the world learning about how people in different countries used technology. They connected almost instantly.

Their first date was the best and the worst Miju had ever had. That's what she told her friends after. To it, she wore her "power outfit." This included brown knee-high boots and a blue sweater with a white shirt underneath. They were clothes befitting the sort of woman she wanted to become. The night rambled. Miju and Xander ended up playing *Skee-Ball* somewhere. They got burritos. They drifted to Miju's favorite bar, the Orbit Room. It has the kind of cocktails adults drink on dates. The bar was in an art-deco building, gold moldings and ivory stucco, like something from the 1920s.

Miju sensed Xander wanted to be there, wanted to listen to the things she had to say. That felt genuine. So what he said at the end hit her heart even harder: "I don't know if I can commit right now."

They kept seeing each other regardless. The Valley boomed. The population grew. The lushness of the city captivated Miju. Up in the hills in the mornings, the eucalyptus trees grow and capture the fog as it rolls off the Pacific. The earth is covered in bark and spear-shaped leaves and smells acidic, like sap. If you turn the right way in the right place, you can see to the other side of the bay, the water dotted with islands, the air moist and salty. Miju wandered through all of this with Xander. He was from there and he knew the best spots. But he kept saying this thing: "I just wish we had met when we were, like, 24." As if 24 were some ripe, old age instead of barely a year or two older than they were right then, kids just out of college. Miju know what he meant, though. They didn't have enough experience dating yet. Couples in San Francisco didn't meet when they were basically children and settle down to get married. Maybe that's what she wanted—although she was embarrassed enough to even admit that she wanted a *relationship*—but that's also what people did back home in Richmond. She'd run from there, done everything she could to get away from that.

She was looking for a solution. She started to think about an open relationship.

On May 3, 2011, the same week Olivia was on that dorm-room date, Aaron was hanging out with The Circle, and Justin would propose to Tara, a book called *The Ethical Slut* slipped into Miju's Amazon shopping cart. It had been popular in the social circles she ran in, often a spicy book club read, but she never thought it would be relevant to her own life. When you look at it, *The Ethical Slut* is in some ways similar to *Case in Point*. It's another guide to doing something difficult that a lot of people might fantasize about but don't know how to do. It was published in 1997 and is stern yet prescriptive. It reads as if it were written by Martha Stewart's way more fun sister.

"Great sluts are made, not born," the book explains, reclaiming the word "slut" as a positive term for anyone who wants and likes sex. "The skills you need to keep you and your partners happy and growing get developed through a combination of conscious effort and frequent practice. There are skills you can learn that will help start your adventure on the right foot and keep it on track." The book is effectively a guide to open relationships. It's polyamory 101. That is the term, according to *The Ethical Slut*, that was coined in 1992 and translates from Greek and Latin roots to mean "many loves." The key to being an ethical slut is to be consensual about sex, to be honest and open about it and not make it a game or a secret. There are bullet points and exercises, including self-affirmations to try:

- I deserve love.
- My body is sexy just the way it is.
- I ask for whatever I want and say no to whatever I don't.
- I can turn difficulties into opportunities for growth.

Looking back, Miju feels the book is already a little dated. The terms "open relationship" and "polyamory" have exploded in popularity in other books, movies, and podcasts since *The Ethical Slut* was written. Dan Savage now talks to people like Ezra Klein about ethical nonmonogamy. The *Wall Street Journal* writes quirky, front-page stories about the challenges of open dating. The conversation has moved forward. But back then, the book helped Miju, because it was the first time she'd seen what success could look like in a different relationship model.

It's hard to know how many people, precisely, are in consensually non-monogamous relationships. Several studies put it at about 4 to 5 percent of the US population, about one in twenty-two people. Despite those relatively small numbers, a recent, nationally representative survey by pollster YouGov showed that about a third of Americans would like their relationship to be nonmonogamous to some degree.[32] As for *non*consensual nonmonogamy, more than half of Americans who have ever been in monogamous relationships say they were cheated on, either physically or emotionally.[33] One in five Americans in a monogamous relationship say they were cheated on by their current partner. A third admit they have at some point in their lives themselves cheated in a relationship.

Which is all to demonstrate how hard it is to maintain a long-term relationship of any sort. A common solution our Boomer parents turned to was divorce. Its rates surged to an all-time high in the 1980s. Back then, books, movies, and television shows presented it as something edgy, a little naughty, frowned upon by conservatives, uncomfortable for sure, but maybe, ultimately, liberating and necessary. Today, non-monogamous relationships surface in plotlines from *The White Lotus* to *Riverdale* in much the same way as divorce did when we were children. There is a sense that Millennials are using open relationships to solve some of the challenges of staying with a partner over decades without ending the whole thing. That sounds good in theory. It did to Miju. Nonmonogamy would allow her to be with someone she was falling in love with but also to live out other experiences she felt she needed. She had desires of her own, parts of her sexuality that had been closeted for a long time. All the same, she had apprehensions. What did it mean to have someone but to let him have others, too?

In San Francisco, yoga teachers are celebrities. I remember going to a class at Yoga Tree myself one Christmas. It was a rarefied studio on the same block in the Castro as one of the neighborhood's most infamous gay bars. Everyone sat giddy on their mats, whispering about how lucky we were that Janet Stone was back in town from Mexico. She was a legend and, said someone on the mat next to me, told "the best guacamole jokes," whatever those were.

Miju found herself at the same studio around the same time, debating her next move with Xander. While she was there, he was going on a business trip. It was to a foreign city, one where he had a friend from college who, Miju knew, was best friends with pop stars. She could only imagine what that handsome, twentysomething guy who said he couldn't commit might do, free from her, on the other side of an ocean, surrounded by celebrities.

"Close your eyes," the instructor said to the class.

He walked around the studio. It was cavernous and bright, looking like an ashram that White people would pay to visit in India for an "authentic" experience.

"And breathe."

That's when the crying started. In eighteen months, Miju had built this incredible life, met this incredible guy, started this incredible adulthood. But it wasn't sustainable. She had to make a choice. She felt sad that Xander couldn't commit, worried that it was because he didn't love her enough. But at the same time, he could have just done what a lot of guys would do and said things to seal the deal, then made her regret it. Ghosted her, ignored her, straight up cheated on her. That happens all the time. It sure as hell happened to me. But Xander wasn't doing that. He was being honest.

It was at some point between the yoga-class cry and Xander's return to San Francisco that Miju decided she could try being in an open relationship.

*   *   *

Today, Millennials vote as full political adults in an environment where trust in government is the lowest it has been at any point since the National Election Study began surveying the question in 1958. Confidence jumped in the Clinton years, rising 25 percentage points, before spiking after 9/11.[34] It fell as the Bush administration mismanaged that trust. But it is worth noting that trust fell during the Obama years, too. He came into office with one in four Americans trusting in government. When he left, just one in five people thought the same thing.[35] That disillusionment came from both sides of the aisle, from red, blue, and purple America.

In the Obama years, it was obvious that the right had it out for the president. Almost as soon as he took office, the snarky #ThanksObama trended first as a right-wing critique of his policies, but then as a way for the left to call out the frequency and sometimes absurdity of such critiques. "The single most important thing we want to achieve is for President Obama to be a one-term president," Mitch McConnell said around the same time, adding, "I don't want the president to fail; I want him to change."[36] In an uglier move, Donald Trump fanned the flames of the birther movement that had begun during Obama's campaign, calling into question whether the president had been born in the United States. (He had.) It was this odd, early crusade that many believe may have sparked Trump's interest in seeking the White House.

Criticism of Obama from the left was less prominent. It was overshadowed in the early years by the collective sigh of relief over the break from the Bush administration. The sigh was so loud, Obama won the Nobel Peace Prize in 2009. For a while, the public outpourings of positivity masked growing frustrations with the Obama agenda. The president's team brought the economy back from the brink, but criticism came from those further left who felt he was simply reincarnating the same laissez-faire system instead of creating a more equitable one. The public perception of race relations hit a high in the first months of Obama's term—44 percent of the country said they were "generally good"—but trended downward, and precipitously so, after the killings of Trayvon Martin in 2012, Michael Brown in 2014, and Freddie Gray in 2015. They got to the point where, in Obama's second term, nearly a third of the country saw race relations as "generally bad."[37] Many Black Americans felt disappointed by Obama's conciliatory language on police brutality.

As Alicia Garza, co-founder of the Black Lives Matter movement put it, Obama "appealed to Black people to look at ourselves and solve the problem of dysfunction in our own communities so that, ostensibly, law enforcement wouldn't find occasion to kill us."[38]

For Tereza, a similar frustration was building up about immigration.

"We've got 12 million undocumented workers who are already here," Obama had said on a *Larry King Live* appearance during his first campaign.[39] "It's absolutely vital that we bring those families out of the shadows and that we give them the opportunity to travel a pathway to citizenship."

Tereza knew those shadows well. So she was dismayed as the years passed and the administration went on to deport more people than any other in history up until that time.[40] Obama shifted immigration policy to rely more heavily on removing people through court orders rather than simply turning people away at the border itself.[41] His team hoped that a focus on deporting people with criminal records would garner bipartisan backing for the sort of immigration reform he had promised.[42] That did not happen.

Washington can feel like a dirty fish tank. There is a fading, white castle in the middle. Moss grows on its sides, and scaly creatures dart into and out of the old structures. Schools of fish meander one way and then the next, left and then right, almost as if nobody in the glass orb has any memory at all. Over the years, at least twenty versions of the DREAM Act have been put before Congress. Not a single one has passed.

If you search through the records of the proceedings of Congress, you'll find Tereza Lee's name mentioned over and over again, particularly by Senator Durbin. "Tereza, would you please stand up?" he asks on June 28, 2011.[43] Hundreds of Dreamers had gone to Washington in support of the DREAM Act, which the Democratic senator was again trying to pass. "Tereza was an extraordinary musical talent who had played as a soloist with the Chicago Symphony Orchestra," he says. "Tereza, you got me started. Thank you for being here." Then there's another about a year later, on June 5, 2012. It's Durbin again, telling her story. "A child prodigy when it came to the piano. She played it so well she had been offered many scholarships, including to the Manhattan Conservatory of Music. When she went to fill out her application, one of the questions was, 'What is your citizenship or nationality?'"

A few days after that, Obama announced the creation of the Deferred Action for Childhood Arrivals program, DACA. It shielded Dreamers from deportation and gave them work permits, but because it was an executive branch memorandum and not a piece of federal legislation passed by Congress, it was temporary. It did not offer a pathway to citizenship, and it would need to be renewed every two years. It changed the lives of millions of people but was far from the original promise.

Durbin kept campaigning, but it was beginning to feel Sisyphean. Still, Tereza's story was front and center. In November 2014, Durbin was again on the Senate floor with a huge, blown-up portrait of Tereza, who had by then gone on to pursue a doctoral degree in music. "This DREAM Act all started with this young lady," he said as he put the massive picture on an easel. He switched to another, a big picture of Tereza with her parents. He explained the accomplishments she'd made, the progress in her degree. "I couldn't be prouder of what she's done with her life."

Tereza was hitting her 30s yet was still a literal poster child. She was billed as this perfect piano prodigy. How could you find fault with someone of such extraordinary talents? Didn't you want this person to be American, too? Fine. But it was also infantilizing. The story people told about Tereza always focused on her childhood: where she was born, what she had done when she had no agency of her own. As she was growing older, she was becoming ever more trapped in someone else's perspective on her story. The real Tereza, the woman, was angry. Her feelings were complex. Of course she was grateful for the help of Durbin and the others who had supported her. But she was tired of other people telling some tale about her that didn't represent the depth of her, her family, the others trapped in limbo.

Tereza was online one day and saw that other Dreamers were going to stage a demonstration in Union Square in Manhattan. A movement had been forming over the years, led largely by young Latino people who wanted first Bush and then Obama to reform the country's immigration laws. The idea for Union Square was to come out as undocumented, show people publicly what it looked like to be a person who by any other measure was indistinguishable from other Americans, save for a little card. Tereza had performed in front of thousands of people by that point. But public speaking wasn't something she'd done much of. There were these huge banners. They said things like "Undocumented and Unafraid." There was a microphone in the middle of the crowd, and people were going up to tell their stories.

Tereza started shaking. Union Square is an intimidating place: the bustling middle of the city, cars rushing by, commuters dashing from one subway entrance to the next. Telling your own story in your own words is frightening—even more when you run the risk of being deported for doing so.

"You don't have to speak," one of the other demonstrators said to her, giving her a big hug.

Tereza knew it was time.

*　*　*

At some point in your twenties, reality begins to settle in. You realize fantasies don't come true unless you make them so. You figure out that what you thought you could achieve maybe isn't possible. We were taught when we were young that we should always try to open up doors, always seek out new opportunities, make ambitious choices. As depressing as the Millennial economy of the 2010s was, an ever-expanding array of apps, games, and networks also made us feel as if we had endless options. There was always a ceaseless scroll of new people to date, new friends to find, new delivery food to order, new ways to distract ourselves on Facebook then Instagram then Snapchat. Even if most of those choices were shallow, papering over bigger problems like the unemployment rate, terror abroad, and an amplified vehemence in politics at home, they were real. But becoming an adult means deciding which doors to shut, which choices *not* to make.

Olivia was wearing grown-up clothes when she agreed to meet up with Giles for the first time since graduation. He was working in a finance job downtown in Manhattan, and she was at an advertising agency in Midtown. She'd officially abandoned her plans of becoming a forensic scientist and had moved into corporate America. Olivia became that person who posts motivational picture quotes on Instagram.

THERE IS NO FORCE MORE POWERFUL THAN A WOMAN DETERMINED TO RISE, she put up one day.

"There are far, far better things **ahead** than any we leave **behind**.—C.S. Lewis," she added on another.

SHE NEEDED A HERO, SO THAT'S WHAT SHE BECAME #MondayMotivation.

"Relax," one of her posts went. "You will become an adult. You will figure out your career. You will find someone who loves you. You have a whole lifetime; time takes time. The only way to fail at life is to abstain."

After graduation, Giles would occasionally text her lyrics to indie songs. Olivia was dating someone else then, and he knew this, but he sent the words anyway. One song was called "Sun & Moon," and it was by a band called Above & Beyond. It's an apology, and in it the band sings:

I'm sorry, baby
You were the sun and moon to me
I'll never get over you
You'll never get over me

Their meeting downtown began with ambiguity but ended with an adult decision. They met in a park unintentionally close to the new One World Trade. Olivia can't remember for sure, but she thinks the building may not have even been finished yet.

In truth, Olivia didn't see a future with Giles anymore. She didn't see white picket fences with him. He was a funny guy who loved to travel, who had an Instagram account documenting toilets he saw on trips abroad. He had helped bring Olivia out of the blur, but any lingering fantasy of them together was holding her back. When they met that day, it became even clearer that it just wasn't going to work. Their relationship was too entwined with old feelings to be just a friendship, but there wasn't enough there to build into something more. They decided to unfriend each other on Facebook and stop talking. Olivia knew she needed to leave behind this thing that had never really even been there so she could move ahead with the rest of her life.

PART IV
THE BRIDGE

The story of a generation is always a dynamic thing. But by the autumn of 2016, the one about Millennial adults, as we largely understand it today, had calcified. It is stubbornly present, frustratingly reductive. I'll call it the "Avocado Toast" thesis.

It came the year "Millennials" peaked as a Google search term.[1] The word "selfie" had entered the lexicon. Newspapers were fanning the flames of a moral panic over whether the people who took such pictures, largely Millennials, were narcissists or not as attractive as they thought they were or even putting their lives at risk if they posed in dangerous spots.[2] (A very unfortunate few had died taking selfies that year, falling from the cliffs and ledges over which they'd aimed to get the best shot.) It was in October of 2016 when a conservative Australian weekend newspaper ran a column that popularized what many of our critics had been thinking but not yet said quite so bluntly. The column's title was "Evils of the Hipster Café," and it focused its ire on a particular brunch item.

"I have seen young people order smashed avocado with crumbled feta on five-grain toasted bread at $22 a pop and more," wrote Bernard Salt, a Boomer, self-described social demographer, and well remunerated partner at the accounting firm KPMG.[3] "I can afford to eat this for lunch because I am middle aged and have raised my family. But how can young people afford to eat like this? Shouldn't they be economizing by eating at home? How often are they eating out? Twenty-two dollars several times a week could go towards a deposit on a house."

Salt's column broke the internet. The backlash was global, and it was furious. "I stopped eating smashed avocado and now I own a castle," mocked one comedian.[4] A major American newspaper calculated that it would take the average Millennial 113 years to afford a down payment on a home if they followed Salt's advice and started eating in the allegedly more frugal manner of the Baby Boomer cohort.[5] Brigid Delaney, a columnist in the *Guardian*, came to the ardent defense of the Millennial bruncher. Her argument rationalizing behaviors Boomers struggled to understand came down to economics. "What do you do when you can't afford to buy somewhere to live?" she wrote. "Well, you decide to live. You get Ubers, you travel, you buy a good phone, you get a laptop, you go for brunch."[6]

Arguments arise when people see the same set of facts but draw different conclusions about them. For our critics, our so-called Millennial habits confirmed what they had feared for a long time: We were selfish. Selfies were evidence. Our seemingly self-centered habit of spending on short-term discretionary goods rather than long-term investments was evidence. So was the fact that we were delaying marriage, childbirth, seemingly adulthood itself. And so, too, was this emerging notion of "cancel culture," often portrayed as spearheaded by Millennials. The idea was that if we didn't like something, even as benign as a few words or as an idea, we wanted it—*poof*—out of our lives. Essentially, our critics could look at our generation and say that our behavior was all about making ourselves feel good in the moment, other considerations be damned.

I'm not going to defend those mostly Boomer critics here. But I am going to point out that their fears about us did come from somewhere. It actually came from themselves—from how they raised us. Their fears were partly based on concerns about a real social experiment that had been conducted on many of us when we were children. It involved self-esteem.

"Low self-esteem," a 1987 piece in the *Los Angeles Times* put the hypothesis of this experiment,[7] "is at the root of virtually every social problem: chronic drug and alcohol abuse, crime and violence, welfare dependency, teen-age pregnancy and more."

The idea had gained traction in the decade many of us were born. A politician in California, Assemblyman John Vasconcellos, popularized it, pushing in the mid-1980s for a so-called Task Force to Promote Self-Esteem and Personal and Social Responsibility. The notion, allegedly backed by research, was that if people simply liked themselves more, they would be less inclined to engage in deviant behaviors, including drinking, drugs, and crime. Hundreds of people applied to be on the task force, more than had ever applied to be on a task force in the state's history.[8] The government selected a diverse twenty-five-member panel to spend three years determining how Californians might improve their self-esteem and, in so doing, society.[9] The report they ultimately filed, which cost hundreds of thousands of dollars, cited valiant examples of self-esteem in history, such as during the American Revolution and during the then recent fall of Communist governments in Eastern Europe. No matter that seven members of the panel dissented from its findings, with some criticizing the use of "anecdotal" rather than scientific knowledge. The panel came up with key principles, goals, and "constructive thoughts" on how to boost self-esteem.[10]

California's task force was a government response to a broader trend. In the same period, hundreds of schools across the country—the ones we were attending—took it upon themselves to gas up the Millennial sense of self. One deputy sheriff toured schools with the goal of reducing drug use by telling students, "You are special. You are a wonderful individual."[11] Teachers stopped using red pens so we'd feel less bad about ourselves if we got answers wrong. A new game (one I remember playing) involved students in a circle throwing a Koosh ball from one to the other, saying a compliment about the person to whom they had just tossed the toy.[12] This was the era when the participation trophy took off. It was when classrooms got mirrors with borders adorned with stenciled-on phrases that said things like, "You are now looking at one of the most special people in the whole wide world!"

All of this stuff was sweet, but it was not based on science. It stemmed from a simple logical fallacy of misplaced causation versus correlation. It wasn't that having high self-esteem prevented people from doing bad things. It was that people who did bad things felt bad about themselves for having done them. In fact, about a decade after the self-esteem craze started, research began showing that people with high self-esteem "pose a greater threat to those around them than people with low self-esteem."[13] The new conclusion, psychotherapist and writer Lauren Slater wrote in 2002, was a fairly obvious one but one that needed to be said, given everything: "Feeling bad about yourself is not the cause of our country's biggest, most expensive social problems."[14]

Yet Boomers remembered the Koosh ball games. They remembered the mirrors that told us we were special. And so only a few years later, as we hit the 2010s and started entering the workforce in large numbers, they began to worry about the side effects of a generation raised on this false savior of self-esteem. They worried our being told we were neat, wonderful, unique individuals would make us entitled and narcissistic adults.

Some data backed them up. Academics found that by the time older Millennials were hitting college age, our scores of narcissism had ballooned 30 percent higher than they had been for similarly aged students in the late 1970s.[15] A *TIME* magazine cover in 2013 proclaimed that "Millennials are lazy, entitled narcissists."[16] The piece was more nuanced than that headline suggests, but it still explicitly linked attempts to build our self-esteem in childhood to a sense of entitlement in adulthood. "All that self-esteem leads them to be disappointed when the world refuses to affirm how great they know they are," the author wrote about us. He quoted a workplace expert who concluded that "this generation has the highest likelihood of having unmet expectations."

And the thing is, that is true. It even forms a major part of the argument I'm making in this book. Millennials *have* been disappointed. But the causes of this sentiment were different from what our critics said they were. We weren't disappointed because we were told we were fuckin' awesome and believed it. We were—and are—disappointed because we haven't achieved the things we aimed for.

Back in the mid-2010s, our disappointment seemed ridiculous to Boomers because in many ways, the world around us was starting to improve. This beclouded their vision of us. A Boomer could look around 2015 and wonder why we were so down about our jobs and stressed about our twenty- and thirtysomething lives. The stock market had recovered some 200 percent from the depths of the recession. Unemployment had fallen from 10 percent in 2009 to under 5 percent. Housing prices were recovering. Technology was again making life seemingly ever-easier and ever-better. The successful stock market debuts of Twitter, Square, Facebook, and even China's Alibaba on Wall Street made America's economy look like an unrivalled global leader in innovation. On the surface, someone who already had a career, a house, and a retirement account could start to feel pretty optimistic again.

For many liberal Boomers, politics reinforced this optimistic feeling. The Tea Party had emerged in politics, peaked, and was seemingly dying out. Polling from Gallup showed support for the movement hit a new low in 2015, with just 17 percent of Americans saying they supported it.[17] Many voters blamed the most right-wing Republicans for the 2013 government shutdown. The 2014 midterms were largely seen as a win for the Republican establishment and an opportunity for the party to chart a new way forward. As *U.S. News & World Report* put it in 2015, "In the long term . . . the Tea Party's rise and the GOP's subsequent ideological split may box the furthest right members of the party out."[18]

"Jeb Bush Is Still the Favorite," a headline in the *New York Times* read that year.[19] As late as June of 2016, Trump was hitting just 38 percent in national polls. Hillary Clinton was at 42 percent.[20] Trump's rise still seemed highly unlikely even in early autumn of that year.

Deeper than the data suggesting the right wing's decline was an idea that many paired with it. It linked back to those posters many of us had hung on our walls, stamped with the words "CHANGE" or "HOPE" or "PROGRESS." It felt like something solidified by the Supreme Court's legalization of same-sex marriage in 2015. It was called the "arc of history," and it was an idea Obama, still president then, loved.

"It's the answer that led those who have been told for so long by so many to be cynical, and fearful, and doubtful of what we can achieve to put their hands on the arc of history and bend it once more toward the hope of a better day," he'd said the night of his electoral victory in 2008.[21]

He talked about the arc of history in 2009 during a graduation at a school in Russia, when Putin had stepped out of the presidency and the country was still seen as a fledgling democracy. Obama told those Russian graduates that "the arc of history shows that governments which serve their own people survive and thrive; governments which serve only their own power do not."[22] He mentioned the arc of history on World Freedom Day in 2010, on Nelson Mandela International Day in 2012, during Hispanic Heritage Month in 2015, at a memorial service for former Israeli Prime Minister Shimon Peres in 2016, and then five times at campaign events for Hillary Clinton late that year.

"In this country, you don't have to be born of wealth or privilege to make a difference," he said at a rally in New Hampshire on November 7, the day before the presidential election.[23] "You don't have to practice a certain faith or look a certain way to bend the arc of history. And that's what makes America exceptional. That's what's always made America great."

It wasn't only Obama who talked about the "arc of history." It was an idea I remember reading about in textbooks as a child about the gradual attainment of freedoms in America. From the country's independence to abolition to civil rights to abortion rights to gay rights, the notion was that history was a constant march toward progress. The phrase itself is likely an adaptation of one used by Martin Luther King, Jr. at a speech he gave at the National Cathedral in Washington in 1968. "The arc of the moral universe is long, but it bends toward justice," he said. Even that is thought to be a harkening-back to a sermon published in 1853 by abolitionist Theodore Parker, who preached, "I do not pretend to understand the moral universe, the arc is a long one . . . but from what I see I am sure it bends towards justice."[24]

Tell that to the families of the women who died after the Supreme Court struck down *Roe v. Wade.*

Yet something like that felt inconceivable in the 2010s. Because there we were in the late Obama era. Never mind polls showing lower turnout in the Millennial crowd or data indicating the earliest rumblings of a divide between older Millennials who skewed liberal and their younger, more conservative counterparts.[25] For a certain Millennial set, it was impossible not to feel a rush of progress ahead. Right?

* * *

Around that time, Miju began to feel society was moving toward greater acceptance of alternative relationship structures. She was. She and Xander had agreed they were going to date each other, but also date other people. They were going to officially become a couple—one that was both open and committed. They went to a discussion group in the Mission for people in open relationships. They were the youngest there by far. There were couples there trying to hold their long marriages together. There were also other people coming together for the first time in an open way. Miju and Xander saw a lot of couples with a lot of different rules, many of which they thought maybe they didn't want to apply to them. Miju and Xander felt that if they were going to do this polyamorous thing, they would "kind of just let what happens happen and then figure out along the way what it was." They wanted to trust each other. They didn't want to do what they saw some others doing, implementing their own "don't ask, don't tell" policies or requiring that the other keep outside relationships purely sexual, ending them if they started to develop feelings. Miju and Xander could tell those types of rules were important for other people, but they were learning that they didn't want them within their own, young coupledom.

A common dismissal of polyamorous people is that they're just bored, rich, and White. They have too much time, too much privilege, too little to worry about, so they go searching for fulfilment where society has told them not to look. But research by a professor at the University of Western Ontario challenges these assumptions.[26] The professor, Rhonda Balzarini, compared 2,428 polyamorous people with 539 monogamous ones. Polyamorous people were more likely to be divorced and actually more likely to make *less* money than their monogamous counterparts. They were, as you might expect, slightly more Democratic than monogamous people, and their ethnic makeup was about the same as the general population.

The participants in the discussion group in the Mission talked about how they didn't need to feel like bad people for wanting to be together but also with other people. They talked about how they didn't need to be ashamed. They also talked about one of Miju's big fears. "What if they leave?" Miju asked someone in the group. "That happens in all types of relationships," a woman told her. "You have to know that if that did happen, you'd be OK."

It would be a lie to say the first year of a nonmonogamous relationship was an easy one for Miju. Generally, that's what polyamorous advice-givers say: It takes about a year or two after opening up a relationship for the waters to still. In the therapy-speak in which many Bay Area residents are conversant, what was happening in Miju's and Xander's relationship at that time was that they were "being avoidant." They had made this big change—allowing one another to date other people—but they weren't always talking about what they were doing with those other people.

Some people in Miju's new world said they didn't feel jealousy. They were happy for their partners to have other partners, and that was that. This was not the case for Miju. It wasn't the easiest thing in the world to enter into a new type of relationship, with new freedoms but also a different understanding of how things would work. That included understandings about the future she had seen for herself. Would she get married? Would she have children? The Dumbledore conversation loomed large.

In that first year, the jealousy hit hardest when Xander traveled for work. There was one trip in particular that just got to Miju. At the time, she was seeing someone in addition to Xander. That was great. But the combination of Xander being far away from her and having suspicions that he was hooking up with someone else on that trip made her feel incredibly jealous. Looking back, Miju now tells me what jealousy is: "It's either an insecurity or an unmet need."

This lines up with advice from *The Ethical Slut*. In the book, the authors encourage readers to inquire into jealousy. They call it an umbrella term for many emotions, ones that might surface when we get the sense our partner is sleeping with somebody else. It "is often the mask worn by the most difficult inner conflict you have going on right now, a conflict that's crying out to be resolved and you don't even know it," the book says. Looking back, it's hard to pinpoint exactly what was bothering Miju so much about Xander on that trip. She called him on video, and they started to talk about it.

Through the screen, Xander looked straight at her and said something that hit home. It hit me when I heard it.

"The person I want to be telling my life about," he said, "is you."

That idea made something inside Miju flip. It made her realize that yes, she and Xander would sleep with other people, date other people, even allow themselves to love other people. But Miju could see that she had a special status with Xander. She was his "anchor partner." Other people didn't have to be threats to her. It was becoming clear that she and Xander would go through life letting themselves try new and different things, sometimes together, sometimes on their own. They would have what Miju calls a "growth mindset." They would talk to each other about what they discovered. But they would always come back to each other.

Miju moved into Xander's apartment. It was fabulous. It had a farmhouse sink she thought was so sophisticated, right near Dolores Park. Moving in reassured her anxieties even further as she discovered that in some ways, Xander's desire for nonmonogamy had perhaps been more about a theoretical freedom than an actual one. Living together, she found that rather than going out every night with a new lover, Xander actually spent many of his evenings in, playing video games with his friends.

They were lying in bed one morning. It was about two years after Miju had cried in Yoga Tree, 2013 or so. She and Xander let their minds wander to the years ahead. It was thrilling thinking about being together in that way. But they also hit upon a reality that many queer Millennials are increasingly facing: Our life milestones may come at different points than those of our straight peers. And no matter how well things are going with your ethically non-monogamous relationship, you still have to grapple with others' expectations of you.

The fact was that Miju's grandmother was dying of Alzheimer's. Before she died, Miju felt she needed her to know she was settled down, that she was making an adult life for herself. In bed that morning, they started talking about having children.

"That means we're getting married," said Miju. "Right?"

Xander proposed at Burning Man. When I found this out, I couldn't believe how Millennial it sounded. Although in recent years Burning Man has started to attract billionaires jetting in on private planes to take Instagram pictures, at its core, Burning Man is still what it's always been: a San Francisco thing. The first one took place in San Francisco itself, on Baker Beach in the city's northwest quadrant, in 1986. There, cofounders Larry Harvey and Jerry James burned an eight-foot-tall effigy of a man made of wood. The story goes that he was using the event to mark the end of a relationship. Those first few years, it was just a group of friends, and they had stellar views of the Golden Gate Bridge. It wasn't until 1990 that it moved to Black Rock Desert.

That night, Xander and Miju were exploring a place called the Deep Playa. It's a part of Burning Man where people don't camp, far away from the places where most people go. They bicycled around that dry lakebed, near the perimeter. There are art installations out there. Some are terrible, but some are great. Miju and Xander parked under one of the great ones, a structure designed so that you could see the underside of a big fire. It was beautiful, witnessing something that in real life you almost never can.

"When are you going to propose to me?" she said.

"How about now?" he said. He took out a dinky ring covered in dust. They agreed.

They would be married. But they would also be open.

They biked off, found their friends, and danced all night together in that huge desert in the middle of nowhere.

I used to think coming out was something you did once. All you had to do was say what you really were, and the world would know your story for the rest of time. Your bigoted enemies would have to grapple with it, but there would also be people like your largely supportive friends and family. In retrospect, that was a childish thing for me to think, even as I lived it. A wise woman said to me when I was young that "you'll come out many times in your life." She was right. For as long as heteronormativity is the expectation, there will always be closet doors to open.

Miju lived this fact, too, in the Castro. Being open gave her a freedom she had never felt. It allowed her to keep an anchor relationship that was important to her but also to fall in love with other people—including women. That was so validating for her. There was a woman at work Miju had grown interested in. But it had been over a decade since her relationship with Willow. For much of that time, she had effectively been convinced she wasn't bisexual.

This changed one night in San Francisco. Miju was out with that woman from work.

At some point, she called Miju's name.

And then she kissed her.

It meant so much. It transported her back so many years. It validated the desire she'd had for Willow when she hardly understood what desire even was. It helped Miju understand herself as someone who, despite what people had said about her, was, is, and would be queer. Miju fell in love with the woman who kissed her.

In those early years, there were moments when being privately polyamorous and queer was challenging to handle in public. There was one time when Miju and the woman from work were walking around the Mission, holding hands, and suddenly bumped into another coworker who knew about Xander. Miju at the time was very much "passing" as straight and monogamous at work and immediately dropped out of the hand holding. Even to this day, Miju says there are some places she's ready to come out and some that she's not. Because the information about her online is so atomized, she feels like people won't always be able to connect the dots between her various identities. She thinks some of her continued separation of worlds has to do with the fact that she came from such a conservative place and had that decade back in the closet.

Yet that bottling-up may have also prompted Miju to take an opportunity to come out in a big, unexpected way. It was 2015, the time when Snapchat was still new. "Discover" had just rolled out, and it was organized and tame. It was a separate screen from the rest of the app that featured tiny colored circles, each of which took you into a separate media outlet's channel. There was the Food Network, National Geographic, ESPN, and CNN. I remember using the app and feeling surprised CNN was on there—it was so formal, Snapchat so not. (In a job I got several years later, I learned why Snapchat wanted formal news organizations on its Discover page: to make the whole operation look more legitimate, with storied brands beside new creators.) I pressed on CNN's little red dot, and a video opened up on my iPhone.

The video, cropped lengthwise for Snapchat but also available in full across the internet and cable news, was entitled, "I have a fiancé, a girlfriend and two boyfriends." It starred Miju.

"How many relationships would you say you're in?" asked the CNN correspondent, sitting beside Miju near a hill in Dolores Park.

"I am in four relationships right now," Miju says, bowing her head a bit, the label on screen identifying her as a product manager, the dream tech job of a certain type of liberal-arts graduate at a moment when Silicon Valley was at its Millennial prime. Miju had already explained that she and Xander practiced partner nonmonogamy, that they were engaged and came first for each other in their hierarchy. "I have been seeing a woman for two years. We say 'I love you' to each other. I also see a man about once a month. And then I have what I like to call my 'distraction spot' for whoever happens to be catching my attention at the time."

As I watched Miju talk, I realized that I actually had a connection with her. This was before we had ever met, before I even was aware that she existed. But I recognized her fiancé, Xander. He featured in a few CNN scenes but didn't say anything. I realized that I had gone to college with him. We weren't close, and I feel comfortable reporting objectively on his wife, who I'd never met until I started reporting for this book. We didn't share social circles. But in college I'd seen Xander at parties. He was wispy, smart, artsy. He was the sort of guy a gay boy would hope deep down might be gay, too. But as so often happens, someone confirmed he wasn't on my team, and so I moved on with life.

Until Snapchat, I hadn't seen him in some five years. In that time, something had started happening in America that I didn't myself understand. In high school, I'd consumed *Will & Grace* clandestinely. I didn't even watch it; I listened to it. On my nightstand I had a radio from Walmart that picked up the NBC television frequency. Hidden as if I needed to keep it quiet from the Stasi, Thursdays at 9 p.m. became my exposure to the idea of what gay men could be. (Little did I know that there were other models.) In college, I came out. I held hands with my boyfriend as we crossed the street in our extremely liberal college town, feeling as if in the privilege and safety of that place, I was some brave, transgressive actor. Edgy.

Now Xander was the more progressive one, alongside his fiancée. I was in a long-distance relationship with my partner and starting to feel like a fuddy-duddy. I even began to use that term to describe myself. In Brooklyn, in my shitty apartment, watching that clip of Miju in her very nice one in San Francisco, I wondered why she would take part in something like this five-minute CNN package when there was so much risk of coming off to so many people, her family and friends included, as bad or wrong, sinful for her relationships and for being so public about something so private. But she did—talking about her four relationships and answering subsequent questions such as, "Can you be analytical about love?" and "What does Cinderella 2.0 look like to you?"

I didn't know a lot about polyamory at the time—anything, really. But Miju stuck in my mind because I thought she'd done a good job with the interview. She was clearly nervous talking to the reporter, but she was so open about something that people would clearly have had a lot of questions about (and, some of them, objections to). Years later, as I sat down to write this book about what happened to a generation of people who came of age amidst a massive transformation in normative understandings about sex, gender, and relationships, it occurred to me that Miju's story might help show what it was really like to live at the forefront of those changes. That's why I called her, and that's why I'm telling you about how she moved from being a closeted girl in Richmond to a woman forging ahead into a different type of family structure in the Bay Area. It takes something deeper than self-esteem to do that.

Miju braced for sharp reactions to her interview. CNN blasted it across social media. But frankly, the internet didn't go as savage as she feared it might. Sure, a Christian blogger wrote that "if you're shocked by her story, know that soon you won't be. Polyamory is the next step in the continued movement of our culture from traditional marriage into whatever people want to do."[27] (As if that were a bad thing.) A less pious but no less opinionated internet commentator argued that "the story presents caricatures from *The Social Network* trying to fit the square peg of love into the round hole of technology and tech marketing with talk of 'optimizing' and 'disrupting' love."[28] And frustratingly, some of the people Miju thought were her polyamorous allies in the Bay Area reacted really negatively to the segment. They picked apart her arguments, also took issue with that word "optimize." (For the record, it was the reporter who used that word first.) But it was worth it, because Miju saw her spot on CNN—maybe a bit like Jon Stewart going on *Crossfire* a decade before—as her own way of trying to fix the world. She wanted to show people that what they thought they knew might be wrong. That there were other ways of living, and that the people who lived those lives were real and mortal.

* * *

On the other side of the country at around the same time, Olivia was on Instagram. She was doing other late-Obama-era Millennial things, too. She'd quit her job. She'd been passed over for a promotion and decided that the advertising industry was not for her. She, like hundreds of thousands of us, had enrolled in graduate school. She was going to become a teacher. Some people use graduate school as a fun but ultimately sad last chance to dress up in the trappings of the careers they fantasize about but know they're unlikely to have. Not Olivia. She slayed her program at Stony Brook University. She was determined, organized, and more serious than a lot of other people around her. Summer 2015 came, and she took a big trip down to Ocean City with her cousin for the Fourth of July to cut loose. They drank, went on pontoon boats, drank, went to a massive Jamaican-themed beach club called Seacrets, drank.

Olivia was feeling good. Optimistic. She liked how she looked, the direction her life was taking. She felt pretty. It was one of those points midway through your twenties where actually, things are starting to go right for once. Swaying to it all by the end of the evening in Ocean City, Olivia did what any self-respecting 24-year-old would have done at the end of a night two decades into the new millennium. She went on social.

And there he was. Riley. Riley was a guy she'd gone to high school with in Sunnydale—that rich guy who'd slammed somebody's head into a microwave in a cafeteria brawl a decade before. The years had been good to him. Microwave Riley had joined the Air Force. He'd served in Afghanistan. He'd literally fought in the war that was started because

Anthony died. That night, he posted something about the Fourth of July, about being deployed in Japan. Olivia sent him a direct message, probably a little trite, but she meant it nonetheless. "Thank you so much for serving our country," she wrote. The bars may have been closing in Ocean City, but thirteen hours ahead in Tokyo, the day was starting. Riley responded. He didn't stop.

That summer, Olivia came to know Riley in a way she'd never let herself know him or his friends in high school. That summer, for many of us, social media still felt really good. It felt like something that could connect us for the better, something that could take us to a grown-up version of the place we imagined we were going when we were children on AIM. Olivia's connection to Riley validated her, gave her a sense that she was taking control of her own life at last. She'd racked up achievements since high school and was proud of them. Connecting with Riley felt like another. Getting back in touch with him helped her reexamine who she was in that blur period of the early 2000s. Maybe then she had been consumed with sadness and loss and had felt like everyone in her hometown was a bitch who excluded her. But maybe it was the other way around. Maybe she had been the bitch.

Olivia and Riley FaceTimed a lot. Fall came, and the Mets were headed to the World Series. The two of them were both thrilled and watched the games together online. The semester progressed, and Olivia was set to graduate. Riley didn't make it back in time for the ceremony—he was due to come home for a longer period of time soon—but he told her to send him the online broadcast of the event. They had that kind of digital intimacy.

He came home in December. They spent New Year's together with his friends. When Olivia went to his parents' house, she pinched herself. There she was in Sunnydale, a place where there were many white picket fences. There were many family traditions. Riley's family was rich and powerful in town. Although Sunnydale was just up the street from Nesconset, the streets themselves told of how different they were. Nesconset's main drag had a CVS, an Ace Hardware, and a 7-Eleven. But on Lake Avenue in Sunnydale, well-preserved women pulled up in big SUVs to stop at places like Goodness Me Deli, which sold tea, tacos, signs that said things like "I work hard so my dog can have a better life," rose-quartz candles that were supposed to promote "unconditional love that carries a soft, feminine energy," and coffee laced with roots and mushrooms. Women came into the bakery and asked if they were planning to sell cookies in the shape of Easter bunnies for the upcoming holiday, like they had done Valentine's cookies a couple months before. Sunnydale was wealth, comfort, community, and continuity. It was the sort of place Olivia could see herself creating the family, community, and continuity she'd longed for in her lonely periods. She couldn't believe she had been invited in.

Before long, Riley was presenting her with a choice. To stay in the Air Force, he had two options: He could take the international route, getting deployed to three countries in three years. Or he could take up domestic life on a base in Maryland. Which would she prefer?

"Wherever you go," Olivia told him. "I'm gonna probably follow you."

They signed a lease in a suburb outside Baltimore. Within days, the girl from Nesconset was packing everything she owned into her orange Dodge Dart, so full she had to turn the TV face-down for it to fit. It was early in the morning when she left home. Her mother—who has always had some clairvoyance about how things are going to turn out—was up to see her off.

"You sure you want to do this?" she said.

There were tears.

"This is my move," said Olivia.

Her mother hugged her, and then Olivia drove out of Suffolk County.

When she made it to Maryland, she put up an Instagram post geo-tagged to her new rental. It showed a picture of an open apartment door. Just beyond were his shoes and hers: worn, brown loafers and aged flip-flops. It was the height of staged social media, when even the everyday Instagrammer could feel pressure to live like an influencer, showing a perfect still from life captured in a single shot on the grid. I cringe thinking about my own much-hashtagged social-media activity from then. Like many, I issued #updates as if they were press releases vetted by both @legal and the @comms team. They showed the lives we wished we could be living already. As such, Olivia's post read almost like a wedding save-the-date.

"So incredibly excited to announce that we will be moving to Frederick, MD this week to start a new adventure together!!!" she wrote. "There'll be an extra bedroom for you to stay in!"

* * *

I picked up on similar feelings of optimism and stability elsewhere in this period. Justin was living a happy but busy married life in Southern California. Aaron got together with someone, and they had a kid. Fatherhood changed him. Quickly he realized his child's mother was in too deep with drugs. He gave her the choice to quit or to leave. She left, he got sober for a while and focused on being a dad. Tereza made it into a PhD program at the Manhattan School of Music. She got married to a really nice jazz trombonist. Their first date was watching *Finding Nemo*. Their marriage meant that she could become an American citizen and would never have to worry about her own deportation again.

Aren't these all nice, shining examples of American progress? They sound as if they fit into an arc of history bending toward the American Dream. The nice guy gets married. The addict beats his biggest challenge.

The woman without a Social Security number gets one. But rarely is anything so easy, so simple, so pat. Bad things take a long time to stamp out. They reemerge to confront us again. They offer us false promises. Beneath the milestones of these lives, between the statistics showing recovery from a recession and hope in the White House, lay fault lines.

If they were hard to see, it's because the American economy was in an aberrational place in the 2010s. Many problems stood hidden from plain sight by an often-misunderstood but increasingly important figure: the federal funds rate. That number is set by the Federal Reserve, the most powerful economic institution in the United States. In the simplest of ways, the rate dictates how much it costs for banks to borrow from one another. But the implications of it are massive. The rate influences everyday facts of life: how much money you make on your savings in the bank, how much your mortgage will cost, what your credit card's APR will be. Broader still, it influences the macro-economy we live in: how the stock market behaves, how likely companies are to hire or fire, how inflation will rise or fall, even how we feel about our prospects—or our "consumer sentiment," as economists call it. And between the years 2008 and late 2015, we were living through one of the most abnormal periods in history for this mysterious but powerful number, which dramatically shaped the way our lives were unfolding and thus how many of us were feeling.

Starting after the Great Recession, the Federal Reserve tested out something new with the funds rate. They would keep it near zero, and they would keep it there for longer than they ever had in history. The goal was to help the country escape the worst financial crisis since the Great Depression. Businesses were either too cash-strapped or too spooked to invest, hire, and grow. Jobs weren't being created. The stock market was crap. The idea was that if it was cheaper for banks to lend to each other, it would in turn become cheaper for businesses to borrow the money they needed to grow. That would create more jobs. More jobs would help companies earn more money, which would benefit their stock prices. Higher stock prices would make people feel richer, and they would spend more, and this would all loop back into a virtuous cycle.

The experiment looked like it worked. Business activity did pick up. Jobs did come back. The stock market boomed. But unusual things happened, too. Because interest rates stayed so low, there were only a few great places for private lenders—rich investors—to get a lot of bang for their buck. They sought out risky investments that were growing out of the Bay Area. This explains why for a while, it seemed like there was a startup for everything. Some of them really worked. It was all happening not long after venture capitalist Aileen Lee in 2013 coined that term "unicorn" for startups that reached billion-dollar valuations.[29] Some of the companies that emerged were smart ideas that would withstand the test of time. Uber, Instagram, Instacart, Airbnb all came out of this period. But others were really dumb, like the startup that promised to deliver people $20 of quarters for $27—you know, for those pesky moments when you didn't have enough coins to do a load of laundry. Investors were willing to throw money at these companies to make them grow, to try to get as many people as possible hooked on them by making them cheap for us to use. The thinking was that once these firms had a big base of customers, they could then charge us more later. To do so, they would subsidize the first few trips on a ride-sharing app or discount deliveries on meal-service platforms. It was something tech journalist Kevin Roose dubbed the "Millennial Lifestyle Subsidy," and it was helping digitally savvy app users live like high rollers with cheap grocery delivery and $6 Lyft rides. "Balenciaga lifestyles on Banana Republic budgets," was how Roose put it.[30]

While low interest rates gave some of us, especially those in cities, a taste of that bourgeois lifestyle, and while they made life pretty good for the well-established, they weren't helping everyone. Low rates are great for those already invested in the stock market. They make mortgages cheaper, which is nice if you already own a home and want to refinance to a lower rate or already have the savings for a down payment. But if you don't have those things, they make it hard to get them, because they make them more expensive. Take housing. Low rates made it cheaper to borrow to buy homes, increasing competition and driving up prices. Lower rates also make saving accounts less appealing because you earn essentially no interest on them.

During the low-rate era, jobs did come back, but they weren't all great ones. The share of temporary positions ticked up, and wages did not. Millennials who graduated in any given year after the Financial Crisis faced a labor market with an employment rate lower than it had been since the 1980s. One study from 2010 found that students who graduate into a recession suffer wage losses of between 1 percent and 13 percent a year. Over 20 years, those can add up to a loss of $80,000.[31] Researchers use a blunt term for people in this category: "unlucky cohorts."[32] In that long slog of years after the recession, we were that.

Inequality rose. So did anxiety. A team of public-health researchers found a steady march upward in anxiety levels in adults in the US between 2008 and 2016. The group with the most significant growth were Millennials.[33]

* * *

Like Obama, Donald Trump talked a lot about history. But he talked about it in a very different way. If Obama referred to its arc marching toward justice, Trump referenced it as a way of creating superlatives, often via Twitter, almost always about himself or someone he hated.

@FoxNews you should be ashamed of yourself. I got you the highest debate ratings in your history & you say nothing but bad . . . he wrote on August 7, 2015, beginning a several-day tirade against that cable network that had been born alongside the youngest Millennials.[34]

President Obama will go down as perhaps the worst president in the history of the United States! he wrote a year later, in the summer of 2016.[35]

A side effect of using so many superlatives is that they start to cheapen the moment. If everything is the most historic thing ever, what isn't anymore? Maybe that was the point. Trump's entire campaign was about making the present seem horrible and his version of the past look better. He made the consequences of not following him sound dire. "This is not simply another four-year election," he said at a speech at the South Florida Fair Expo Center in October 2016.[36] "This is a crossroads in the history of our civilization that will determine whether or not 'We the People' reclaim control over our government." He'd taken the *us-versus-them* rhetoric of the Bush era and magnified it. He called not just for "us" to defend freedom or American interests abroad, as Bush had done. Trump pushed for a fight to reclaim some vague but ominous idea of "our civilization" under threat. He won the White House doing so.

*　*　*

In the first year of Trump's presidency, Tereza reflected a lot on an idea implicit in many of Obama's speeches about the arc of history, but maybe not understood widely enough. His point wasn't that you can just sit there and let history happen. It's not laissez-faire. You have to do something if you want change or progress. The arc of history won't bend on its own; you have to shape it.

Tereza was trying to do that. Late in 2017, she had lodged herself into a revolving door forming part of a blockade on Third Avenue. Holiday decorations sat just behind her in the foyer of Chuck Schumer's Manhattan offices, across from a Citibank branch and a Smith & Wollensky steak house. It was just under a year into the first Trump presidency, and there was a chance that maybe—if people like the senator from New

York demanded it—the DREAM Act could be included in a forthcoming spending bill.

"I can't get into my building to work," snapped a woman in a pea coat who tried walking through the blockade.

That was the point. The stakes were high. The Trump administration had just announced plans to phase out DACA, the executive branch memorandum issued by Barack Obama in 2012. The passage of the DREAM Act in Congress would obviate the need for DACA, which had only ever been a stopgap anyway, and end the uncertainty for good. There were maybe a dozen protesters in Tereza's group. They had the look of the politically engaged during the early Trump administration: homemade placards, beanies, hooded sweatshirts, a T-shirt here or there with a hammer and a sickle. Tereza held up her sign, #NoDreamNoDeal.

There were nearly sixty thousand protests in the United States during Trump's first presidency.[37] Somewhere between twenty-one and thirty-one million people took part in them, many for the first time in their lives. Analysts have now calculated the most common themes had to do with racism, policing, or the presidency itself. At first, the media reported on the outpouring of protests with awe, headlining stories about demonstrations that seemed to pop up "out of nowhere" in reaction to incendiary policy shifts.[38] But over time, there were so many events in so many parts of the country it was hard not to describe them as some form of the new normal, or to describe the country, as the *Washington Post* did, as a "rallying nation."[39] There was the Women's March, the Travel Ban protests, the March for Science, the March for Our Lives. It wasn't purely a left-wing habit. The number of pro-Trump counterprotests grew over time. So, too, did protests that didn't really have much to do with the president directly, if at all. In Oklahoma, West Virginia, and Kentucky, verified red states, teachers started protesting by literally walking off their jobs because of pay, something more or less unseen since the 1990s.[40]

By this point, Tereza had become a full-fledged activist herself. She'd grown dismayed by the surging number of deportations during the Obama presidency and found community in the tight-knit group of Bernie Sanders supporters around her in New York City. She rallied for legislation protecting immigrant rights—not just the DREAM Act, but other more local policies as well. She helped in churches that functioned as sanctuary spaces for undocumented immigrants, creating a modern version of an Underground Railroad for migrants. Of course, her life had grown and shifted outside of her activism work, too. She started teaching at the Manhattan School of Music and the Church Street School for Music & Art downtown. And there was her marriage. With her wedding, the worst of Tereza's fears about her own deportation vanished. Her husband threw her a surprise party. But the actual, real, nuanced feeling was bittersweet. Tereza's citizenship ceremony came a day after yet another of the many attempts to pass the DREAM Act failed in Congress. It felt wild to Tereza that one piece of paper, nine digits of a Social Security number, could wield so much power over her entire life. And in her heart, there was a clenching: She'd gotten her papers. But what about the others? Her own mother and father, her friends, the other activists she'd come to know and work with over the years.

It was in this era that a slew of stories started to bother her.

Tereza Lee, the original Dreamer[41]

Why The 'Original DREAMer' Remains Hopeful Amid DACA's Uncertain Future[42]

The Original DREAMer Recalls 'All Pervasive' Fear as an Undocumented Child[43]

Tereza would ask journalists not to use the term "original DREAMer" when they wrote about her. But it was a label that was too hard for them to resist. The problem with the name "DREAMer," Tereza points out, is that it divides undocumented immigrants into two camps. There are the deserving ones, the children brought to the country against their will, often painted by the well-intended but naïve journalist as innocent, angelic minors. The label automatically casts the others by contrast as undeserving, having come to America knowing what they were doing, not against but by their will. Were the DREAMers supposed to cast them aside in pursuit of their own goals?

"Hi, my name is Tereza Lee," she said to the crowd gathered that day on Third Avenue. She told her story. Cabs honked on the wide avenue. Delivery guys on bikes sped by. Christmas lights shone across the way. Of course the DREAM Act was flawed. But at the time, with Trump in the White House and DACA hanging in the balance, what other options did they have?

The protestors tried walking into the building, but a security guy sent them away. He gave them a number to call for the senator's office. They called, but the only person who came down was a nervous-looking staffer named Jackie in a bright blue coat. They wanted to see Schumer.

"Do you guys have something I could bring to the senator?" she said. "Paperwork or a flyer? We'll definitely tell him about this demonstration."

It turned out Schumer was on the Senate floor that day, 228 miles away.

A woman in the crowd took her cell phone camera out and started a livestream on Facebook. She asked Jackie to clarify Schumer's position on the DREAM Act and the spending bill. The woman had been given some positive-sounding assurances from the Binghamton office but wanted Jackie to state them on camera.

"Thank you all so much for coming." Jackie clasped her hands together. "It really is important to make your voices heard."

There was a creeping sentiment at that time, a year or so into the first Trump administration, when millions of people had already protested in thousands of demonstrations, backed up online by countless posts. It was this harsh fear, one you might read now as a foreshadowing: Who was listening?

A cynic could look back at the first four years of the Trump presidency and wonder where those sixty thousand demonstrations got us. As you know, he is back in the Oval Office now. A less-than-generous interpretation could cast the protests aside as mere virtue signaling. A more forgiving person with a long historic memory might look back further to the 1963 March on Washington and wonder why it and other protests led to the Civil Rights Act in 1964—with the guarantee of equal voting rights and the banning of discrimination against Black Americans in public places like restaurants and theaters—but the sixty thousand demonstrations of 2016 to 2020 showed little concrete legislative change. Why has it become so hard to replicate the results of the past now?

A clue comes from the Seattle protests of 1999, the ones that coincided with Britney Spears's birthday. Although they managed to shut down parts of the city and gain worldwide media attention, they did not have the long-term political impact one might have expected from such a sizeable demonstration. The sociologist Zeynep Tufekci, who studied the Seattle protests and many since, points out that modern movements tend to be broad but not deep. It's true that with the advent of the internet and then social media, it has become easier than ever to organize a mass event, but that means these events come together quickly, before the institutional structures are in place to affect lasting change. (This can even happen with hastily organized presidential campaigns.) Some movements will go on to develop those crucial structures and have long and effective political lives. Others won't. The fact of the matter is that in prior generations, it could take years of work and relationship-building to convince people to go march on Washington in droves. In that time, activists would have been busy working in tandem on other means of bringing about change. Today, protests happen at a different point in the movement's lifecycle: at the beginning. So even if it looks like the protests of today are less effective than those from the past, it's because, as Tufekci says, they form earlier.

Even "slacktivism," the much-derided form of Millennial protest that comes in the form of likes, retweets, and Instagram posts, plays a role in the evolution of a movement.[44] Posts and comments don't carry the same gravity as chaining yourself to a tree, and neither do hashtags. But recently, psychological research has shown that such activity helps create what's known as "consensus mobilization." That is the process through which activists help convince an otherwise apathetic member of the general public that they should care about a cause. A mass of posts cluttering a feed helps spread a movement's theses beyond their original proponents, carrying them from the personal into the ideational.

"Protests sometimes look like failures in the short term," notes Tufecki.[45] "But much of the power of protests is in their long-term effects, on both the protesters themselves and the rest of society."

So, what happened in those early Trump years was not for nothing.

People who study protest movements say that demonstrations—even quickly arranged ones—are particularly effective when they take place at a politician's office. A goal of mass demonstration, Tufecki says, is to show politicians that the people have reached a point where they won't take any more. It's one thing when these events burst out into the streets. It's another when they indicate the level of organization it takes to show up united at a politician's office.

For Tereza, there was historical potency to standing outside Schumer's office in particular. More than thirty years before she sat in the building's doorway, it was Schumer, then a 35-year-old Democratic congressman, who became crucial to the passage of Reagan's 1986 Immigration Reform and Control Act—the one that had, for the first time in American history, made it illegal for employers to hire undocumented immigrants. Schumer was one of the Act's main advocates in Congress. In the mid-1980s, he pointed out that the immigration situation in the country had grown untenable. He had some concerns but was willing to take a risk with the more draconian measure. "The bill is a gamble, a riverboat gamble," he said back then. "There is no guarantee that employer sanctions will work or that amnesty will work. We are headed into uncharted waters."[46]

That winter day in late 2017 outside Schumer's office, there was some debate about what to do. Three of the protestors decided they would block the entrance to the office. But should they all block one of the three revolving doors together, or split up? Solidarity was a good look, but it would leave two doors open for people to go into and out of. They decided to each block their own door.

"I'm not afraid of getting arrested," Tereza said to a reporter on the scene, who approached her where she sat in the doorway. "We've been suffering for way too long. And I'm doing this for the eleven million undocumented people."

In a few minutes, the police came. They had plastic handcuffs that looked like zip ties. They wrapped them around Tereza's wrists to arrest her. Two marched her away from the revolving door, and as she walked, she chanted to the others.

"What do we want? DREAM Act. When do we want it? Now. If we don't get it, shut it down."

*　*　*

A related consequence of the Trump presidencies has been a widespread challenge to the status quo. Elon Musk as a grand vizier. Fox News hosts in the cabinet. We know that part of Trump's enduring appeal—and his danger—is his willingness to jackhammer through norms politically and culturally. It was once considered prohibitively unpresidential to brag about groping women or to criticize private citizens via tweet or to be convicted of thirty-four felony counts by a jury of one's peers. But when everything is getting shaken up at the top of the country, things start to shake up further down, too.

One norm that was questioned for the better early in 2017: Maybe powerful men who used their positions of authority to get sex shouldn't be able to do that. That autumn, a *New York Times* investigation found that Harvey Weinstein, one of the most powerful producers in Hollywood, had reached at least eight settlements with various women for sexual harassment and unwanted physical contact. The guy who had produced so many film and television mainstays of our childhoods— *Good Will Hunting*, *Shakespeare in Love*, even *Project Runway*—had also done things like send Ashley Judd up to his hotel room and ask her to either give him a massage or watch him shower.[47] Five days after the *Times* piece came out, Ronan Farrow published a story in *The New Yorker* that included allegations from three women saying that Weinstein had raped them.[48] Gwyneth Paltrow and Angelina Jolie shared their stories of abuse by Weinstein, and others like Lady Gaga began telling similar stories about other aggressors in the entertainment industry. Alyssa Milano from *Charmed* tweeted, "If you've been sexually harassed or assaulted write 'me too' as a reply to this tweet." The #MeToo movement was born.

That is, at least, the story as most people know it. In reality, a Black woman named Tarana Burke had started the #MeToo movement for survivors of sexual abuse a full decade before.[49] She started a nonprofit called Just Be and in working with survivors had discovered how powerful the phrase "me too" can be. It lets the survivor know they are not alone and helps with something that Burke calls "empowerment through empathy." In many ways, those early proclamations online by celebrities in 2017 felt like yet another example of White America shamelessly, ignorantly appropriating from Black America. Burke watched on her screen that fall as the actresses, mostly White, began hashtagging. The phrase exploded. The famous men fell quickly. After Weinstein came journalist Mark Halperin, fired by NBC on October 30.[50] On November 9, five women accused comedian Louis C.K. of sexual misconduct.[51] CBS and PBS fired broadcaster Charlie Rose on November 21.[52] And then on November 29, NBC fired Matt Lauer.[53] One woman said he had asked her into his office under the guise of talking about a story. Once she arrived, he locked the door by pressing a button under his desk. He asked her to unbutton her shirt. He then bent her over a chair and had sex with her. That was in 2001, not all that long after his "Silent Night" Christmas-tree lighting interview with Britney Spears in Rockefeller Center. The one where he said he felt like her dad.

Accountability is a good thing. But at the time, Burke was concerned.[54] Her fear was that the campaign might turn into just another social-media flash in the pan. Movements, we know, start earlier now and don't always last. Burke worried the campaign might put pressure on survivors who weren't ready to share their stories to come forward, or to feel guilty if they didn't. She worried that the wealthy celebrities telling their stories might not be ready for what comes after disclosure of a painful secret. Everyday people might not be ready, either. Healing from sexual abuse doesn't come from a single public statement. She and Milano eventually met, and Burke recognizes the promotional help celebrities gave the movement. But she made and continues to make a solid point: Moving on from sexual abuse requires continual support over the very long term. "People need hope and inspiration desperately," Burke has said. "But hope and inspiration are only sustained by work."

Did that work happen? A year after #MeToo started, my editor told me and my colleagues to walk around town at lunchtime asking "young people" about its effects. Most people I interviewed didn't know what the phrase even meant. It's now a perennial article idea, every fall, for newspapers and magazines to ask "Did #MeToo Do Anything?" In 2024, New York's highest court stunned survivors when it overturned the rape convictions that had put Harvey Weinstein in prison. (The court said the judge in that case had violated Weinstein's rights by calling witnesses who could testify about Weinstein's abuse but not about the particular charges he was being tried for in that case. Weinstein still faces a sixteen-year sentence in California.)

But there is no doubt that #MeToo changed the Millennial workplace. It unfolded in a time when all of us were working age. It did not stamp out every sexual abuser in the labor force, and it did not bring about immediate, systemic change. But #MeToo did force a reassessment of power and privilege at work—even beyond issues of sexual misconduct.

Miju saw this happen in her own life. She had turned into a Silicon Valley success story, the sort of person you see on LinkedIn and maybe get jealous of as you scroll past. You wonder how they became so successful at such a young age. She had hopped to a software company—a big, billion-dollar unicorn that most engineers know intimately, but the everyday internet user won't necessarily be familiar with. Someone she'd worked with at a previous job had referred her to a C-suite executive at the company, and that executive liked her. She got hired. It was the first time Miju felt like an "industry insider," someone with a reputation, someone a newspaper might call "a source familiar with the matter." (Because Miju still works in tech, I won't name the unicorn where she worked in order to allow her to speak to me more freely.)

Long story short, Miju rocked her new gig. She pitched projects her managers loved. She pulled them off. She was asked to deliver a keynote speech just after her CEO's speech at a huge conference in San Francisco. For professionals of a certain age, being asked to deliver a keynote was *the* sign of having made it in Silicon Valley—maybe in life. Keynotes are modeled on the ones Steve Jobs used to do, where he'd wear all black and deliver exciting product updates in a casual-but-no-nonsense manner, complete with sharp hand gestures. Getting to do one was getting a vote of confidence from the company. They said, "We trust you enough and think you are presentable enough to announce an important thing to our customers, the media, the universe. We're choosing you specifically to do this."

The tech conferences where they happened often felt like rock concerts. The one for Miju's keynote did. The lighting was flawless, the stage dark and sleek, the audience packed, the CEO famous. He spoke about collaboration that could make "everyone in the world" win, a world where we could take all the data that's out there and "make everyone better." What he said sounded a lot like tikkun olam, the idea that had motivated Miju years before to go to Cameroon. It was the idea of fixing the world. It permeated Silicon Valley in the Obama years, losing some sheen when Trump came to power, even more when Elon Musk bought Twitter and then became Trump's apparently most trusted adviser in 2024. But the dream of tech as something that could fix the world still drifted through San Francisco. It made well-meaning liberal tech workers feel like they were doing good things for the world. Because they were . . . weren't they?

The rock music played. Miju stepped out in red heels, wearing all black. Whoever wrote the Williams College guide to dressing professionally would have been so proud: "Keep it simple, but feel free to pick accessories that show your personality," it says.[55] Along with her dark tech executive outfit, she wore a solitary necklace with silver metal stacked jaggedly. She stopped in the middle of the stage, smiled, and started talking.

"Hello, universe," she began.

The keynote was a pinnacle for Miju. In a few months, she would walk away from the firm.

Tensions had already been brewing in the background. Miju's company, the media reported, was in the middle of a "full-blown culture war." A few years before, a female software engineer had gone public about the firm's allegedly "meritocratic culture" that actually just let men bully and disrespect women. Its then CEO resigned. The company brought in an executive to help diversify the place, but then after a few years, that person resigned, too.

Miju felt as if the tempestuous debates rocking the country—a mix of #MeToo and the broader reckoning with privilege, race, and politics—had landed with force in her own workplace. She was one of few executives of color at the company, and people who were not straight White men sometimes consulted with her about their problems. She listened. She felt protective. Often, what they described were the sort of micro-aggressions you now are warned about within the first few minutes of a company's HR training. Senior-level women who were asked to do secretarial tasks. Male managers who took credit for ideas women came up with in meetings. Miju had seen some of this herself. At one point, she asked a male colleague why he hadn't consulted with her about something since they were the same level of seniority.

"Well, you know, I hadn't seen any good work from you," he said.

This was after the keynote, around the time Miju's team won a major industry award—what she says is the "closest to a Grammy I'll ever get." Her project was ranked one of the top ten software developments of the year by the industry publisher *InfoWorld*. Miju Han is a feedback person. She is so much of one that it might make you feel uncomfortable sometimes. While I was interviewing her, there were points where she'd correct me as I asked questions and tell me why what I'd just said was wrong. In the moment, I really didn't like it. I'm not used to getting immediate commentary about myself. But after the fact, I often came to appreciate her thoughts because I felt like she was trying to teach me something or at very least being honest with me in a way most people aren't. Miju has been featured in tech media as someone who literally goes to feedback retreats, where she sits face-to-face talking with people about her ideas and thoughts in the moment, subjecting herself to immediate input from those listening to her. It's like going to the career center to watch how you performed in a mock job interview, just a lot more real.

The importance of feedback is one of the noble truths of Silicon Valley. The irony is that the Millennial heroes of technology have all told us how important it is, but rarely tend to explain how to give or respond to it. "We all need people who will give us feedback," says Bill Gates. "That's how we improve." Tim Cook claims he "religiously" looks at customer feedback every morning, starting at 5 a.m. "You have to get real feedback," says Sheryl Sandberg. "You have to be open to feedback, you have to ask for feedback. You have to build in a culture where, when I think you need to do something better or you think I need to do something better, we tell each other, and tell each other directly and work it out."

It was in the context of all this chief executive chatter on the importance of feedback that Miju wrote the email. In her mind, her higher ups were totally mature enough to hear helpful feedback. She was going to be a bridge. She'd link the people who found themselves crying at work to the management team, who, she thought, just needed to know how their behavior was upsetting people. Then maybe they'd fix it. Most of the trouble was coming from her counterpart, the guy who allegedly "hadn't seen any good work" from her. Miju wanted to *prevent* another big culture-war scandal at the company and felt like she could do that by being transparent and telling management how things should change. So she listed the things people were saying and offered herself as a resource to help the guy—and the company—understand what was going on. She emailed her counterpart, and she forwarded it to HR, thinking that might be useful, even transformative. It was a move based on the way many companies painted their workplace cultures: Remember that in Silicon Valley, HR departments bill themselves not as the corporate ass-coverers they are, but as change-makers, cultural-agenda-setters, "chief people officers."

"Hey," she wrote to HR, optimistically. "I think we need to talk about this."

But the thing is, people in upper management almost never actually find themselves in a position to take that kind of feedback. And as a result, when they do, they don't do so very well. It's ironic. Emphasizing how important you find feedback is a really good way, if you're in a position of high power, to get away with telling people some very nasty things, usually sans repercussions. The highest-ranking people are usually shielded by their seniority, so they get to dish it out, positioning themselves as people who can take it as well, but in actuality they very rarely have to. And when they do, they are shocked.

In retrospect, Miju now sees she could have been a little more careful communicating with the powers that be. She knows now that people often really need to believe that they're good, and that people in power can especially struggle to hear anything to the contrary.

"Oh, no. You don't understand," her problematic counterpart said to her when she confronted him. "I'm a champion for women in tech. I mentor female founders."

"That wasn't feedback," an executive at Miju's company said regarding her email. "That was a takedown."

Miju's bosses were, she feels in hindsight, worried that she was trying to start a public culture war at the company. Unbeknownst to Miju, right around the same time, another woman at the firm was preparing to sue the company for discrimination. What's more, the world's largest software company was considering acquiring the company, making its reputation more important than ever. The bosses ended up reprimanding Miju for the feedback, and she went back to her duties.

But going to work after a dispute with your bosses is chilling. It feels terrible to walk in the door as you dig through your bag for that fucking badge to tap in. It feels terrible to slink to the elevator, hoping you won't get stuck beside anyone awful as you shoot up to the floor where you must pass at least eight respectable hours doing things on a computer. Smiling at people sometimes. Attending meetings. It feels like a victory to make it through a day avoiding the awful men you fear, but it feels weak, too, because you're avoiding the problems instead of confronting them head-on.

And you can't confront them head-on. That right has been, it's made clear, reserved for the truly powerful. So all you can do is get through the day and deflect until the other people start zipping up their laptop cases from TJ Maxx, emptying their "Keep Calm and Keep Coding" coffee cups in the sink, Google Mapping their commutes home. Wishing the same thing weren't going to happen ad nauseam until retirement.

In other words, Miju was miserable.

Her mentors told her to leave. "Why are you still working there?" they'd ask.

She wanted to navigate the situation. Solve the problem. In essence, get back to that incredible peak she'd scaled in late 2017. It's a Millennial tendency to think we can find the solution if we just Google hard enough. But it wasn't working this time.

"You need to go to therapy," her husband told her.

She didn't. Her email inbox transformed from a stream of productivity into an idle pool she just stared at, as if she were daring it to attract larvae. She didn't answer messages. She felt stagnant.

It wasn't until 2018 that Miju finally left. She went to therapy. She reflected on what she now describes as the "small 't' trauma" of that period of her life. She updated her LinkedIn profile, got jobs at other companies. She loved the people she met. She climbed the ranks again. But she didn't feel like she was finding the same traction that led her up to that keynote peak. She felt something was missing.

When it came to Millennials in the 2010s workplace, two tropes stemming from our ostensible participation-trophy childhoods lingered. (In many ways, they still do.) The first was that as products of the self-esteem movement, we would be so used to getting praise for doing nothing that we would be horrible employees. "Managers must tread lightly when making a critique," one author advised employers around that time in the *Wall Street Journal*.[56] (The author had literally written a book called *The Trophy Kids Grow Up*.) "This generation was treated so delicately that many schoolteachers stopped grading papers and tests in harsh-looking red ink. Some managers have seen Millennials break down in tears after a negative performance review and even quit their jobs." But Miju's experience shows that for some of us, the opposite happened. Many of us were given so much meaningless praise growing up by teachers, parents, and coaches that we learned to see through it in the way you can see straight through the cheap plastic faux-crystal of a participation trophy to the "Made in China" sticker affixed to the bottom. Some of us grew to desire something deeper than praise. Like Miju, we wanted real, honest feedback.

The second idea about us was that we would struggle with failure. And I think this one was more accurate. Around the time Miju quit her job, lots of management publications and business books were offering tips for leaders on how to handle a supposed Millennial fear of failure. "Millennials have a complicated relationship with risk," went one such piece in *Inc.* magazine.[57] "They've grown up in a connected world where failure is more public and permanent. One wrong move and the Internet can immortalize one's failure." And that pressure to show the world the best version of our workplace selves was certainly part of why we developed a unique relationship with failure. Baby Boomers didn't have frenemies on LinkedIn or Twitter watching their every career move online. We did.

Even more than that, though, I think what has made the idea of failure hard for us is that we were told to cast ourselves as the lead characters in our careers. In that sense, the self-esteem movement did help put us in the middle of everything. Around the time we entered the work world, the cofounder of LinkedIn published a book called *The Startup of You*, with stress-inducing, self-oriented quotes like "if you're not moving forward, you're moving backward." The people we were meant to see as career role models were not collaborators who saw the bigger picture, but self-centered, rule-breaking entrepreneurs like Mark Zuckerberg and Elon Musk. So we focused on ourselves at work. That can have a harsh flip side. When things go badly, we unhelpfully blame ourselves, even if some of the failures that befell us were the result of others, of a system, of history.

I get the sense Miju did this during her struggles at the software company and afterward. She blamed herself for not finding what she calls that "magic combination" that would propel her back up toward the top of a corporate ladder. Never mind that in world around her, interest rates were ticking up, making startup investments less attractive. Business confidence was ticking down. Trump had initiated an international trade war targeting China, but with a series of policies that created blowback for the US economy, including slowed growth, hiring, and business investment.[58] What's more, the breakneck pace of change that had exhilarated Silicon Valley in the early 2010s was cooling. Uber, Twitter, Facebook, and Google were maturing. The opportunities for exponential growth in one's career, including in Miju's, were slowing down. That wasn't her fault.

*　*　*

Justin left his job within a few months of Miju leaving hers. Different, though: He didn't just leave a company. He left the labor force completely.

It's part of a trend that has been building in the United States since the 1960s. Back then, 97 percent of men ages 25 to 54 took part in the labor force. Today, that figure is around 88 percent. Nobody can say exactly why. *Bloomberg* columnist Allison Schrager calls it "one of the big economic mysteries of our time."[59] She shows that recessions amplify the trend, but she also points to a range of other theories that could partially explain it: the decline of manufacturing jobs, the difficulties men have in school compared with women, the opioid epidemic, even the rise of more involved video games. Schrager finds that when men out of the labor force get asked why they aren't working by the Census Bureau, small proportions of them cite things like illness, family responsibilities, lack of training, or the fact that they couldn't find other work. But the most common answer, cited 36 percent of the time, is just "other."

When I ask Justin why he left, what he tells me boils down to math. There was no way he and Tara were going to be able to afford the life they wanted, emotionally or financially, if he kept working.

Every year since 2003, demographers have been asking Americans how they spend their time. Married Americans say that, on average, they spend about four-and-a-half hours a day with their spouses, not including sleeping. Research shows that the more time spouses spend with each other, the more satisfied they are with life.[60] Looking back, Justin remembers his early married years as a point when he and Tara were so busy with work, they were spending barely an hour together each day. Their schedules were staggered: Tara had gotten a job at a financial services company, and it started early and ended early, Monday through Friday. Justin's hours, meanwhile, were mostly later in the day and on weekends, since martial arts academies work around kids' school schedules.

Their one night together was Thursday. They'd go to this place, what Justin calls "our *Cheers* bar." Its name was the Blarney Stone. It is 1,500 square feet of anachronistic Ireland plopped into a shopping center in San Diego. No matter that its neighbors are the tiny, glass-fronted Tobacco Emporium and the very plain-looking Blush Hour Nails & Spa. It advertises out front "A bit of Olde Ireland" in Gaelic script and has wooden beams over the stucco that look like Tudor-style wattle and daub. It had been around for years, two lots over from the strip mall where White Dragon was located, and it was across the street from an apartment Justin and Tara rented for a while. They'd gone in from time to time. But it reached *Cheers* status the Thursday night before their wedding. It was a relatively dead night, but there was a guy performing on stage with a guitar and a harmonica. Eventually, he found out what Justin's and Tara's party—there were about eight or nine of them—were celebrating. Others did, too, and they kept buying everybody shots and drinks. After that, it turned into a Thursday night ritual.

"Thursday night at the Stone? I think so!" Justin and his friends would post on Facebook, back when it was still the platform you used to organize nights out.

"I'm not drunk, you're drunk!. . . . . ok, I might be drunk."

"If you're reading this, come get silly with us at the Blarney Stone Pub tonight and watch an AMAZING Irish band play all night!"

But they couldn't stay in the Blarney Stone forever. It was, after all, a Disneyland kind of place, fun but obviously not real. They wanted to spend more time with each other, like they used to, back in their early days. Time kept slipping away from them as they were trying to do something important: grow up.

It was totally contradictory to those critiques of Millennials as selfish failures to launch. But it was what many of us were saying, increasingly so. We did want to grow up, get married, buy homes, and have children. It was just that the goalposts we typically assign to adulthood had become harder to reach. Jobs had become more difficult to land and harder to keep. Low interest rates meant you earned nothing on your savings. It also meant that those who did have savings invested them in assets that could actually earn money, like stocks and housing. This drove the prices of both of those up, making it even harder for those without them to get there.

Justin and Tara felt that pinch on housing. They were working their asses off, hardly seeing one another, but also hardly seeing their savings for a down payment grow. All the while, housing in California was only growing more expensive. In 1980, the average price for a home in San Diego was $55,000.[61] By 2018, it was $338,000. No amount of economizing on avocado toast was going to get them there. This wasn't just a California or a coastal problem. That same year, the average sale price of a home in the US in general had shot up to nearly $380,000. The trend came from larger, structural problems in the American housing market that started in the wake of the Great Recession. Remember: In the early 2000s, home prices were shooting up. To make money, developers started building homes like crazy. But when the recession hit, they racked up major losses on properties nobody could afford to buy or even keep living in. As a response, they stopped building. So the supply of housing shrank, and it remains far lower today than what the country needs. Meanwhile, the US population has continued to expand. This sent home prices up sharply and kept them well out of sync with wages, which have not increased at the same rate. This has become a particularly acute problem as Millennials age into the part of life when they form families and need larger places to live.

That included Justin and Tara.

One night, Tara invited Justin out to dinner at one of their favorite restaurants. She handed him a little card with the news on it. She was pregnant. He was thrilled.

Parenting in the age of Millennial social media is filled with joys but also stressful contradictions. It begins before birth. On Facebook, Justin and Tara posted a picture of their two dogs, each one sitting behind a chalkboard with a sign on it. "Our parents are getting us a human," one chalkboard read. "Guard dog duty begins May 2017," read the other. The gender-reveal post came 22 days later. "It's a boy!" was the caption. Two tiny, blue Chuck Taylor shoes sat on a box in the picture. The birth post arrived 176 days after that. Their baby was wrapped in a small blanket. The post said he was born at 7:46 p.m. on Memorial Day. "Perfect in every way," Justin wrote. "Mom and baby are happy and healthy. Just catching up on much-deserved rest."

But social media is a two-way street. You post, but you also compare. It's not just the superficial stuff about whose kid is cuter or whose house is bigger. The comparisons go on endlessly, raising the bar for how to be the smarter, better, more clued-in parent. It's never been easier to research and research and research the "best baby stroller" or "when my kid should be talking" or even what ever-changing trends are suddenly essential. Then, armed with information, you can compare on social media to see who is doing it all right and all wrong and all better than you. And don't forget comparing yourself to friends who don't even have kids yet, who are seemingly having way more fun than you are.

It was a few months after their son was born that using Facebook started to hurt for Justin and Tara, for some of those reasons. It's hard to tell who felt it before whom; they didn't talk about it the first, second, or maybe even the third time it arose. But this thing was definitely happening, and Justin is sure it was on Sundays, because those are the days that follow the fun, reckless Saturday nights of the child-free, when their photos go up online.

"Hey," Justin or Tara finally said. "Did you get invited to that?"

"No," the other replied.

They realized that they, the only parents amongst their still-young-ish friends in their late twenties and early thirties, weren't getting invited to things anymore. There was a loneliness to that. All the while, time was rushing by. They were still working all the time. But Justin's career trajectory was starting to look like it had a ceiling, well enough as he was doing, much as he liked the guys at White Dragon. There were only a handful of White Dragon academies in the area, and to get the chance to run one could mean waiting decades. Then there was Tara's career. Her company's headquarters had moved to Charlotte. The economy there was booming.

Justin and Tara were at their son's three-month checkup in 2017. They were both looking out the window. Work was out there—all the expectations. So were the friends having fun without them. Something had to change.

A thought came to Justin.

"Well," he said. "What's going on with the Charlotte office?"

The last day of Justin's career at White Dragon—one he had built over a decade, from the time he was a teenager through the Great Recession and into fatherhood—ended with him giving a student a kung fu test. He'd administered hundreds by then, and it could have been like any other, one student hoping to move up a rank. (It was a pass.) When it finished, he changed clothes, walked across the padded training floor one final time, pushed open the glass front door into the sunshine that falls on California evenings even in the late autumn, and walked two lots over to the Blarney Stone.

Friends came in and out to say goodbye. Justin and Tara had been planning the move to North Carolina for months by then. Justin had sold his truck, and they'd had yard sales many weekends in a row. They wanted to leave the place they had been their entire lives in the right way.

"What are you going to do out there?" the people who trickled into the bar kept asking.

Justin wasn't sure. He knew he was leaving the next day on a road trip across those two thousand miles to the apartment waiting for them in Charlotte. He knew the stops along the way already. He was going to do the drive with his best friend and brother-in-law. Tara would fly out with their son and her sister to meet him later. To save money, he had booked all the hotels in advance, putting the exact amount of cash he'd need for each reservation in separate envelopes. But he wasn't sure what he'd do for work in Charlotte while Tara worked in finance. Justin's plan was to get out to North Carolina, rest a bit—he'd been working ever since leaving high school—and figure it out later.

The friends said goodbye around 10:30 p.m. Justin got a burrito for dinner, then he made his way back to the small ranch home he rented with Tara, by then largely empty.

When morning came, he got into Tara's Mazda SUV with the guys, and they headed across the Sonoran Desert to the Arizona border, leaving California behind.

It's a move many Millennials have made, quitting high-priced coastal cities for places where housing is cheaper. And those houses are springing up rapidly in places like Charlotte, where neighborhood names give clues to what was there before: Oak Forest, Hickory Grove, Bradfield Farms, Eagle Lake. Driving around town, it's impossible to miss the modern farmhouse subdivisions of cul-de-sacs, the brand-new hipster-inspired/industrial-chic hotels, and the fast-casual restaurants alongside intricate on-ramps and off-ramps that lead to super centers and big box warehouse extravaganzas.

The reason for this growth is an explosion of jobs. There were many big companies headquartered in Charlotte already: Bank of America, Lowe's, Duke Energy, LendingTree, Bojangles. The list of companies moving their headquarters to the city in recent years is long. Honeywell moved down from New Jersey a few years ago. Truist came from Atlanta, after a merger. The railcar company TTX came in from Chicago. Columbus McKinnon even more recently relocated from Buffalo. In press releases, their CEOs usually say the moves have to do with "wanting everybody to be in the same place" without really explaining why that place needs to be Charlotte. The big reason: North Carolina now has the lowest corporate tax rate of any state that levies corporate taxes in the United States. (South Dakota and Wyoming don't subject companies to income taxes, but they don't have the same pull factors—proximity to the university Research Triangle, connectivity to other large cities, abundance of leisure activities.)

When jobs appear, people follow. In 1990, the population of Charlotte was 426,984. Thirty-four years later, in 2024, it hit 923,164—bigger than San Francisco, Seattle, Denver, Nashville, Boston, Portland, Atlanta, or Washington, D.C. And that population is sprawling outward. It goes all the way down to the South Carolina border and north to towns that were once separate and distinct just a few years ago, like Concord and Monroe. The people who come are young. America's median age is 39; Charlotte's is 34. Justin, when he arrived, was 30.

In their first hours there, he and his friends roamed the city. It was a new adventure, a new world for someone who had lived in the same city his entire life. They went to the Bank of America Stadium, where the Carolina Panthers play. They found a brewery they'd heard about and had a few beers. They went back to Justin's new apartment and rolled out sleeping bags. The beds hadn't come yet, and Tara and the baby wouldn't be there for a few days, so they slept on hardwood floors.

Tara and the baby arrived. They settled in. Christmas came, and so did the New Year. As the weeks passed, Justin and Tara came to feel something difficult: Sure, housing prices in the greater Charlotte area were lower than they were in California. But the costs of paying someone to watch their son while both of them worked were still unmanageable. As is the case in thirty-seven states and the District of Columbia, infant care costs more in North Carolina than the annual in-state tuition for a four-year public college. Tara's job paid well. In California, it had been responsible for boosting their combined household income into that coveted six-figure range. (In California, though, that six figures still only got them to a place where they were living paycheck to paycheck.) But for Justin to get a job, they would need childcare.

They ran the numbers. The average salary of a martial arts instructor in Charlotte is $38,406. Justin's salary had been higher than that in California, but the industry isn't plug-and-play. It takes years to build enough trust to become a chief instructor at a new studio. And childcare was expensive, sometimes totaling more than rent. Justin's take-home pay wouldn't be enough to justify paying a stranger to watch his son all day.

So he joined the ranks of a small but growing group of American men: He became a stay-at-home father. At recent count, they numbered around 2.1 million—enough to populate a city the size of Houston. At-home dads make up about 18 percent of all stay-at-home parents, up from 10 percent in 1989. Still, they're a hard group to count, in part because of lingering societal ideas about what a man should be doing with himself during the day. Some men who stay home to take care of their children don't admit to it in surveys. Others say that they're staying at home because of job loss or disability or being retired but just happen to watch the kids while they're there. Justin was straightforward about it. To get what he and Tara wanted—to save money but also raise a family with adequate childcare—he was going to have to stay out of the workforce.

Ultimately, this isn't unusual. Findings from a smaller set of qualitative interviews with at-home fathers show that they may take up the role for economic reasons.[62] Some reported going through a transition period of a year or so getting used to a job that not many American men have, struggling with conceptions of masculinity as it relates to parenting. There are things at-home fathers report doing to help with some of this. They look to their past accomplishments as a source of pride. They conceptualize their current roles as jobs that, like any other, help support the household. They may see their new positions as an opportunity for a new direction in life. Yet they still report finding the role isolating, not only in practice but in social impact. It's the split-second double takes you get at grocery stores and post offices and in other informal settings that can make you feel like a foreigner.

For Justin, the hardest part about giving up his career was psychological, especially in that first year. He'd climbed the ladder of White Dragon over many years and was used to being impressive: a chief instructor. In this new role, he was on the bottom of the social pecking order. The introduction "Hi, I'm Justin and I'm a stay-at-home dad" got a very different reaction from the one that ended with ". . . and I'm the chief instructor of a martial arts academy."

There were a lot of things that were hard that first year in Charlotte. Arriving in the city, Justin and Tara had about $2,000 to their names. They'd spent most of what they had on the cross-country move. They knew almost nobody in town, and didn't really know the town at all. What they did know is that they only wanted to rent for a year. They were sick of it. So they spent 2018 trying to spend as little as possible. In a way, it was sort of a preview of 2020's lockdowns. They mostly stayed at home. When they went out for fun, they'd just drive around looking at their new city, thinking about the future.

Above all, that year, Tara worked. Justin threw himself into his new role, too. He sees the position as a job, one that brings in the amount of money the family would otherwise spend on childcare, plus more: the convenience of not having to drop a kid off somewhere, the peace of mind of not having to vet a stranger to watch their son. It's not perfect. The "Mr. Mommy" comments at playgrounds are annoying. So are the assumptions that come at times when, say, he's running some errand like getting his hair cut and the barber knowingly beams, seeing a father with his son, and says, "Taking the day off work to be with your son, are you?" Justin has begun stopping people who say this, explaining, "This is what I do for work now."

If being a stay-at-home parent is a job, though, it's not one a person can punch into and out of, forgetting about when the clock strikes five. There are unannounced performance reviews from friends and family. Justin's son, for instance, was a late talker. He didn't say his first word until he was around 2½. The undertones in family members' comments could be painful. There were times when they seemed to suggest that Justin was doing something wrong.

There were nights when Justin would tell Tara he needed to go to bed early, at 7 o'clock. He'd just stare up at the wall for a while until he drifted off to sleep.

Taking on the role of managing the family's money became a way for Justin to find meaning and deal with any insecurities of being a provider. In those early Charlotte months, he came up with a plan he now calls "zeroing out." Each month, Tara got paid on the first and the fifteenth. They'd pay off their bills on the first, and then do what Justin calls "zeroing out to five": They'd leave $500 in their checking account, and everything else left they'd put into savings. When the fifteenth rolled around, they'd keep $500 for checking again, but that time, because bills weren't due, there'd be a lot more to put into savings. By the end of the month, they'd usually have about $1,400 socked away.

That's how they got the house. The year ticked by. There was an online portal where new houses would list at 7 a.m., and they checked it each morning. One morning, a three-bed, three-bath with a big, green lawn came up. Justin just knew it was the one. He called Tara, and they put in an offer that night. The price was $178,000. The deposit was $9,500. The offer was accepted the next day at 1 p.m. when Justin and his son were strolling around a grocery store. Finally, after thirteen years together, the formation of two careers, a child, a cross-country move, and many sacrifices, Justin and Tara had become American homeowners.

* * *

I'll just cut to it: Aaron started using again. He started getting a real falling feeling around the same time the new steel tariffs took effect. Trump had announced those in 2018, pulling a page from the Bush playbook, pandering to voters in steel country by pledging to make American steel cheaper domestically than its foreign competitors. It was a desperate move. The Bush tariffs hadn't saved steel country in 2003. Why weren't there any better ideas all these years later?

It's hard to talk about Aaron's down years. He wasn't at his best. Frankly, the years between 2018 and 2020 don't make him look great. But Aaron wants to tell me the truth about what happened to him. He thinks it will help people because it shows that the road out of addiction isn't a straight line; it's a bending one that leads to ups and downs, into sobriety, often out again, and then hopefully back once more. More people need to understand this hard journey if we're going to end the opioid crisis. Comfort with uncomfortable memories is something that I really respect about Aaron: He looks me in the eyes and takes responsibility for the stories about the good times in his life, but also the bad ones. He owns his mistakes. He doesn't like excuses.

Aaron tells me about the Kia incident to show how the toll of his usage and dealing was getting steeper as the years went on. It weighed on his relationship with a new girlfriend, who didn't want him using. They had a nice home life, with his son and a daughter they had together, plus his girlfriend's other children. Aaron was inspired by his father to be a good dad, too. But some of the comfort they had established came from the fact that Aaron was lying about what he was doing. He didn't like it, but it felt like he couldn't help it. Physically, he was addicted to drugs, and addiction makes us do things we know we shouldn't.

One day in 2019, Aaron said he was going out to play basketball. In reality, he drove from Alliance to Akron to pick up a load of pills for a friend. It was a drug deal. But when he was getting back on the I-76 eastbound, elevated over Akron, a semitruck swerved into him, knocking his vehicle into the median and totaling it so badly that a million tiny shards of glass splattered across the road.

This is the sort of moment when Aaron talks about how twenty-nine-year-old him, addict him, used to think he had nine lives. He wasn't hurt, but he was shocked. Before he knew it, the police were approaching. He was quick enough in hiding the pills that they didn't see them, and he didn't get in trouble for that. But the semitruck driver was being a dick, pretending he didn't know what had happened, that he hadn't hit Aaron's car. As this was going on, the police questioning him, the truck driver acting dumb, Aaron was temporarily deafened by the onrushing wind of the highway. In the back of his mind, he knew he'd have to call his girlfriend to tell her what happened, and that meant telling her where he'd been. There was no hiding this one. His car was totaled. Aaron tried hard to be a good boyfriend, a good father. But because he was addicted to opioids, a lot of times that meant masking what he did. This was one of those painful moments when he was going to have to call home and fess up.

"What the fuck?" Aaron's girlfriend said on the other end of the line. "You said you were going to go play basketball."

He felt bad about the lie. He felt crushed like that Kia, the first real, adult purchase he had made in his life. He was in so much trouble with the woman he cared about more than anything. And it would only get worse.

Midway through the Trump era, the demographics of the opioid epidemic started to shift. A crisis that had been growing exponentially among White men was suddenly starting to hit Black men in greater numbers. Only a few years before, in 2015, Black men had been at less risk than White men of dying from overdose. But between that year and 2020, Pew research calculates that the death rate for Black men more than tripled, increasing 213 percent. In the same time period, it rose just 69 percent for White men.[63] A recent paper by researchers at the Howard University College of Medicine and the National Institute of Allergy and Infectious Diseases attributed some of this change to a shift away from underreporting. For years, White overdose deaths were more likely than Black deaths to be recorded as such.[64] Some of this has to do with perceptions that arose out of a race-based lag in prescribing, wherein young, White Americans "were more likely to receive opioids for pain management than Black counterparts of any age." The authors also pointed to data showing "that Black people are disproportionately dying from drugs adulterated with fentanyl or its derivatives." The cause of death for someone who dies after using fentanyl-laced cocaine may be mischaracterized and not counted as an opioid death even if it was.

This creates a damaging feedback loop. If opioid deaths are under-counted, it makes opioid treatment options seem less necessary in Black communities. But that lack of treatment options just leads to more deaths. So perceptions of the crisis as more of a White, rural problem can have fatal consequences. But recognition brings problems, too. The concern starting around 2018 was that as politicians clocked the racial changes of the epidemic, they would stop being as sympathetic as they had been in its early stages. Already that year, Trump had begun to suggest using the death penalty on dealers.[65]

No matter what our parents might have thought, when people do bad things, it's obviously not just because they have low self-esteem. In recent years, pundits have been giving new attention to the work of a French pioneer of sociology named Émile Durkheim. Over a century ago, Durkheim was worried about what technology might do to society. His concern was that an increasingly complex economy could weaken the social ties we feel toward each other. He observed that when a society changes quickly, old norms are harder to achieve. We start to feel a sense of distress that we can't get what we thought we could or should. We feel a lack of purpose, like there's no point to striving or trying hard. Recent writers have used these ideas to help explain why Trump won the American presidential election twice and to explore what we might do to keep democracy alive in America.[66]

Durkheim's views influenced what is now known as "strain theory," which posits that people do things like break the law when they have been socialized to think they need to achieve certain goals but are structurally unable to achieve them. It gets worse as inequality increases. As we were growing up, this started happening with the American Dream. We were raised with the idea that we needed to get good jobs, get good houses, and raise good families. That has gotten harder to accomplish, but the pressure remains. This disconnect helps explain the sense of insecurity many of us feel, no matter our income or station in life. It drives us to feel anxious, always behind, like we're missing out. In a way, this is strange, because so much of the new technology we have gained over the course of our adulthoods was pitched as a way of bringing us together. Mobile phones were supposed to connect us. The internet was supposed to make work faster and easier. Social media literally has the word "social" in it. But as Millennials grew up, many began to realize that these technologies were not inherently positive, much as Silicon Valley would want us to think they are. At best, they are neutral, and their overuse can ironically create a sense of greater disconnection than anything else.

That was how Aaron felt on a cold day late in February 2019 when he thumbed into Facebook and saw that Ronnie had died.

Aaron would have none of it. This was "fucking White people" Ronnie. Ronnie of the rundown duplex where they did stupid shit. This was some prank. Ronnie was a goofball. This wasn't real. He couldn't be dead.

The doorbell rang. Brittany, from The Circle, was downstairs. She'd heard from Mike's wife, and she didn't have to say anything; Aaron knew that if Brittany was standing at his front door, it was serious and the stupid post he saw on Facebook was actually true. The consequences of using and dealing were suddenly there, real and heavy. All of this pain Aaron had been keeping inside himself over the past decade as he'd ridden up and down and around on the addiction rollercoaster rose out of some dark place until his breathing constricted. It felt like his esophagus was closing up, and his face got hot as if it were overcome with fever. He just fucking broke down. He broke down in a way he had never done before in his adult life.

Aaron went to the duplex, not far from where he lived. But by then, he was just confirming a fact he already knew would weigh on his heart for the rest of his life. For each day of 2019, an average of 137 people died of a drug overdose in the United States. Ronnie was one of those 137 for the day of February 23.

There was a visitation on the first Friday of March between 6:00 p.m. and 8:00 p.m. at the Gednetz-Ruzek-Brown Funeral Home. It's a small, old brick building that looks like a house connected to a chapel with an American flag dangling out front. A gathering of friends and family was scheduled for the next morning. And after that, Ronnie—the big soft guy, the guy who line danced at country bars, whose job was at a place called Quikrete where he packed concrete, the funny guy who always wanted to lighten the dark, who loved a dog called Lunchbox—went into the earth beneath a grave with a picture of a Mustang on it at Highland Memorial Park. That's in Beloit, a little village six miles to the east of Alliance, just off US Route 62. It's a road that stretches straight as can be for miles and miles into the Ohio country, with all its rolling hills and little farms, creeks and streams and trees that droop over the way, with a gentle sameness.

After Ronnie died, things deteriorated quickly. Aaron and his girlfriend broke up. His drug use intensified. He ran, he says: He tried leaving Alliance for a while and got a job working at a toy factory near St. Louis, living close to a friend. Aaron came back to Alliance for a visit to try and show everybody that he was better, but instead, anxious at a birthday party, he overdosed for the first time. His friends and family rallied around him but told him he had to fix this problem. "Do you want to be alive?" his mother asked. "I don't want you to leave," said Spike, the friend he'd lived with in high school and had been in the military with.

Aaron went to rehab for sixty-four days. The goal was to get better and, hopefully, to get back together with his girlfriend.

He got better, for a while. After leaving rehab, Aaron was given a drug called Suboxone, a treatment for opioid use disorder, which itself contains a milder opioid that helps ease withdrawals. It's like Nicorette but for a way worse drug. It worked great for Aaron, but there was a hitch: The clinics that give patients Suboxone are—and this is something reformers say needs to change if we're truly going to end the opioid epidemic—overly punitive. To get Suboxone, you often need to prove you are entirely clean of all other substances. Part of this has to do with safety, part of this has to do with a hangover from the idea that drug users just need more willpower to beat their addictions, when in reality, their brain chemistry has been altered so much that willpower alone may not be enough to get better. In one urine test, Aaron tested positive for weed. He was promptly cut off Suboxone. "You were born bored, in the wrong place, in the wrong time," his nurse said to him.

Soon thereafter, Aaron relapsed again.

*   *   *

In 1986, New York Senator Daniel Patrick Moynihan gave a speech at Harvard outlining two divergent but important viewpoints on American life.

"The central conservative truth is that it is culture, not politics, that determines the success of a society," he said. "The central liberal truth is that politics can change a culture and save it from itself."

It's difficult not to wonder about the tension between these ideas in the Trump era. Conservative politicians who criticized Trump's influence on culture, who said they would never back him, eventually did. CEOs of America's largest companies steered clear of making any supportive comments of him in his first race, but then started opening up their factories to him for photo ops, showing up in Washington to lobby their causes. If there had been any semblance of a cordon sanitaire against an antidemocratic populist, it unspooled, revealing itself as made from the kind of thread they'd used in the emperor's new clothes.

This is what happens in countries where democracy is backsliding. A figure that political scientists call a "norm breaker" bursts onto the scene. The norm breaker does the sorts of things that Trump did to American political and even popular culture, ripping apart old understandings of how things work simply because they can. One common democratic norm that tends to fall quickly is mutual tolerance between opponents. It's the sort of tolerance you have to maintain on something as simple as a bowling league. In healthy democracies, "the other team" isn't the enemy, it's just the other team. Sometimes they win and sometimes they lose, and they're usually pretty irritating, but their mere existence isn't a crisis. Norm breakers, however, recast the populace's perspective. They polarize us. They don't respect the restraint expected of someone in a powerful office, and they don't respect the outcomes of elections. As what may have been unthinkable before becomes normalized, the norm breaker usurps ever more power. Such figures usually self-destruct before they rise to maximum power. Mainstream politicians typically don't back norm breakers because of the damage they could wreak on the system, and the lack of oxygen extinguishes them.

Ruin comes to those who think they can play with fire. In one of the most influential political books of the Trump era, *How Democracies Die,* Steven Levitsky and Daniel Ziblatt use decades of research on the collapse of more fragile democracies to explain how backsliding started in Trump's America, how damaging it has been that Republican politicians enabled a character they could have nipped in the bud time and time again. There is a passage when they quote an aristocratic politician from Germany in 1933, deciding to cut a political deal with a dictator-in-waiting. "Within two months, we will have pushed Hitler so far into a corner that he'll squeal."

Trump was another norm breaker who politicians with more experience thought they could use. Instead, he used them. Twice. He refashioned the Republican Party in his image and stamped out intellectual diversity within the American conservative sphere. His influence was even bigger, though. His norm-breaking was more than political, it was also cultural. To get what they wanted, Republicans ignored the bombastic things he said and cast aside their worries about his morality and propriety so they could get what they wanted: power.

I couldn't help but see a similar cultural dynamic playing out in Olivia's relationship with Riley, too. There was a price Olivia learned she would need to pay for an Instagram-perfect life. She began to register it not long after they moved in together in Maryland. Cracks started showing as their previously long-distance relationship moved from online to the real world, from the zeroes and ones to the everyday. It's one thing to be in a long-distance relationship with someone. Communication tends to be asynchronous. You write a text, he writes back a few hours later, it continues. But when you move in together, suddenly, you're in real time. You don't see the rehearsed version of somebody. You see the warts and all. It turned out Riley had a lot of those.

Olivia got a job at a middle school in Baltimore. It was in a tough neighborhood, and the kids did not make her job easy. Compared to the theoretical space of graduate school, it was real and it was exhausting. A lot of days, Olivia came home doing the thing many people do as they land out of graduate school and into the real labor market: She cried.

Video games were an escape. Olivia grew up watching Anthony play low-res games like *Duke Nukem* and *Grim Fandango*, so this felt like a tradition of sorts. She'd bonded with her father playing these games, and now she was bonding over them with someone who, if things went right, might be the father of her own children. She and Riley played those multiplayer games you compete in with other people from the internet. But he'd get irrationally angry if he ever felt like Olivia wasn't completely and utterly on his side, if he even suspected that she was allying with other players in the game.

"Dude," he'd say to her, the TV screen bathing their two faces in cool blue light. "You need to tell them I'm your fucking boyfriend."

"You're supposed to fucking side with me," he'd say. "Even if I'm fucking wrong."

Once, Riley got so mad playing, he punched a wall.

Riley was a military man who had seen combat and watched his friends die on foreign soil. Olivia was sympathetic and wanted to be a dutiful girlfriend. So she looked away from the hole in the wall, absorbed the comments, promised to side with Riley even when she knew he was wrong. She also disregarded the beer. It was the type of unwelcome surprise a person notices when they move in with someone: She's worried about how much time he'll think she spends in the bathroom and rushes through her daily grooming to avoid seeming high-maintenance; he casually disregards her as he brings home a twelve-pack of beer daily.

"I really think you should chill it with the beer," she said one day. "You drink a lot."

He told her it was either her or the beer. And the beer was always going to be there.

"So either get over it," he said, "or leave."

Olivia stayed. She stayed even as it got weirder. Riley didn't like Olivia being friends with other men. He didn't like her going to work happy hours. If she did go, she'd have to ask everyone if it was OK to take a few selfies with them to send back to him so he'd know who was there. He started calling her names she couldn't unhear. But if she looked past the ridiculous things he said and just focused on what was happening, she could mostly be fine with it. He'd been promoted. They left the rented apartments to live on base. It was a prestigious posting. Olivia formed a group on Snapchat of women that called themselves the "Still Not Yet Military Wives Club." They were all young, dating guys on base, and it made her feel like she had a place to fit in there. The pictures she posted online didn't look too dissimilar to those of the other women from Syracuse, women who were married already. The pictures were of things Olivia was proud of. Things she thought Anthony would have been proud of, including going to a military Christmas party at the White House.

That night, Olivia wore a red dress. It made her feel like Jacqueline Kennedy. It was a Rent the Runway number with a giant bow on the back. Trump had just suffered a blow in the midterm elections: Democrats had captured the House. The federal government was nearing its longest shutdown in history over the president's demand for nearly $6 billion to build a wall at the Mexico border. More information was coming to light about how Russians had used social media to influence Americans in the 2016 election. It was looking like there wouldn't be snow in Washington for the holidays. And there was a question people of all ages had been asking, in conversation but also in anxious op-eds.

"Where are the grown-ups?" a *San Jose Mercury News* editorial had asked about Trump's foreign policy.[67] That fall, the *New York Times* editorial board published an anonymous guest essay by a staffer claiming to be part of "the resistance" inside the Trump administration. These sentences in it were supposed to be reassuring: "Americans should know that there are adults in the room. We fully recognize what is happening. And we are trying to do what's right even when Donald Trump won't."[68]

It was an especially strange feeling to hear the question *Where are the grown-ups?* from Boomers and Gen Xers as a new Millennial grown-up, the youngest of us having only entered that club a few years before. In some ways, it was the same question that always happens in that twentysomething, thirtysomething stage of life, when you look around the room, don't see any other adults, and have to reckon with the fact that *you* are the one making choices and dealing with the consequences, for better or for worse. It just doesn't usually happen when people of other generations are lamenting the fact that there is someone with the temperament of a child setting the tone for the culture of the country from the highest office in the land.

Yet through those four years, we kept reaching milestones, like the one Olivia was about to reach at age 27. She was in full "adulting mode," running around the house, trying to prepare for the guests she knew were about to arrive. The plan was for all of the military couples to travel together to the White House. Yes, Trump was a child. But it was the *White House*. He was *the president*.

The guests arrived, and Olivia met them downstairs. But she couldn't find Riley. When she did, he said he was having a problem with their dog. "I gotta put him in the crate," he said. Olivia wondered why he hadn't done that well before. The crowd was growing larger and more impatient. "My teeth," he said when he came down again. Again, being so forgetful. "I gotta brush my teeth."

By then, everyone was there, the excitement of the impending party building as the winter chill of nightfall arrived. Riley came out a third time. As if on cue, everyone crowded around.

"You look beautiful," he said to Olivia, the guests watching. The benefit of someone who gets so angry all the time is that they create demand for the moments when they speak kindly.

He got down on one knee.

"Oh my God," Olivia said.

"You look beautiful," he said. "But I think you'd look better with this." He took out a box.

Olivia dropped her purse when her hands flung to her face.

Stability. Tradition. The basement apartment beneath her grand-parents' place where Anthony, her unwed mother, and she first lived in 1991. The stepparents and half-siblings. The weekends shuttling between the suburbs of Long Island. The loneliness and the longing. Giles's indie lyrics. A single salary versus a double. The prospect of a perfect life with this son of Sunnydale.

"Say yes," everyone kept telling her.

Someone was filming.

Olivia stood silently in the falling night.

"Say yes," everyone kept saying.

That was the Christmas that Melania Trump decorated the East Colonnade with blood-red trees. Dozens of red topiary cones lined the green carpet of the long hall. They were ridiculed online by people who compared them to trees from a nuclear site, trees that appeared to have been imported from Soviet Russia, trees that looked like the costumes from *The Handmaid's Tale*.[69] It was not a good look for American culture. It was not clear politics could save it from itself.

Riley and Olivia set their wedding date for November 20, 2020. If you have made it this far through this book, and if you also made it through the COVID-19 pandemic, I trust that you have the reasoning skills to deduce that their relationship did not endure to their wedding day.

Talking about the pandemic is challenging. That is partly because we have an odd cultural amnesia about much of it. First and foremost, it is almost sociopathic that 1.1 million Americans died of COVID from the beginning of the pandemic to its declared ending in 2023 and we don't talk about it more. Politicians have little interest in relitigating what they did wrong. The rest of the country seems ready to move on, too. Bosses no longer want to make the accommodations they were making in the days of remote work. People want to forget about the worst memories of death, uncertainty, and boredom—quite literally, in fact. Some of the country's largest newspapers have all written in-depth reports on why we have been forgetting some of the worst parts of COVID. "Because of information overload and the monotony of pandemic life," says the *Washington Post*.[70] "Forgetting protects us from this debilitating anxiety not by deleting memories but by quieting their emotional scream," says the *New York Times*.[71] "Acts of God are less memorable than wars and other disasters caused by humans," says the *Wall Street Journal*, classifying COVID as an act of God.[72]

But an unplanned freezing of society as some of us hit forty had implications for our generation that will last the rest of our lives. A potent interpretation of the 2024 election is that it was actually an election about the effects of COVID—lingering inflation from snarled supply chains, a post-pandemic surge in migration across the globe, anxiety and insecurity about the future—that was never explicitly stated. We will be living with the outcomes of that election for decades. But even away from politics and economics, the effects continue in our cultural lives. I never want to do a Zoom baby shower again. I quit a job and started a new one from the same desk, just by signing out of and then in to a different Slack account. I realize that I was lucky. Many people lost parents, grandparents, friends, partners, jobs, a sense of security.

A lot of experts talked during the pandemic about how it was a "great accelerator." They meant that the pandemic sped up the adoption of trends that had already been happening in society: more remote work, remote socializing. It all made an AIM generation even more enmeshed in digital communication.

The pandemic also accelerated our relationships. It was like a pressure cooker that made us confront hard truths about our partners, homes, and jobs faster than we otherwise would have. In part that was because we had nothing else to do. It was also because it felt like the whole world had changed dramatically and would keep doing so. There was a new future that was going to come after COVID, and it would be different from the one before. Bitcoin was going to rule the world. We were going work in an economy based on NFTs. Mark Zuckerberg changed the name of his company from Facebook to Meta and actually said this about a metaverse future that was supposed to arrive soon: "In this future, you will be able to teleport instantly as a hologram to be at the office without a commute, at a concert with friends, or in your parents' living room to catch up. This will open up more opportunity no matter where you live. You'll be able to spend more time on what matters to you, cut down time in traffic, and reduce your carbon footprint."[73] Outside tech, the future looked like one in which we might have smaller social circles in the real world, one in which we'd have to isolate and distance, if not forever, at least for a very long time. Some feared that travel, concerts, and sporting and other community events would never be the same again.

With all of that strangeness, it's no wonder that Olivia started to question things with Riley. Through the Instagram window into their life, they looked #blessed. She had accepted Riley's marriage proposal. Riley left the Air Force and started working at his uncle's company on Long Island. His parents bought them a home. It was so close to the beach, you could walk. Olivia got her "big girl job" a couple towns over, teaching science at a high school. She got a Honda CR-V in which she imagined driving her future children home from the hospital.

But when COVID came, it amplified the parts of Riley's proposal that had made Olivia hesitate. He got worse. During lockdown, Olivia says he threw furniture, called her a bitch, embarrassed her in front of his family, drank so much. That was another area of loss during the pandemic: people whose personalities shifted and never returned. Some grew anxious and haven't been able to embrace life again. Others fell for the strangest conspiracy theories. Olivia's last straw with Riley was the day they had a fight and she had to take the gun out of their home because she worried about what he might do with it. Olivia knew she had to get away from him.

One of the central challenges of Olivia's young adulthood was learning how to lose people. This is an existential challenge for all of us; we will all eventually lose everything and everyone. But sudden loss doesn't tend to happen to people so young. Her hunt for stability and tradition seems like a way of coping with that trauma of loss. But as we grow older and life becomes more complex—as we transform into adults—our coping mechanisms stop working. We can't just dwell on our biggest problems: We have to confront them. And so Olivia leaving Riley, losing that Instagrammable life she thought she wanted, must have been hard. But it was an important step in her growth.

She told me it felt like getting divorced. It was late August, the birch and elm leaves still green and heavy after the last hot summer rain in Sunnydale. Her grandfather; her stepdad; and her uncle, Anthony's brother, drove over with a U-Haul to help pack up what had looked like a fairy tale of a life. As Olivia boxed things up, dividing them between his and hers, she noticed how many of the items in her life with Riley she had bankrolled, how little he had contributed.

When she was outside shuttling boxes to the truck, a neighbor called over to her from his side of the fence to remark on the hubbub.

"You guys moving out?"

"Actually," Olivia said. "I'm leaving him."

The neighbor paused for a minute. He just looked at her from across the fence.

"Took you long enough," she remembers him saying.

After Olivia's family left with the U-Haul, she went back inside one last time. She put bills, the keys, and a final letter to Riley in an envelope. The only way to leave the house locked up without her keys was to exit through the garage door.

"Of course," Olivia thought as she did that. Of course her dramatic departure from the relationship would be punctuated with a meditation on the cursed date of her wedding. She punched in that garage door code one last time: 11/20/2020, the date of the ceremony she was going to need to cancel.

She sat in her car for a minute alone. She cried. When she was ready, she turned out of the driveway and down the charming streets of Sunnydale. Olivia got to the highway. She accelerated, leaving the town behind her, heading south. She was losing a future she thought she had claimed. But as she moved forward, fast, she couldn't believe how much freer she felt already.

* * *

"You think you know," Britney Spears said, her big smoky eyes trained on the camera, nude lip curling into a smile. "But you have no idea."

It was her very own episode of MTV's *Diary*. Each one, as you'll remember, began with that famous tagline. Spears's began in June of 2001, our last normal summer before the change of an era. Shaky, home video–style footage showed her recording a voiceover for her first movie, *Crossroads*. Then there was footage of her working with Max Martin, the Swedish producer who has worked on scores of Millennial pop anthems since, by everyone from the Backstreet Boys to Taylor Swift. In the episode's footage, Spears laid down a track that was supposed to characterize her purported metamorphosis: "I'm Not a Girl, Not Yet a Woman." She opened up about it: "You're just in that transitional stage in your life where you're just figuring yourself out," she said to the camera in the reality TV show–confessional style that has become a standard of the genre. "Life doesn't always go my way."

It didn't. Three years after *Diary*, Spears got drunk in Vegas and married a childhood friend in a union that lasted fifty-five hours. A few months after that, she met dancer Kevin Federline in a hot Hollywood club called Joseph's Café. She and Federline wed within weeks. They had two children and talked a lot about being happy together. In truth, they weren't. They filed for a divorce in 2006 that rocked Spears's life. The story culminated for the public on February 16, 2007, when she walked into Esther's Haircutting Studio, a cozy salon in the San Fernando Valley across the street from a strip mall with a Vons, a Pet Food Express, and a Starbucks. Inside Esther's, Spears grabbed a sideburn trimmer and shaved off all her hair. She ended up in rehab and then, for thirteen years after that, under the hermetic seal of a conservatorship controlled by her father. It dictated everything from how often she could see her children to whether or not she could get married again. Spears told a Los Angeles court in 2021 that under the arrangement, she had been drugged, forced to work against her will, and required to stay on birth control.

I remember a manager at my awful first job hanging a poster on her cubicle that said, "If Britney Spears can make it through 2007, I can make it through this day." At the time, it was the kind of thing people found funny. But since she has become free—the conservatorship ended in 2021—and has started telling her own story, it's become clear that it's mostly just sad. Sad for her, of course; that's obvious. But it's also a sad reflection on us: that we laughed at the things she was doing, which in isolation maybe did look ridiculous but that taken together should have been an indication she was in the depths of a severe mental-health crisis.

Britney Spears is doing better now. If you go online and look at her social media presence today, you will notice something else: how much she looks like somebody you might know. A former member of your high school cheer squad figuring out her forties, say, or a zany dance instructor you met on a Carnival cruise. On Instagram, Britney Spears posts a lot of pictures of herself in bikinis and sun dresses, ruminations on writing, happiness, intermittent fasting, love.

All things truly WICKED START from INNOCENCE, she put up one November day, quoting Ernest Hemingway.

The most dangerous animal in the world is a silent smiling woman, she added on another.

Her attitude is savage, but her heart is gold, she posted not long ago.

I think Britney Spears is happy. She says she is never going back to the music business. I'm sure she has a lot more money than pretty much any of us ever will. Even so, when I look at her, I see something familiar. Visualize with me, for a moment, just one of the fourteen million Furbies sold the same year Britney Spears turned 18. Imagine that particular Furby's AA batteries died, shutting its cute/creepy eyes for twenty-five years. Say its owner then shoved some batteries back in, opening up those eyes that I swear can actually see. That Furby would clock a very different Spears today. But it would also clock a very different you. What that Furby would see is that Spears no longer represents us. Rather, she has *become* one of us. And in an odd twist of fate influenced by the economic, social, and technological changes of our time, we have become a lot more like her.

After all, isn't she just another Millennial, trying to tell the internet her story, articulating the fact that things didn't totally go her way but that she is making sense of it nonetheless? Unresolved expectations like these are not unique to Spears, or to us. Every generation has to confront society's evolving assumptions about growing up. A Boomer's experience of being 18 was not a Gen Xer's was not ours. Boomers were raised in an upswing of optimism after World War II that ended up colored by Vietnam, Watergate, and a string of early-career recessions. Gen X had to learn the internet on the job, start saving for retirement amidst a gigantic shift from traditional pensions to 401(k)s, and navigate their peak earning years during a pandemic. Now Gen Z faces the uncertainty of an AI future in an angry, populist world, with Gen Alpha close behind.

Despite all this, there was something unique about *our* expectations. About the way they butted up against *our* reality. I've outlined a lot of reasons for that. We live in an age of chaos. There are no more jobs for life. Business cycles last for weeks rather than decades. Uncertainty and anxiety are rife. Our understandings of family, gender, race, and power are shifting in ways maybe we don't even understand yet. On top of it all, between cable news, reality TV, and the ever-growing FOMO-fest of social media, we are surrounded by stories of how our lives should look at the same time as we're told to put our own on display. We post updates about moments as prosaic as drinking in strip-mall Irish bars or as private as childbirth, as personal as our first moves into apartments with our romantic partners and as sanctified as our marriages. It's the kind of attention only celebrities used to get. Britney Spears does it. We do it. We are all storytellers now.

There is something romantic about that notion. In some ways, it can be comforting to think of our stories as part of broader narratives. We're Giants fans, we're Geminis, we're stay-at-home parents; we're ESFJs, Swifties, Millennials. This sense of belonging is part of why stories about generations captivate so many people; such groupings help explain things in an age of confusion and loneliness. Remember, nearly one out of every three Millennials say they have zero best friends. We have to find our communities somewhere.

Still, today's new preponderance of story causes problems. We've seen what happens when people become *too* trapped in their own lore about themselves and about others. Social and political camps become unwilling to see each other's humanity. Government gets stuck, then turns to brinkmanship. Everyday people get left behind.

I think about how our stories can trap us—even our most inspiring ones—when Olivia tells me of the hundreds of messages she gets every year on September 11. Social media acts as a living record of the things we've said and done to the point where changing course often gets called "rebranding." Social media and texting and messaging help us keep in touch with people from the many periods of our lives. That feels good for a while, but it also keeps us tethered in a new way to those who only really know older versions of ourselves. Case in point: Every September 11, Olivia is inundated with messages saying things like, "Your story is so inspiring." "I'm thinking about you and your family." "I always remember you on this day."

She understands that these digital notes come from a good place. But they also represent the Millennial experience of transitioning to ubiquitous connection that arose in the formative period when we were becoming adults. Boomers and Gen Xers in their twenties and thirties could stop answering letters, unplug their landlines, even slam shut their flip phones. It was normal for them to vanish for a while, deal with their shit, and then reemerge. On the other end of the spectrum, Gen Z grew up constantly tethered to the mobile social internet, their expectations since childhood centered on constant connection in what author Jonathan Haidt describes as a phone-based life. This brings with it extraordinary problems, but also an extraordinary amount of focus on those issues and possible solutions for them. Millennials are something of a bridge, raised analog but increasingly digitized. We now exist in what can feel like a never-ending high school reunion we weren't prepared for, sort of like our very own eternal episodes of MTV's *Diary*.

At the same time that's all happening in our individual lives, something frustrating has happened to our generational story on a broader level. It was told so often and so loudly in the early days of the social internet that everyone thinks they have our plot points down. Millennials? We need self-esteem. We eat too much avocado toast. We love selfies and social-media attention. We were screwed by Boomers, by the Great Recession, by the system. We're less interesting than Gen Z. Google searches for Gen Z spiked in 2020 and have only headed upwards since, while interest in us has lurched in the opposite direction. We are now officially 60 percentage points less interesting than Gen Z, according to Google traffic data. It's as if everyone has moved on and there is nothing new to tell.

But our lives continue. And increasingly, we are the only adults in the room. Others may have lost interest, but we're still here, still living, still reconciling an optimistic start with the clusterfuck of a journey that has followed, whose twists and ramblings never cease to surprise. Others may think they know our story—that the headlines of yesterday will remain the same indefinitely. But as they have tuned out, we are the only ones really left paying attention as we keep rewriting our story.

My point is that this is a very good thing. When we're watched closely, it's constricting. It can make it hard to grow. We feel it on an individual level with social media: You can't fumble your way to a better future if you're always worried about how doing something new might make you look. Not everything in life is going to follow a neat, narrative path. This is true for our generation, too. Collective time out of the limelight gives us a chance to rework our yarn.

The stories of the five Millennials in this book show how we might do that. Each person reexamined the narratives they were given about themselves, figured out which they liked, which they couldn't stand, which needed to be recast.

Take Miju. It has been well over a decade since she first decided to be in an open relationship, nearly as long since she went on CNN to talk about it. What I gather from our conversations over the years is that it was one thing to be a successful, attractive, polyamorous woman in San Francisco in the 2010s, in her twenties and early thirties. But it means something very different at middle age. Miju's career has progressed. She climbed back up the ranks of the big tech firms. Life got busier. She and her friends, who once roamed the Castro with the ceaseless time horizons of twentysomething Millennials, started not just to *think* about milestones, children, and families, but to make them real. That required challenging old norms, laws, even real estate zoning requirements that favor homes for nuclear families but not large groups of people who want to live together. Miju and her friends formed a chat group called "Coho," which stands for "Cohousing." They started looking for a big place where they could all be together: friends, maybe sometimes more than friends, definitely together.

It turns out the architecture of the American city is still designed for the nuclear family. At first, Miju and her friends rented a couple units in a big building near Lake Merritt in Oakland. The views looking back at San Francisco were stunning, and it felt special for them to reflect on a city where they had been coming together for the better part of a decade. It was where Miju had landed when she was still closeted, where she arrived not knowing Silicon Valley's location on a map. But the living space was ultimately limiting. They'd rented two apartments right next to each other, but the third was a couple floors down. The friends who lived in the adjoining apartments benefited from proximity, random interactions like the kind you'd have in the dining hall of a college dormitory. It was hard to establish that kind of intimacy across floors.

The group scattered during the pandemic. Miju and Xander had their first kid. But as the virus started to subside, she and her friends began looking for a home again—a real one this time, one that could truly suit what Miju called her chosen family. They were people she wanted in her life who weren't necessarily even sexual or romantic partners, but friends she wanted to be close to her in an intentional way. She sends me links to podcasts featuring authors like Rhaina Cohen, who wrote a book called *The Other Significant Others*. It's about how we spend all this time fretting about and naming our sexual relationships, but don't spend enough time or energy examining, inquiring into, and caring for our platonic friendships.

Miju is guarded when she talks about her chosen family. It was important to her to mention that they exist; I felt she wanted to show the world that what she was doing wasn't hurting anybody. Actually, she often talked about how living in a large household of partners and friends that went beyond the scope of a nuclear family might provide answers for more people at a time when Millennials are lonely and stretched both for time and money. But she wanted to protect the privacy of her family, too, most notably that of her children.

She does tell me that her family found a place in the East Bay. It was sold as a single-family home but was actually two large apartments stacked on top of each other with a small unit in the basement. It was perfect for a group of couples and friends who wanted to live together but also have some privacy. Over the course of my interviews with Miju, she was pregnant with and eventually had her second child.

I get the sense that changes and challenge will confront Miju as she navigates the private and public realities of a different type of family structure. But Miju has practice telling her story. After all, she came out to a cable news network. But that doesn't make it easier, and it doesn't mean it's done. I gather that the woman who got the rare consulting job during the Great Recession, climbed high up the tech ladder, gave a keynote speech for a unicorn, and then left on her own terms is gearing up for a new chapter. As she does, though, she is still coming out. She will be doing so for the rest of her life. There is no bullet-pointed list for this. And that's fine.

Justin is writing a new chapter in his love story that grew into a family one. I saw it playing out one midday not long ago in Charlotte. Tara was at work, and Justin's son was at kindergarten. Justin and his two-year-old daughter, born during the pandemic, went to the post office and for a walk around the block. She had lunch, and then went down for a nap.

Justin and Tara made hard choices to land their version of the American Dream. Two kids, two cars, a house in the pretty suburbs of a nice city. While the myth of avocado toast is bullshit, it is true that they didn't eat out at a lot of brunches as they were saving up. Justin had to make the hard call of stepping out of a career he had spent years building.

But now he's making another sacrifice. In that slot of two hours while his daughter is napping, Justin doesn't nap, too, as much as he sometimes wants to. He uses the time to push toward what he wants to be next: a writer. Walking the sidewalks of his tidy neighborhood, Justin thinks about how "you just have to write the big one." One big book that could be a hit. There would be financial freedom in that. The freedom to work wherever and whenever his parenting duties call. Freedom from those delayed glances he gets when he introduces himself as Justin, stay-at-home parent. He'd become Justin, writer. Barbara Kingsolver wrote her first book, *The Bean Trees*, when she was pregnant with her daughter and couldn't sleep. She later won a Pulitzer.

There is a closet upstairs that Justin has converted into his office. He's a movie buff, and there are old DVDs and Blu-ray discs around. They inspire him. There are no windows, really just a desk and a computer. It's cold in there. On the wall is a picture taped up that his son drew in kindergarten; it's of him and Justin. This is where Justin writes.

There was a moment in the pandemic, after the vaccines came out but before normality returned, when Justin had the seeds of a story in the back of his mind. But as anyone who has ever sat down at a laptop on a Wednesday night with a glass of Malbec and a novelistic dream knows, writing is hard. Especially after the meal prep, the dishes, the trash you took out, and the kids you put to bed. The blank Word screen dares you to tame the blinking cursor, and often, in your exhaustion, the cursor wins.

Justin has a friend he met in the Charlotte Dads Group, an organization he now runs. Dads in the area get together to hang out, talk, trade war stories. Some dads come just once and then move on. Others are regulars. Justin's friend recently moved away to Kansas. He's a writer, too, but he has a little more freedom. His wife works in social media for Panera and sometimes travels for business. When she does, he stays up until 1 a.m. just writing. Justin can't stay up that late. It would throw his entire household schedule out of whack. But sometimes Tara covers for him. She lets him check into a nearby hotel and just write, alone in a room with a laptop for a few days. Between the writing at the hotel and what he gets done at home, Justin has managed to finish the first draft of a novel. The style is urban fantasy. The protagonist is tending tables and working the door at a speakeasy. He dreams of starting his own investigative business, solving mysteries and crimes. One day, he is offered a case, and it's much bigger than he ever could have imagined.

A gray-green light falls through the three sash windows to the rear of the stage. Outside is Tribeca, a neighborhood where the average home costs $3.5 million and you can see the Freedom Tower down the street, standing tall where the Twin Towers once came down. Inside, rows of black chairs fill with twittering Millennial parents, hair-spraying their offspring's bangs. Parents pose their children in front of the piano for Instagram shots before the concert begins, others arrive from work in tailored blazers. There are tiny violins carried by boys in bowties. There are more iPhones in the room than children as they begin to play. Their parents watch through their screens, saving or broadcasting videos for viewers somewhere else to watch, too.

Tereza claps for her students. She even takes out her own iPhone and snaps some footage of one plodding through a rendition of "Twinkle, Twinkle Little Star."

The concert ends. Tereza thanks all fifty or so attendees for coming. She directs them to a small foyer where there are cookies and juice. She smiles and moves about politely yet determinedly in a black power suit. The vibe she gives is lady in charge. She's become a smooth talker with a loud voice, an iron fist behind a velvet glove. She is telling her story now, in charge of the way it plays out. Tereza is a director at the Church Street School for Music & Art now, a nonprofit academy in lower Manhattan that is not dissimilar to the Merit School she once attended. After her students' parents—many of whom don't know Tereza's story; she doesn't hide it but doesn't make it a central part of her working life—have filed out, back into Tribeca, away to their apartments and play dates, expensive dinners and yoga sessions, I ask Tereza if she has a moment to catch up. We go downstairs and sit on squeaking chairs.

As of the writing of this book, the DREAM Act has still not passed. Immigration was used as a convenient, ever-present scapegoat in the 2024 presidential election. At the same time, the US immigrant population is reaching a record peak. Some 14 percent of the population is now foreign born.[74] That's more than forty-six million people, more than the population of Canada. America is home to more immigrants than the next four most-popular immigrant destinations—Germany, Saudi Arabia, Russia, and the United Kingdom—combined.[75] A central challenge for the rest of our adult lives will be determining how we live up to the promise of our country as a nation of immigrants while managing a large population influx and the pattern of bad actors who blame them for problems they didn't cause. All the while, there are still as many as 3.6 million DREAMers in the US.[76] There are eleven million undocumented people. They are growing older, having American children, living American adulthoods. What sort of lives are we going to let them lead?

I see in Tereza a shift I have been seeing in a lot of Millennials lately. Yes, we still want big change. Yes, Tereza wants comprehensive immigration reform. But big changes, the ones that shape the arc of history, aren't solved in the timeframe of a single protest, news cycle, or even presidential administration. They are composed of many smaller changes, choices individuals make each day that eventually add up to something bigger. In her role every day, Tereza thinks often of Ann Monaco, the woman who pushed her to apply to college. Now, Tereza is building the Church Street School's own scholarship program, like the one Ann used to run. Tereza continues to advocate for immigrant rights, to protest, to help. But she has also learned the power of incremental change. She knows what can happen if she gives music to just the right person.

Everyone who agrees to talk to a journalist does so for a reason. Aaron's reason is he wants people to know that the Millennials of the duplex, the people of The Circle, were good people. They were people who had fun, and they were people who cared for each other. They weren't perfect. Sometimes, they were people who got into trouble. Once, Ronnie had to serve twenty hours of community service and pay $100 for speeding. Another time, Brittany got arrested at Walmart on a Saturday night for (allegedly) leaving the store without paying for some pictures she got developed. Aaron got into his share of trouble, too.

But they were people. And Aaron wants you to think about the lives they each lived before so many of them became data points on the mortality chart of the opioid crisis.

It felt like everything collapsed when it happened to Brittany. Aaron found out about her death in August of 2020. That summer, it was hot in Alliance. It was boring, and the air felt so strange, it could have been haunted. There was anger all over. People were sick of COVID. Trump was acting like a fool. Black Lives Matter was out protesting the death of George Floyd, and more angry people were counterprotesting, saying things that to this day bother Aaron, things like "all lives matter" that are so obvious that they are obviously just intended to inflame.

It was a bad month. It was made worse when he got a call from Dawn, the good girl in The Circle, the one who didn't use but who still came around sometimes. She was Brittany's sister.

"Hey," Dawn said. "She's gone."

Aaron had known Brittany since those days when he was a big reader at Liberty Elementary School. She was the little blonde girl who ran around on the playground, whose parents bowled on a league with his. She'd overdosed. And now she was reduced to a statistic and a few obituary lines.

Brittany M. Wheeler, 33, of Alliance passed away on Monday, August 31, 2020 at Aultman Alliance Hospital. Brittany was born on March 17, 1987 in Canton, Ohio. Brittany was a graduate of Alliance High School and was going to school to become a chef.

She had a passion for cooking and enjoyed playing softball, tennis and the violin. Brittany's greatest joy in life was spending time and being a mother to her son.[77]

Brittany's funeral was at the same place where Ronnie's had been, that small funeral home a few towns over. Her pastor, a man named Dale Gruver, officiated.

"The sun is shining outside but inside of our world it is dark," he said to a packed room of dozens, throats tight, eyes wet. "Today, Lord, we need your light."

Brittany, who in her twenties used to make them all chicken alfredo. Brittany, who wanted to be more than just a cook, who was training to become a real chef. Brittany, who once, when Aaron was struggling, stopped by his house to give him some stuff from the store, just to lighten his load.

Pastor Gruver read Psalm 23:4:

Though I walk through the valley of the shadow of death,
I will fear no evil;
For you are with me;
Your rod and your staff, they comfort me

That's the same psalm Bush read the night of September 11, the day Anthony died, the day Millennial life was set on its current course.

After that terrible summer, autumn came to Alliance, and something in Aaron snapped. He knew he had to change. Really, truly change. He had too many loved ones gone. He needed to transform—for the people who were still in his life, so he wouldn't leave them behind, but also for the people he'd lost.

Not long before this book went to press, Aaron celebrated yet another year of sobriety. On the phone, he talks about being "addicted to success." Since that summer, he has kept busy. This, plus the support he gets from his family, keeps him sober. For a while, he worked as a welder. He's tried his hand at studying cybersecurity on the side so that he might become an IT guy. He coaches a youth basketball team. It reminds him of his high school glory days. Aaron feels guilty about his lost years, the time he spent drunk and high and away from the people he loved.

Over the course of our interviews, Aaron was always applying for different jobs. He used to joke about having nine lives, and I think he could imagine nine hundred different versions of how his new sober life would play out. But as I mentioned way back at the start of this book, he ultimately landed a great role at a VA hospital as a drug and addiction counselor. He loves that he gets to help people. The job is changing his life, too. He always wanted to work hard at something like this. His parents are proud of him. His children are thrilled. Aaron had been working nights in his previous jobs, but now his more regular schedule means he gets to spend more time with them, playing with them, giving them the sort of love and attention his own father gave him.

Aaron's story forms part of the meta-narrative of the epidemic that has plagued America since Millennial adulthood began. We are likely to feel its aftereffects for the rest of our lives, and in unexpected ways. Four out of ten Americans say they know somebody who has died of a drug overdose, according to a recent study by the nonprofit think tank RAND.[78] Since the beginning of the new millennium, overdoses have killed more Americans than any war in which the country has fought over the same period.[79] That is to say nothing of those still living. There are some forty-eight million Americans currently struggling with substance abuse disorders. They are haunted by the memories of the friends, family, and former versions of themselves that the crisis has claimed.

More of us need to know that the path out of addiction is not a straight line. It does not have a clear beginning, middle, and end. There will be successes and failures on the road away from it. For the millions of Millennials who fell into the opioid crisis, addiction will be a lifelong battle. It is for Aaron. Stories of the people he loved still follow him around his small town.

"It's hard for me not to think about those people," he says. "When I'm passing these familiar landmarks that I know they used to reside in."

We cannot fight this epidemic with words alone. But the stories of those it claimed and of those who survived now form a permanent part of Millennial memory. They remind us of what others—sometimes silently, sometimes in deep pain—were witnessing, of what the luckiest overcame, and of how much work there is still left to be done.

Near the end of our Sunday brunch in Long Beach, I get the sense that Olivia's story is about to change.

Sunnydale is ancient history now. Olivia is living by herself in an apartment nearby. She's learning to be alone. She's open about the fact that she goes to therapy, every Tuesday, 2:45. Recently with her therapist, she's been working through what her expectations for adulthood were versus what they turned out to be. She doesn't own a home. She doesn't have children. She's not married yet. She's reclaiming herself after Riley. It's a slog. It's not always easy, but Olivia has a sense of humor about it. She's deftly done her own "rebranding." Olivia pulls up her own profile and scrolls down the grid to a photo of herself in a scarlet dress, barefoot and alone at the beach. It's a temporal marker for her, even if it's from a few years ago. She flips her phone around for me, and I see the date:

November 20, 2020, the date her wedding was supposed to be. I read the caption. It's so long it could be a five-paragraph essay.

"I have always loved you. Since the day I saw you I knew you'd be important to me. Little did I know how truly important you'd be to me," goes one paragraph. I'm worried the whole thing is a digital offering to Riley, her pleading with him to take her back or something. But as it goes on, I start to realize who she's really talking about. "And I sit here today, reflecting on how much of yourself you lost and yet here you are, standing on two feet after so much of life has knocked you down. I will never again think you're incapable of anything. I will never again let you become a villain like you once were. I look in the mirror and I see you for exactly who you are." Turns out, Olivia's Instagram post from a decade before was right. Her #MondayMotivation actually panned out. She needed a hero, so that is what she became.

As she's holding out her phone, I spy a tattoo on her wrist. We need to leave the restaurant, but quickly I ask if I can take a picture of it.

"Sure," she says.

I get out an old camera. Like an aging hipster, I use the disposable kind we had when we were kids. I focus it on the cursive marked in ink on her left wrist:

Anthony Perez

The bench with his plaque is a couple blocks from the restaurant, facing the beach. We go there and talk about a bizarre milestone she's about to hit. Next year, Olivia will turn 33 and officially be older than her own father ever was. There's this weird thing happening in pictures of him now. She grows older. But in photos, he is starting to look younger.

We get in her car and drive east. We leave the built-up neighborhood and glide down parkways that wind through marshy bays and along beaches facing the Atlantic. We talk about other people's weddings and babies. We talk about how Olivia has turned off Instagram notifications and how good that has been for her sanity. We talk about how she is dating a teacher from the school where she works. He's nice and he loves the real her. He originally teased her for buying Costco wine—now they drink it together on weekends. And then when Olivia starts to talk about her father, I realize I am hearing a change in her voice. It's different from how it sounded in our early calls, and it comes as we near the water. I hear Olivia speaking with the quiet grace of someone who has learned to lose a person as important as Anthony. It's something I can't imagine yet, and I feel a profound sense of admiration for her.

We loop through an intersection. We shift gears. And then suddenly, before us, there stands the Great South Bay Bridge. It's the one Olivia told me about the first time I called her. It's where she used to drive with her father when she was young. It's a place she still comes sometimes to speed over, just to feel free. Olivia hits the accelerator, and we pick up pace. Sixty to seventy to eighty miles per hour over that miracle of New York State infrastructure. It feels as if we are flying.

What happened to us? I wish I could give you a simple answer. An easy hot take that makes great headlines and explains our entire generation to the world. The truth is, there are millions of answers to that question, because there are millions of versions of us. There are seventy-two million American Millennials, and even more iterations of the people we have become. If you freeze the frame at any single moment over any one of those lives, the ultimate takeaway will be different from the one that came before. I've spent this book talking about what it means to be a Millennial, but when you get down to it, one of the only ongoing truths of the human experience is that we change.

In the beginning, the story others told about "Gen Y" was that we would be free, safe, all but perfect as we slid through the end of history. When it became clear that wouldn't be the case, the narrative about us changed. It became one in which we were troubled, a "Me" generation that needed plastic trophies and satin ribbons just for showing up. We supposedly became obsessed with selfies, social media, expensive brunch items, ourselves.

But enough of all that. The story isn't true anymore; it no longer fits.

Take the woman standing on a boat beneath the Great South Bay Bridge. It's the weekend, and the guy she's dating has brought her out, veering into the channel, against the current, anchoring beneath the bridge. When the wind blows across the water, chilling her skin, is she still CoolBlue91? Waves batter the craft. Her boyfriend bends down on one knee. What happened to that girl who, a quarter century before, sped across the bridge in a car with Anthony above the same spot where she stands now? Her boyfriend takes out a ring.

People will always tell their own stories about us, will always try to fit us into their own understandings of how history is happening. They did it with Olivia. For a long time, they spun this sad elegy of her: 9/11 Girl, damaged yet oh so brave. For many years, Olivia accepted that that's who she was. Then she grew. It took a while, but she began to define herself in relation not only to the tragic events of a single day but also to the people around her, to the new things that befell her. In reality, Olivia is still 9/11 Girl; she always will be. But what has let her grow and live and be happy has been deciding that one part of her life doesn't need to dictate the rest of it. She can decide what her full story will be.

In their own ways, Justin, Miju, Tereza, and Aaron have done this, too. Justin knows what other people think the role of a husband and father should be. He also knows he has become a provider in his own right. Miju is well aware of the story people tell about Bay Area liberals, about tech, ethical nonmonogamy, open relationships. She also knows she wants a family, that she's not afraid to talk about it and is even less afraid to defend it. As a young woman Tereza's story was used to support someone else's dream. Now she knows the limits of that approach and is pushing forward with her own. Aaron tells me something I feel other people might say about him in a disparaging way: He will always be an addict. But he says he needs to admit this to himself because even if it is true, it is also true that he doesn't have to use the substances from his past. He doesn't have to run from his old life. He can face the memories he carries with him and forge a new future for himself and the people around him that he loves.

People tell a lot of stories about us, about Millennials. We were the future once, until we weren't. We were the Tamagotchi Generation before the avocado-toast one. Some of the things people said about us were very premature. Some were rude, bizarre, unnecessary, or false. But some of the things people said about us were true—and some still are. Part of growing up is deciding which elements of your story you keep and which you cast aside.

I went out looking for the story of a generation. I heard memories of hope and failure, love found then lost, weakness built to strength, AIM names gone offline but honestly, still there deep within us. What I found from all this is that to make it through the strangeness of these times, the best way is to stop believing the story other people think they know about you—and to start living the one that only you know.

ACKNOWLEDGMENTS

Olivia, Aaron, Justin, Tereza, and Miju: Thank you for speaking to this reporter on the record. Thank you for the time, the patience, and the trust. Your stories made me laugh, cry, reflect, and grow—may they do the same for the world.

Jamison Stoltz and Abby Muller, you brought this project to life with Abrams in a way nobody else could. Eve Attermann, you've been making me laugh so hard since 2013, and I'm ever thankful to count you as my friend and agent. Rivka Bergman, I see you, too. A huge thank you to the whole team at WME. Sonya Maynard, I am indebted to you for the thorough fact-check.

This book would not have happened without the incredible support of the Bloomberg newsroom. Thank you to my colleagues for making it the best place I have ever worked. Craig Giammona, I'm lucky to call you my boss—just keep your flag pin on. Brian Chappatta and Sree Vidya Bhaktavatsalam, I would badge in every day for you. Pratish Narayanan, Pierre Paulden, and Caroline Gage, thank you for hiring me in the middle of a pandemic. Francine Lacqua and Dani Burger, thank you for those early on-air opportunities. David Gillen, your talent knows no bounds. Misyrlena Egkolfopoulou, we will forever have A$$ Coin. Maggie Shiltagh, Loukia Gyftopoulou, Claire Ballentine, Brian Wall, and Stephen Carroll: Those voice notes were crucial, but please delete them all. I owe you, Zeke Faux. And a huge thank you to Bloomberg's unrivaled newsroom leadership.

To the journalists who taught me what I know and kept me going when I wasn't sure. My mentors at *The Wall Street Journal*: Larry Rout, Cristina Lourosa-Ricardo, and Emily Nelson, your words live in me. *The Economist* was where I learned the power of opinion, and Zanny Minton Beddoes shaped mine. Brian Moylan and Abby Phillip, thank you. I am indebted to the journalists, authors, and academics I quote in this book for helping me bring the story of the past 25 years to life. David Wiegand, I know you rest in peace and style. Writing is a solitary craft, but some people made it less so. Jake McAuley and Mark Bergen, thank goodness for you both and for that Baker Street Chinese banquet. Kevin Burrows, this is for your patient reading, and for the 805. Emily Graff, you make magic happen.

Some people help strangers in hopes of changing the world. I always carry gratitude for Peter and Susan Solomon: What I learned and put in this book, you nurtured. I am proud to count myself a Solomon Scholar. I am thankful for Benjamin A. Trustman, his family, and legacy; I swore there was a book in that Trustman Fellowship—it just took a little longer than planned. Professors Daniel Ziblatt and Andrew John Boyd Hilton, thank you for your advice and mentorship. Joe Hubbell, Laurie Decker, Donna Kandel, and Robyn Metchik: You made me. Thank you to Tuesday's Children, Minority Veterans of America, the Charlotte Dads Group, and City Dads Group for your introductions. And I need to take a moment to thank all of the Millennials out there—or Millennials at heart—who helped me and heard me out through this process.

Finally, I would be nothing without my family. Kim Wells, your voice guides everything I do. Tom Wells, you will always be my first and best editor. Lori Orozco, you taught me the right way to tell a story. Doug Lagen, I'll never forget your support. Amy and Ian Wells, you are my best friends. Elyssa, thank you for always making me feel at home; I will always love that we were friends first. Clark, thank you for always being there. Carol Jeanson and Ira West, I am so thankful to have you in my life. 할머니, 항상 사랑합니다.

And to Adam Peter McWilliams: No words can ever thank you enough for the adventure you began with me along Mill Road very long ago at a little place called Kohinoor.

NOTES

You Think You Know

1. Linda Lee, "Attack of the 90-Foot Teen-Agers," *New York Times*, November 9, 1997, https://www.nytimes.com/1997/11/09/style/attack-of-the-90-foot-teen-agers.html.

2. Amelia Hill, "Thumbs are the new fingers for the GameBoy generation," *Guardian*, March 24, 2002, https://www.theguardian.com/uk/2002/mar/24/mobilephones.games.

3. Jean M. Twenge, *Generation Me: Why Today's Young Americans Are More Confident. Assertive. Entitled—and More Miserable Than Ever Before*, updated ed. (New York: Atria, 2014); and Joel Stein, "The Me Me Me Generation," *TIME*, May 20, 2013, https://time.com/247/millennials-the-me-me-me-generation/.

4. Jamie Ballard, "Millennials are the loneliest generation," YouGov, July 30, 2019, 2019, https://today.yougov.com/society/articles/24577-loneliness-friendship-new-friends-poll-survey.

5. M. Heron, "Deaths: Leading Causes for 2017," *National Vital Statistics Report* 68, no. 6 (June 2019).

6. Amanda Montei, "Can a Sexless Marriage Be a Happy One?," *New York Times Magazine*, April 17, 2024, https://www.nytimes.com/2024/04/17/magazine/sexless-marriage.html.

7. Khristopher J. Brooks, "It's taking Americans much longer in life to buy their first home," CBS News, August 15, 2023, 2023, https://www.cbsnews.com/news/average-homebuyer-age-millennial-data-realtor/.

8. Vanessa Friedman, "How Can I Update My Millennial Style?," *New York Times*, February 12, 2024, https://www.nytimes.com/2024/02/12/style/millennial-gen-z-style.html.; and Hillary Hoffower, "Are you a geriatric millennial? It depends on how comfortable you are with TikTok, and whether you remember MySpace," *Business Insider*, September 15, 2021, https://www.businessinsider.com/typical-geriatric-millennial-age-digital-skills-communication-2021-7.

9. James C. Davies, "Toward a Theory of Revolution," *American Sociological Review* 27, no. 1 (February 1962), https://louischauvel.org/DAVIES2089714.pdf.

10. "Millennial," Britannica, updated February 1, 2024, https://www.britannica.com/topic/millennial.

11. Louis Menand, "It's Time to Stop Talking About 'Generations,'" *New Yorker*, October 11, 2021, https://www.newyorker.com/magazine/2021/10/18/its-time-to-stop-talking-about-generations.

12. Bobby Duffy, *Generations: Does When You're Born Shape Who You Are?* (London: Atlantic Books, 2021).

13. Rebecca Onion, "Against Generations," Aeon, May 19, 2015, https://aeon.co/essays/generational-labels-are-lazy-useless-and-just-plain-wrong.

14. "How Pew Research Center will report on generations moving forward," Pew Research Center, May 22, 2023, https://www.pewresearch.org/short-reads/2023/05/22/how-pew-research-center-will-report-on-generations-moving-forward/.

15. Josh Zumbrun, "A Millennial Puzzle: More Diverse but More Segregated," *Wall Street Journal*, May 19, 2023, https://www.wsj.com/articles/a-millennial-puzzle-more-diverse-but-more-segregated-f8db5ae2.

16. Ipsos, "US Millennials are most likely to identify as 'working class,'" March 16, 2016, https://www.ipsos.com/en-uk/us-millennials-are-most-likely-identify-working-class.

Part I: Countdown

1. "Happy Birthday Britney: Spears Celebrates 18 In Style," MTV News, 1999, https://www.mtv.com/news/tud77i/happy-birthday-britney-spears-celebrates-18-in-style.

2. Samantha Stark, Joe Coscarelli, and Liz Day, "Britney Spears Quietly Pushed for Years to End Her Conservatorship," *New York Times*, June 22, 2021, https://www.nytimes.com/2021/06/22/arts/music/britney-spears-conservatorship.html.

3. Jim Rutenberg Ellen Gabler, Michael M. Grynbaum, and Rachel Abrams, "NBC Fires Matt Lauer, the Face of 'Today,'" *New York Times*, November 29, 2017, https://www.nytimes.com/2017/11/29/business/media/nbc-matt-lauer.html.

4. "NBC Christmas in Rockefeller Center," NBC, 1999, https://www.youtube.com/watch?v=4Ml5U6-fSfo.

5. Jesse McKinley, "Out for a Night In Search Of the In," *New York Times*, May 28, 2000, https://www.nytimes.com/2000/05/28/style/out-for-a -night-in-search-of-the-in.html.

6. Alex Diaz, "Rare photos show fresh-faced Britney Spears cuddling up to Justin Timberlake at her 18th birthday party," *Daily Mail*, February 22, 2021, https://www.dailymail.co.uk/news/article-9286589/Rare-photos -Britney-Spears-cuddling-Justin-Timberlake-18th-birthday-party.html.

7. "The Great Telecoms Crash," *Economist*, July 18, 2002, https://www .economist.com/leaders/2002/07/18/the-great-telecoms-crash.

8. Sam Howe Verhovek and Steven Greenhouse, "National Guard Is Called to Quell Trade-Talk Protests; Seattle Is Under Curfew After Disruptions," *New York Times*, December 1, 1999, https://www.nytimes.com/1999 /12/01/world/national-guard-called-quell-trade-talk-protests-seattle -under-curfew-after.html.

9. Zeynep Tufekci, *Twitter and Tear Gas: The Power and Fragility of Networked Protest* (New Haven: Yale University Press, 2017), x.

10. David E. Sanger, "Talks And Turmoil: The Overview; President Chides World Trade Body In Stormy Seattle," *New York Times*, December 2, 1999, https://www.nytimes.com/1999/12/02/world/talks-turmoil-overview -president-chides-world-trade-body-stormy-seattle.html.

11. Frank Bruni and Richard W. Stevenson, "Bush Tax Cuts Are Assailed As Too Little or Too Much," *New York Times*, December 2, 1999, https:// www.nytimes.com/1999/12/02/us/bush-tax-cuts-are-assailed-as-too -little-or-too-much.html.

12. Vicky Spratt, "Why Are Millennials the Most Nostalgic Generation Ever?," *Grazia*, March 28, 2016, https://graziadaily.co.uk/life/opinion /millennials-nostalgic-generation-ever/; "Why Millennials Are Afflicted with "Early Onset Nostalgia,'" Digiday, June 15, 2015, https:// digiday.com/marketing/early-onset-nostalgia-surge-cola-mad-libs -renaissance/; and Kalhan Rosenblatt, "Millennial nostalgia sells. Just ask these influencers making their livings off it," NBC News, September 16, 2022, https://www.nbcnews.com/pop-culture/pop -culture-news/millennial-nostalgia-sells-just-ask-influencers-making -livings-rcna47736.

13. John Tierney, "What Is Nostalgia Good For? Quite a Bit, Research Shows," *New York Times*, July 8, 2013, https://www.nytimes.com/2013 /07/09/science/what-is-nostalgia-good-for-quite-a-bit-research-shows .html.

14. Paul Taylor, "Nonmarital Births: As Rates Soar, Theories Abound," *Washington Post*, January 21, 1991, https://www.washingtonpost.com

/archive/politics/1991/01/22/nonmarital-births-as-rates-soar-theories
-abound/9bcc65f3-6c64-4012-b2da-fbe6eeaf0090/.

15. George A. Akerlof, Janet L. Yellen, and Michael L. Katz, "An Analysis of
Out-of-Wedlock Childbearing in the United States," *Quarterly Journal of
Economics* 111, no. 2 (1996), https://doi.org/10.2307/2946680, http://www
.jstor.org/stable/2946680.

16. Rebecca Greenfield, "How Much Did All of Those AOL CDs Cost?,"
Atlantic, December 28, 2010, https://www.theatlantic.com/technology
/archive/2010/12/how-much-did-all-of-those-aol-cds-cost/68600/.

17. Kurt Andersen, "The Best Decade Ever? The 1990s, Obviously," *New
York Times*, February 6, 2015, https://www.nytimes.com/2015/02/08
/opinion/sunday/the-best-decade-ever-the-1990s-obviously.html.

18. U.S. Census Bureau, "Real Median Household Income in the United
States," https://fred.stlouisfed.org/series/MEHOINUSA672N.

19. Jeanna Smialek, "Are We in a Productivity Boom? For Clues, Look to
1994," *New York Times*, February 21, 2024, https://www.nytimes.com
/2024/02/21/business/economy/economy-productivity-increase.html.

20. N. R. Kleinfield, "For Girls Only: Glimpse of Workaday World," *New York
Times*, April 29, 1993, https://www.nytimes.com/1993/04/29/us/for-girls
-only-glimpse-of-workaday-world.html.

21. Bureau of Labor Statistics, "Employee Tenure in 2022," updated
September 22, 2022, https://www.bls.gov/news.release/tenure.nr0.htm.

22. Robert P. Rogers, *An Economic History of the American Steel Industry*,
Routledge Explorations in Economic History, 42 (London: Routledge,
2009), 193.

23. Rogers, *An Economic History of the American Steel Industry*, 161–64.

24. Adrian Bejan, "Why the Days Seem Shorter as We Get Older,"
European Review 27, no. 2 (2019), https://doi.org/10.1017/S106279
8718000741, https://www.cambridge.org/core/product/2CB8E
C9B0B30537230C7442B826E42F1.

25. Tressie McMillan Cottom, "We Weren't Wrong to Love 'The Cosby
Show,'" *New York Times*, February 14, 2022, https://www.nytimes.com
/2022/02/14/opinion/cosby-show-documentary.html.

26. Joy Horowitz, "Snookums! Steve Urkel Is a Hit," *New York Times*, April 17,
1991, https://www.nytimes.com/1991/04/17/news/snookums-steve-urkel
-is-a-hit.html.

27. Rashawn Ray and William A. Galston, "Did the 1994 crime bill cause
mass incarceration?," Brookings Institution, August 28, 2020, https://
www.brookings.edu/articles/did-the-1994-crime-bill-cause-mass
-incarceration/.

28. Katharine Q. Seelye, "Fiscal Year Ends With U.S. Surplus, First In 3 Decades," *New York Times*, October 1, 1998, https://www.nytimes.com /1998/10/01/us/fiscal-year-ends-with-us-surplus-first-in-3-decades .html.

29. "How Big Is the Prospective Budget Surplus?," Brookings Institution, 2000, https://www.brookings.edu/articles/how-big-is-the-prospective -budget-surplus/.

30. "Counting Their Chickens," *Economist*, February 4, 1999, https://www .economist.com/united-states/1999/02/04/counting-their-chickens.

31. Jackie Calmes, "GOP Front-Runner Defends Tax Plan as Both Parties Take Shots at Bush," *Wall Street Journal*, December 2, 1999, https://www .wsj.com/articles/SB94409523462381176.

32. Peter Baker, "Mourning 'Compassionate Conservatism' Along with Its Author," *New York Times*, February 10, 2023, https://www.nytimes .com/2023/02/10/us/politics/michael-gerson-memorial-compassionate -conservatism.html.

33. "Text from Debate Among Republicans," *New York Times*, December 14, 1999, https://archive.nytimes.com/www.nytimes.com/library/politics /camp/121499wh-gop-debate-text.html.

34. "Text of Bush's Victory Speech," *Wall Street Journal*, December 14, 2000, https://www.wsj.com/articles/SB976764797598003263.

35. Eric Schmitt, "Bush Says Plan for Immigrants Could Expand," *New York Times*, July 27, 2001, https://www.nytimes.com/2001/07/27/us/bush -says-plan-for-immigrants-could-expand.html.

36. Jesús A. Rodríguez, "The Supreme Court Case That Created the 'Dreamer' Narrative," *Politico*, October 31, 2021, https://www.politico.com/news /magazine/2021/10/31/dreamers-undocumented -youth-forever-children -516354.

37. *Senate Congressional Record Vol. 147, No. 110.*

38. "The Story of DACA and the Original Dreamer with Tereza Lee," Divided Families Podcast, September 8, 2021, https://dividedfamiliespodcast .medium.com/the-story-of-daca-and-the-original-dreamer-with-tereza -lee-136738d7809e.

39. "Tereza Lee, an Original Dreamer," *Hyphen Magazine*, September 17, 2012, https://hyphenmagazine.com/blog/2012/9/17/tereza-lee-original -dreamer.

40. Chris Fuchs, "'Original Dreamer' Still Fights for Undocumented Immigrants 16 Years After First Dream Act," *NBC News*, March 30, 2017, https://www.nbcnews.com/news/asian-america/original-dream er-still-fights-undocumented-immigrants-16-years-after-first-n7 40491.

41. Julie Young, "Profile of Tereza Lee," Korean American Story, November 16, 2017, https://koreanamericanstory.org/written/profile-of-tereza-lee/.

42. "The Original DREAMer Recalls 'All Pervasive' Fear As An Undocumented Child," interview by Mary Louise Kelly and Dick Durbin, NPR, June 20, 2018, https://www.npr.org/transcripts/622002025.

43. James Truslow Adams, *The Epic of America* (New York: Blue Ribbon Books, 1941).

44. Neil Howe and William Strauss, *Millennials Rising: The Next Great Generation* (New York: Vintage Books, 2000).

45. Howe and Strauss, *Millennials Rising*.

46. Howe and Strauss, *Millennials Rising*.

47. "Anthony Perez," https://www.legacy.com/obituaries/name/anthony -perez-obituary?pid=132278&view=guestbook&page=4.

48. Stephen Engelberg, "Terrorism's New (and Very Old) Face: It's Not the Kind of War the West Fights Well," *New York Times*, September 12, 1998, https://www.nytimes.com/1998/09/12/arts/terrorism-s-new-and-very -old-face-it-s-not-the-kind-of-war-the-west-fights-well.html.

49. Hannah Hartig and Carroll Doherty, "Two Decades Later, the Enduring Legacy of 9/11," Pew Research Center, September 2, 2021, https://www .pewresearch.org/politics/2021/09/02/two-decades-later-the-enduring -legacy-of-9-11/.

50. "Trauma," *APA Dictionary of Psychology* (updated April 19, 2018). https:// dictionary.apa.org/trauma.

51. Judith Lewis Herman, *Trauma and Recovery*, [new ed.] (London: Pandora, 2001), 1.

52. Herman, *Trauma and Recovery*, 188.

53. G. Hirschberger, "Collective Trauma and the Social Construction of Meaning," *Frontiers in Psychology* 9 (2018), https://doi.org/10.3389/fpsyg .2018.01441.

54. Herman, *Trauma and Recovery*, 242.

55. ABC News, "Poll: Bush Approval Rating 92 Percent," ABC News, October 10, 2001, https://abcnews.go.com/Politics/story?id=120971&page=1.

56. Doherty, "Two Decades Later, the Enduring Legacy of 9/11."

57. Doherty, "Two Decades Later, the Enduring Legacy of 9/11."

58. "The Campus Attitudes towards Politics and Public Service (CAPPS) Survey," Harvard Kennedy School Institute of Politics, Fall 2001, https:// iop.harvard.edu/youth-poll/2nd-edition-fall-2001.

59. Attorney General John Ashcroft, "Prepared Remarks for the US Mayors Conference," news release, October 25, 2001, https://www.justice.gov /archive/ag/speeches/2001/agcrisisremarks10_25.htm.

60. Office of the Inspector General, "The September 11 Detainees: A Review of the Treatment of Aliens Held on Immigration Charges in Connection with the Investigation of the September 11 Attacks," June 2003, https:// oig.justice.gov/sites/default/files/archive/special/0306/press.htm.

Part II: 13/F/VA/BI

1. David E. Sanger, "The Struggle For Iraq: The White House; Bush Backs Away From His Claims About Iraq Arms," *New York Times,* January 28, 2004, https://www.nytimes.com/2004/01/28/world /struggle-for-iraq-white-house-bush-backs-away-his-claims-about -iraq-arms.html.

2. David E. Mosher and John V. Parachini, "Rereading the Duelfer report : Iraqi insurgents and weapons of mass destruction," *New York Times,* November 15, 2004, https://www.nytimes.com/2004/11/15/opinion /rereading-the-duelfer-report-iraqi-insurgents-and-weapons-of-mass .html.

3. Brian Knowlton, "Iraq war justified, Bush insists again," *New York Times,* October 7, 2004, https://www.nytimes.com/2004/10/07/world/americas /iraw-war-justified-bush-insists-again.html.

4. Jeremy Egner, Dave Itzkoff, and Kathryn Shattuck, "Jon Stewart and 'The Daily Show': 9 Essential Moments," *New York Times,* August 4, 2015, https://www.nytimes.com/interactive/2015/08/04/arts/television /jon-stewart-daily-show-9-essential-moments.html.

5. "CNN Crossfire Ad," https://www.youtube.com/watch?v=-WDlqqy9JFk.

6. "Britney Spears: 'Trust our president in every decision'," CNN, September 4, 2003, https://edition.cnn.com/2003/SHOWBIZ/Music /09/03/cnna.spears/.

7. "What are the current swing states, and how have they changed over time?," USAFacts, June 16, 2023, https://usafacts.org/articles/what-are -the-current-swing-states-and-how-have-they-changed-over-time/.

8. Hank Whittemore, *CNN: The Inside Story* (Boston: Little, Brown and Company, 1990), 5.

9. William A. Henry III, "Shaking Up the Networks," *TIME,* August 9, 1982, https://content.time.com/time/subscriber/printout/0,8816,925663,00 .html.

10. Whittemore, *CNN: The Inside Story,* 4.

11. Gabriel Sherman, *The Loudest Voice in the Room: How the Brilliant, Bombastic Roger Ailes Built Fox News—and Divided a Country* (New York: Random House, 2014), xix.

12. Montanaro, D., "Super Tuesday Was Created to Nominate Someone Moderate. It Backfired," NPR, February 29, 2020, https://www.npr.org/2016/02/29/468253626/a-history-of-super-tuesday.

13. Eben Shapiro and Elizabeth Jensen, "Fox Launches Its News Channel, But Manhattanites Can't Get It," *Wall Street Journal*, October 8, 1996, https://www.wsj.com/articles/SB844732515488228500.

14. Ken Auletta, "Vox Fox," *New Yorker*, May 19, 2003 https://www.newyorker.com/magazine/2003/05/26/vox-fox.

15. Lawrie Mifflin, "At the new Fox News Channel, the buzzword is fairness, separating news from bias.," *New York Times*, October 7, 1996, https://www.nytimes.com/1996/10/07/business/at-the-new-fox-news-channel-the-buzzword-is-fairness-separating-news-from-bias.html.

16. Auletta, "Vox Fox."

17. Gabriel Sherman, "Chasing Fox," *New York*, October 1, 2010, https://nymag.com/news/media/68717/.

18. Sherman, *The Loudest Voice in the Room*, 137.

19. Jim Rutenberg, "War or No, News on Cable Already Provides the Drama," *New York Times*, January 15, 2003, https://www.nytimes.com/2003/01/15/business/media-business-advertising-war-no-cable-already-provides-drama.html.

20. Sherman, *The Loudest Voice in the Room*, 261.

21. Matthew Rose and John J. Fialka, "Even With More Play-by-Play, Truth Remains Elusive in Iraq," *Wall Street Journal*, March 31, 2003, https://www.wsj.com/articles/SB10490593338723500.

22. Egner, Itzkoff, and Shattuck, "Jon Stewart and 'The Daily Show': 9 Essential Moments."

23. "Jon Stewart's America," *Crossfire*, October 15, 2004, https://transcripts.cnn.com/show/cf/date/2004-10-15/segment/01.

24. "Ad Questions John Kerry's Duty in Vietnam," *Fox News*, August 6, 2004, https://www.foxnews.com/story/ad-questions-john-kerrys-duty-in-vietnam.

25. *Crossfire*, hosted by Donna Brazile and Tucker Carlson, aired August 6, 2004, on CNN. https://transcripts.cnn.com/show/cf/date/2004-08-06/segment/00.

26. Matt Hines, "Jon Stewart 'Crossfire' feud ignites Net frenzy," CNET, May 5, 2006, https://www.cnet.com/culture/jon-stewart-crossfire-feud-ignites-net-frenzy/.

27. David D. Kirkpatrick, "Rally Against Gay Marriage Draws Thousands to Capital," *New York Times*, October 16, 2004, https://www.nytimes

.com/2004/10/16/us/rally-against-gay-marriage-draws-thousands-to
-capital.html.

28. Greg Hitt and Jacob M. Schlesinger, "Bush Supports Constitutional Ban
    On Gay Marriage," *Wall Street Journal*, February 25, 2004, https://www
    .wsj.com/articles/SB107763526982637731.

29. Congressional Budget Office, "Employment During the 2001–2003
    Recovery," August 2005, https://www.cbo.gov/sites/default/files/109th
    -congress-2005-2006/reports/08-05-jobs.pdf.

30. Terence M. McMenamin, David S. Langdon, and Thomas J. Krolik, "U.S.
    labor market in 2001: economy enters a recession," *Monthly Labor Review*,
    February 2002, https://www.bls.gov/opub/mlr/2002/02/art1full.pdf.

31. Louis Uchitelle, "Spending Stalls and Businesses Slash U.S. Jobs," *New
    York Times*, October 25, 2008, https://www.nytimes.com/2008/10/26
    /business/26layoffs.html.

32. Congressional Budget Office, "Employment During the 2001–2003
    Recovery."

33. Nancy Whitaker, "Workers Get the Bad News," *Alliance Review*,
    February 9, 2002.

34. Whitaker, "Workers Get the Bad News."

35. "Contents," *Alliance Chronicle 2004–2005*, https://www.alliancememory
    .org/digital/collection/p16335coll4/id/36313/rec/15.

36. Herman, *Trauma and Recovery*, 51.

37. "Full text: George Bush's victory speech," *Guardian*, November 4, 2004,
    https://www.theguardian.com/world/2004/nov/04/uselections2004
    .usa17.

38. George W. Bush, "Address to a Joint Session of Congress and the
    American People," September 20, 2001, https://georgewbush-whitehouse
    .archives.gov/news/releases/2001/09/20010920-8.html.

39. George W. Bush, "Remarks by the President at Bush-Cheney 2004
    Luncheon," https://georgewbush-whitehouse.archives.gov/news
    /releases/2003/12/20031205-1.html.

40. Bethany McLean and Joseph Nocera, *All the Devils Are Here: The Hidden
    History of the Financial Crisis* (London: Viking, 2010).

41. George W. Bush, "President Calls for Expanding Opportunities to Home
    Ownership," *Remarks by the President on Homeownership*, June 17, 2002,
    https://georgewbush-whitehouse.archives.gov/news/releases/2002/06
    /text/20020617-2.html.

42. Brooks, "It's taking Americans much longer in life to buy their first
    home."

43. National Association of Realtors, "The Average Age of First-time U.S. Homeowners Is 38, an All-time High," November 5, 2024, https://www.nar.realtor/newsroom/in-the-news/the-average-age-of-first-time-u-s-homebuyers-is-38-an-all-time-high-cnbc; and Zillow, "Today's First-Time Homebuyers Older, More Often Single," August 17, 2015, https://zillow.mediaroom.com/2015-08-17-Todays-First-Time-Homebuyers-Older-More-Often-Single.

44. Jonathan Kaplan, "Bank of America 2023 Homebuyer Insights Report," December 4, 2023, https://institute.bankofamerica.com/content/dam/bank-of-america-institute/economic-insights/uneven-housing-market.pdf.

45. Scott Carpenter, "US Housing Market Is So Stressful That Buyers Are Left in Tears," Bloomberg News, June 2, 2022, https://www.bloomberg.com/news/articles/2022-06-02/buying-a-home-americans-say-stress-of-purchase-process-is-making-them-cry.

46. Emmie Martin, "Millennials agree on the best way to invest—but they're wrong," CNBC, July 18, 2019, https://www.cnbc.com/2019/07/18/millennials-say-real-estate-is-the-best-long-term-investment.html.

47. Catherine Thaliath, "Why Are Millennials So Risk-Averse?," *Take On Payments*, January 22, 2019, https://www.atlantafed.org/blogs/take-on-payments/2019/01/22/why-are-millennials-so-risk-averse.

48. Paulina Cachero, "Lots of US Homeowners Want to Move. They Just Have Nowhere to Go," Bloomberg News, July 30, 2023, https://www.bloomberg.com/news/articles/2023-07-30/housing-market-is-stuck-as-homeowners-with-low-mortgage-rates-stay-put.

49. Michael Kolomatsky, "The Gen-Z Advantage in Housing," *New York Times*, April 25, 2024, https://www.nytimes.com/2024/04/25/realestate/the-gen-z-advantage-in-housing.html.

50. Naomi Klein, "Disowned by the Ownership Society," *Nation*, February 18, 2008, https://www.thenation.com/article/archive/disowned-ownership-society/.

51. Klein, "Disowned by the Ownership Society."

52. U.S. Census Bureau, "Homeownership Rate in the United States," May 21, 2024, https://fred.stlouisfed.org/series/RHORUSQ156N.

53. George W. Bush, "Remarks by President Bush and Senator Kerry in Second 2004 Presidential Debate," October 9, 2004, https://georgewbush-whitehouse.archives.gov/news/releases/2004/10/text/20041009-2.html.

54. David Wessel, "The Fed Starts to Show Concern at Signs of a Bubble in Housing," *Wall Street Journal*, May 19, 2005, https://www.wsj.com /articles/SB111645643190837423.

55. James R. Hagerty and Ruth Simon, "As Prices Rise, Homeowners Go Deep in Debt to Buy Real Estate," *Wall Street Journal*, May 23, 2005, https://www.wsj.com/articles/SB111680569071440252.

56. Sarah Zhao, "Subprime Lending," American Predatory Lending, Duke University, https://predatorylending.duke.edu/wp-content/uploads /sites/9/2021/10/Subprime-Lending-Products.pdf.

57. Caroline Bologna, "What Happened To The 'Going-Out Top'?," *HuffPost*, March 16, 2023, https://www.huffingtonpost.co.uk/entry/going-out-top -what-happened_l_608836cee4b04620270016e1.

58. Rutgers Center for American Women and Politics (CAWP), "Gender Gap: Voting Choices in Presidential Elections," https:/cawp.rutgers .edu/gender-gap-voting-choices-presidential-elections; John J. DiIulio Jr., "Biden, Trump, and the 4 categories of white votes," Brookings Institution, April 15, 2024, https://www.brookings.edu/articles/biden -trump-and-the-4-categories-of-white-votes/.

59. "Election 2024: Exit Polls," CNN, https://edition.cnn.com/election/2024 /exit-polls/national-results/general/president/20.

60. Ezra Klein, "The Men—and Boys—Are Not Alright," *New York Times*, March 10, 2023, https://www.nytimes.com/2023/03/10/opinion/ezra -klein-podcast-richard-reeves.html.

61. Richard Reeves, *Of Boys and Men: Why the Modern Male Is Struggling, Why It Matters, and What to Do About It* (2022), x.

62. Reeves, *Of Boys and Men*.

63. Bureau of Labor Statistics, "Highlights of women's earnings in 2020," *BLS Reports*, September 2021, https://www.bls.gov/opub/reports /womens-earnings/2020/.

64. Klein, "The Men—and Boys—Are Not Alright."

65. Reeves, *Of Boys and Men*, 9.

66. Frank Newport, "Seventy-Two Percent of Americans Support War Against Iraq," Gallup, March 24, 2003, https://news.gallup.com/poll /8038/seventytwo-percent-americans-support-war-against-iraq.aspx.

67. Bruce Riedel, "9/11 and Iraq: The making of a tragedy," Brookings Institution, September 17, 2021, https://www.brookings.edu/articles/9 -11-and-iraq-the-making-of-a-tragedy/.

68. Carroll Doherty and; Jocelyn Kiley, "A Look Back at How Fear and False Beliefs Bolstered U.S. Public Support for War in Iraq," Pew Research

Center, March 14, 2023, https://www.pewresearch.org/politics/2023/03/14/a-look-back-at-how-fear-and-false-beliefs-bolstered-u-s-public-support-for-war-in-iraq/.

69. Philip Shenon and Christopher Marquis, "Panel Finds No Qaeda-Iraq Tie; Describes a Wider Plot for 9/11," *New York Times*, June 17, 2004, https://www.nytimes.com/2004/06/17/politics/panel-finds-no-qaedairaq-tie-describes-a-wider-plot-for-911.html.

70. Doherty, "Two Decades Later, the Enduring Legacy of 9/11."

71. Doherty and Kiley, "A Look Back."

72. Pew Research Center, "Public Trust in Government: 1958–2023," September 19, 2023, https://www.pewresearch.org/politics/2023/09/19/public-trust-in-government-1958-2023/.

73. Charles A. Henning and Lawrence Kapp, "Recruiting and Retention: An Overview of FY2006 and FY2007 Results for Active and Reserve Component Enlisted Personnel," Congressional Research Service, February 7, 2008, https://www.everycrsreport.com/files/20080207_RL32965_04f747950f4d6da0b22fec0a1953e44dc6e73a7a.pdf.

74. Henning and Kapp, "Recruiting and Retention."

75. Jeremy K. Saucier, "Mobilizing the Imagination: Army Advertising and the Politics of Culture in Post-Vietnam America" (PhD diss., University of Rochester, 2010), http://hdl.handle.net/1802/12399.

76. Dan Savage, "Episode 1," *Savage Love Podcast*, October 26, 2006, https://savage.love/lovecast/2006/10/26/welcome-to-the-very-first-savage-love-podcast-in-this-episode-the-woes-of/.

77. Arjen M. Dondorp et al., "The Relationship between Age and the Manifestations of and Mortality Associated with Severe Malaria," *Clinical Infectious Diseases* 47, no. 2 (July 2008): 151–157. https://doi.org/10.1086/589287.

78. Mark Whitehouse, "As Data Point to Slowdown, Housing Market May Land Harder Than Economists Predict," *Wall Street Journal*, August 7, 2006, https://www.wsj.com/articles/SB115491028400528328.

79. Michael Greenstone and Adam Looney, "Unemployment and Earnings Losses: A Look at Long-Term Impacts of the Great Recession on American Workers," *Brookings Institution*, November 4, 2011, https://www.brookings.edu/articles/unemployment-and-earnings-losses-a-look-at-long-term-impacts-of-the-great-recession-on-american-workers/.

80. U.S. Bureau of Labor Statistics, "Job availability during a recession," *Issues in Labor Statistics*, https://www.bls.gov/opub/btn/archive/job

-availability-during-a-recession-an-examination-of-the-number-of
-unemployed-persons-per-job-opening.pdf.

Part III: The Cupcake Economy

1. Alexis de Tocqueville, *Democracy in America*, ed. Harvey C. Mansfield and Delba Winthrop (Chicago: University of Chicago Press, 2000), 511–14. https://press.uchicago.edu/Misc/Chicago/805328chap13.html.
2. Satya Doyle Byock, *Quarterlife: The Search for Self in Early Adulthood* (London: Penguin Books, 2024), 38.
3. Dennis Jacobe, "More Than Half Still Say U.S. Is in Recession or Depression," Gallup, April 28, 2011, https://news.gallup.com/poll/147299/half-say-recession-depression.aspx.
4. Zachary M. Seward, "RIM renames itself BlackBerry: Here's how that name came to be," *Quartz*, January 30, 2013, https://qz.com/49115/rim-renames-itself-blackberry-heres-how-that-name-came-to-be.
5. Simon Romero, "The Right Connections: The Simple BlackBerry Allowed Contact When Phones Failed," *New York Times*, September 20, 2001, https://www.nytimes.com/2001/09/20/technology/the-right-connections-the-simple-blackberry-allowed-contact-when-phones-failed.html.
6. Jeff Zeleny, "For a High-Tech President, a Hard-Fought E-Victory," *New York Times*, January 22, 2009, https://www.nytimes.com/2009/01/23/us/politics/23berry.html.
7. Hugo Miller, "BlackBerry Stands by Hardware as Sales Slip to 2007 Level," Bloomberg News, December 18, 2013, https://www.bloomberg.com/news/articles/2013-12-18/blackberry-s-chen-stands-by-hardware-as-sales-slip-to-2007-level. and{Goldman, #336}
8. Laura G. Knapp, Janice E. Kelly-Reid, and Scott A. Ginder, "Enrollment in Postsecondary Institutions, Fall 2011; Financial Statistics, Fiscal Year 2011; and Graduation Rates, Selected Cohorts, 2003–2008," National Center for Education Statistics, December 2012, https://nces.ed.gov/pubs2012/2012174rev.pdf.
9. "Anthony Perez Obituary," PennLive, https://obits.pennlive.com/us/obituaries/pennlive/name/anthony-perez-obituary?pid=132278.
10. Byock, *Quarterlife: The Search for Self in Early Adulthood*, 108.
11. Barack Obama, "Transcript: Obama's Speech Against the Iraq War," NPR, October 2, 2002, https://www.npr.org/2009/01/20/99591469/transcript-obamas-speech-against-the-iraq-war.

12. Brian Stelter and Jennifer Preston, "Turning to Social Networks for News," *New York Times*, May 2, 2011, https://www.nytimes.com/2011/05/03/business/media/03media.html.

13. Rick Rojas, Larry Gordon, and Christopher Goffard, "Osama bin Laden's death removes a cloud that enveloped a generation," *Los Angeles Times*, May 4, 2011, https://www.latimes.com/local/la-xpm-2011-may-04-la-me-bin-laden-generation-20110504-story.html.

14. "Gallup Daily: Obama Job Approval," Gallup, https://news.gallup.com/poll/113980/Gallup-Daily-Obama-Job-Approval.aspx.

15. James Dao and Dalia Sussman, "For Obama, Big Rise in Poll Numbers After Bin Laden Raid," *New York Times*, May 4, 2011, https://www.nytimes.com/2011/05/05/us/politics/05poll.html.

16. "Modest Declines in Positive Views of 'Socialism' and 'Capitalism' in U.S.," Pew Research Center, September 19, 2022, https://www.pewresearch.org/politics/2022/09/19/modest-declines-in-positive-views-of-socialism-and-capitalism-in-u-s; Jamie Ballard, "How much power do Americans think the president has on the economy?," *Economist and YouGov*, September 13, 2020, https://today.yougov.com/politics/articles/31891-economy-presidents-poll-data.

17. "Unemployment Rate [UNRATE]," Retrieved from FRED, Federal Reserve Bank of St. Louis, https://fred.stlouisfed.org/series/UNRATE.

18. David M. Cutler and J. Travis Donahoe, "Thick Market Externalities and the Persistence of the Opioid Epidemic," *National Bureau of Economic Research Working Paper Series* No. 32055 (2024), https://doi.org/10.3386/w32055, http://www.nber.org/papers/w32055.

19. CDC, "Injuries and Violence Are Leading Causes of Death," https://www.cdc.gov/injury/wisqars/animated-leading-causes.html.

20. Maia Szalavitz and Khary K. Rigg, "The Curious (Dis)Connection between the Opioid Epidemic and Crime," *Substance Use and Misuse* 52, no 14 (December 2017): 1927–31.

21. Cutler and Donahoe, "Thick Market Externalities."

22. Alvin Powell, "How friends helped fuel the rise of a relentless enemy," *Harvard Gazette*, May 3, 2024, https://news.harvard.edu/gazette/story/2024/05/how-relationships-have-fueled-the-u-s-opioid-crisis-epidemic/.

23. US Government Accountability Office, "Drug Misuse: Most States Have Good Samaritan Laws and Research Indicates They May Have Positive Effects," Mar 29, 2021, https://www.gao.gov/products/gao-21-248.

24. Jules Netherland, Helena Hansen, and David L. Herzberg, *Whiteout: How Racial Capitalism Changed the Color of Opioids in America* (Oakland: University of California Press, 2023).

25. Richard Fry, "Millennials Aren't Job-Hopping Any Faster than Generation X Did," Pew Research Center, April 19, 2017, https://www.pewresearch.org/short-reads/2017/04/19/millennials-arent-job-hopping-any-faster-than-generation-x-did/.

26. Sarah Green Carmichael, "Millennials Are Actually Workaholics, According to Research," *Harvard Business Review*, August 17, 2016, https://hbr.org/2016/08/millennials-are-actually-workaholics-according-to-research.

27. "2024 Gen Z and Millennial Survey," Deloitte, May 29, 2024. https://www.deloitte.com/global/en/issues/work/content/genz-millennial-survey.html.

28. "Martial Arts Studios in the US: Market Size, Industry Analysis, Trends, and Forecasts," IBISWorld, December 2024, https://www.ibisworld.com/united-states/number-of-businesses/martial-arts-studios/4187/.

29. Carolina Aragão, Richard Fry, Kiley Hurst, and Kim Parker, "In a Growing Share of U.S. Marriages, Husbands and Wives Earn About the Same," Pew Research Center, April 13, 2023, https://www.pewresearch.org/social-trends/2023/04/13/in-a-growing-share-of-u-s-marriages-husbands-and-wives-earn-about-the-same/.

30. Michael S. Kimmel, *Manhood in America: A Cultural History* (New York; London: Free Press, 1996), 18.

31. Kimmel, *Manhood in America: A Cultural History*, 19.

32. Linley Sanders, "How many Americans prefer non-monogamy in relationships?," YouGov, February 21, 2023, https://today.yougov.com/society/articles/45271-how-many-americans-prefer-nonmonogamy-relationship.

33. Oana Dumitru, "How Many Americans Have Cheated on Their Partners in Monogamous Relationships?," YouGov, October 4, 2022, https://today.yougov.com/society/articles/43605-how-many-americans-have-cheated-their-partner-poll.

34. Pew Research Center, "Public Trust in Government: 1958–2024," June 24, 2024, https://www.pewresearch.org/politics/2024/06/24/public-trust-in-government-1958-2024/.

35. Pew Research Center, "Public Trust in Government: 1958–2023."

36. Glenn Kessler, "When did Mitch McConnell say he wanted to make Obama a one-term president?," *Washington Post*, January 11, 2017, https://www.washingtonpost.com/news/fact-checker/wp/2017/01/11/when-did-mitch-mcconnell-say-he-wanted-to-make-obama-a-one-term-president/.

37. Michael Dimock, "How America Changed During Barack Obama's Presidency," Pew Research Center, January 10, 2017, https://www.pewresearch.org/social-trends/2017/01/10/how-america-changed-during-barack-obamas-presidency/.

38. Alicia Garza, *The Purpose of Power: How to Build Movements for the 21st Century* (London : Black Swan, 2021), 113.

39. "Interview With Barack Obama," *Larry King Live*, March 19, 2007, https://transcripts.cnn.com/show/lkl/date/2007-03-19/segment/01.

40. Sarah Gonzalez, "No One Expected Obama Would Deport More People Than any Other U.S. President," WNYC, January 19, 2017, https://www.wnyc.org/story/no-one-thought-barack-obama-would-deport-more-people-any-other-us-president/; Sarah Pierce, Muzaffar Chishti, and Jessica Bolter, "The Obama Record on Deportations: Deporter in Chief or Not?," *Migration Policy Institute*, January 26, 2017, https://www.migrationpolicy.org/article/obama-record-deportations-deporter-chief-or-not.

41. Dara Lind, "Removals vs Returns: How to Think about Obama's Deportation Record," *Vox*, April 11, 2014, https://www.vox.com/2014/4/11/5602272/removals-returns-and-deportations-a-very-short-history-of-immigration.

42. "All Presidents Are Deporters in Chief," editorial, *New York Times*, July 13, 2019, https://www.nytimes.com/2019/07/13/opinion/sunday/trump-deportations-immigration.html.

43. Senate Hearing 112-941 – The Dream Act, June 28, 2011, https://www.congress.gov/event/112th-congress/senate-event/LC57434/text.

Part IV: The Bridge

1. "Google Trends Results: "Millennial"," Google Trends, https://trends.google.com/trends/explore?date=all&geo=US&q=%22millennial%22&hl=en-US.

2. Jonathan Jones, "Those taking selfies with Hillary Clinton aren't narcissists—but our best hope," *Guardian*, September 26, 2016, https://www.theguardian.com/commentisfree/2016/sep/26/taking-selfies-hillary-clinton-not-narcissists. Adam Boult, "People who take selfies regularly 'overestimate how attractive they are': study," *Telegraph*, May 20, 2016, https://www.telegraph.co.uk/science/2016/05/20/people-who-take-selfies-regularly-overestimate-how-attractive-th/; and Bryn Lovitt, "Death by Selfie: 11 Disturbing Stories of Social Media Pics Gone Wrong," *Rolling Stone*, July 14, 2016, https://www.rollingstone.com

/culture/culture-lists/death-by-selfie-11-disturbing-stories-of-social
-media-pics-gone-wrong-15091/.

3. Bernard Salt, "Evils of the Hipster Cafe," *Australian Weekend Magazine*,
October 16, 2016, https://www.theaustralian.com.au/subscribe/news/1
/?sourceCode=TAWEB_WRE170_a_GGL&dest=https%3A%2F%2Fwww
.theaustralian.com.au%2Fweekend-australian-magazine%2Fmoralisers
-we-need-you%2Fnews-story%2F6bdb24f77572be68330bd306c14ee8
a3&memtype=anonymous&mode=premium&v21=HIGH-Segment-2
-SCORE&V21spcbehaviour=appendend.

4. "How row over mashed avocado toast is dividing Australian generations,"
BBC, October 18, 2016, https://www.bbc.co.uk/news/world-australia
-37693375.

5. Linda Qiu and Daniel Victor, "Fact-Checking a Mogul's Claims About
Avocado Toast, Millennials and Home Buying," *New York Times*, May 15,
2017, https://www.nytimes.com/2017/05/15/business/avocado-toast
-millennials.html.

6. Brigid Delaney, "Baby boomers have already taken all the houses, now
they're coming for our brunch," *Guardian*, October 17, 2016, https://www
.theguardian.com/commentisfree/2016/oct/17/baby-boomers-have
-already-taken-all-the-houses-now-theyre-coming-for-our-brunch.

7. Beth Ann Krier, "Checking In With the State's Task Force . . . : The Quest
for Self-Esteem," *Los Angeles Times*, June 14, 1987, https://www.latimes
.com/archives/la-xpm-1987-06-14-vw-6995-story.html.

8. Ibid.

9. Will Storr, "'It Was Quasi-Religious': The Great Self-Esteem Con,"
Guardian. June 3, 2017, https://www.theguardian.com/lifeandstyle/2017
/jun/03/quasi-religious-great-self-esteem-con.

10. Katherine Bishop, "A Study On Feelings Creates Bad Ones," *New York
Times*, February 20, 1990, https://www.nytimes.com/1990/02/20/us
/california-journal-a-study-on-feelings-creates-bad-ones.html.

11. Storr, "'It Was Quasi-Religious.'"

12. Jesse Singal, "How the Self-Esteem Craze Took Over America," *Cut*,
May 2017, https://www.thecut.com/2017/05/self-esteem-grit-do-they
-really-help.html.

13. Lauren Slater, "The Trouble with Self-Esteem," *New York Times
Magazine*, February 3, 2002, https://www.nytimes.com/2002/02/03
/magazine/the-trouble-with-self-esteem.html.

14. Slater, "The Trouble with Self-Esteem."

15. J. M. Twenge et al., "Egos inflating over time: a cross-temporal
meta-analysis of the Narcissistic Personality Inventory," *Journal of*

Personality 76, no. 4 (July 2008), https://doi.org/10.1111/j.1467-6494
.2008.00507.x.

16. Joel Stein, "The Me Me Me Generation," *TIME*, May 20, 2013, https://
    time.com/247/millennials-the-me-me-me-generation/.

17. Jim Norman, "In U.S., Support for Tea Party Drops to New Low," Gallup,
    October 26, 2015, https://news.gallup.com/poll/186338/support-tea-party
    -drops-new-low.aspx?version=print.

18. Gabrielle Levy, "Tea Party Losing Its Potency," *U.S. News and World
    Report*, Oct. 26, 2015, https://www.usnews.com/news/blogs/data-mine
    /2015/10/26/tea-party-support-falls-to-lowest-point-ever-gallup-says.

19. David Leonhardt, "Jeb Bush Is Still the Favorite, the Markets Say," *New
    York Times*, June 15, 2015, https://www.nytimes.com/2015/06/16/upshot
    /jeb-bush-is-still-the-favorite-the-markets-say.html.

20. "FiveThirtyEight 2016 Election Forecast," FiveThirtyEight, https://
    projects.fivethirtyeight.com/2016-election-forecast/national-polls/.

21. Barack Obama, "Address in Chicago Accepting Election as the
    44th President of the United States," American Presidency Project,
    University of California, Santa Barbara, November 4, 2008, https://www
    .presidency.ucsb.edu/documents/address-chicago-accepting-election
    -the-44th-president-the-united-states.

22. Barack Obama, "Remarks at a Graduation Ceremony at the New
    Economic School in Moscow, Russia," American Presidency Project,
    University of California, Santa Barbara, July 7, 2009, https://www
    .presidency.ucsb.edu/documents/remarks-graduation-ceremony-the
    -new-economic-school-moscow-russia.

23. Barack Obama, "Remarks at a Campaign Rally for Democratic
    Presidential Nominee Hillary Rodham Clinton in Durham, New
    Hampshire," American Presidency Project, University of California,
    Santa Barbara, November 7, 2016, https://www.presidency.ucsb.edu
    /documents/remarks-campaign-rally-for-democratic-presidential
    -nominee-hillary-rodham-clinton-durham.

24. Susan Ratcliffe, ed., *Oxford Essential Quotations*, 5th ed. (Oxford
    University Press, 2017). https://www.oxfordreference.com/view/10.1093
    /acref/9780191843730.001.0001/q-oro-ed5-00008165.

25. {TK—Bauerlein, #411}

26. Rhonda N. Balzarini, Christoffer Dharma, Taylor Kohut, et al.,
    "Demographic Comparison of American Individuals in Polyamorous
    and Monogamous Relationships," *Journal of Sex Research* 56, no. 6
    (July–August 2019): 681–94.

27. Jim Denison, "'I have a fiancé, a girlfriend and two boyfriends'," Denison Forum, January 30, 2015, https://www.denisonforum.org/biblical-living /christianity/i-have-a-fiance-a-girlfriend-and-two-boyfriends.

28. Joey deVilla, "CNN's painful piece on polyamory in San Francisco," *The Adventures of Accordion Guy in the 21st Century*, January 27, 2015, https:// www.joeydevilla.com/2015/01/27/cnns-painful-piece-on-polyamory-in -san-francisco/.

29. Farhad Manjoo, "Unicorn: A Fitting Label for Its Time and Place," *New York Times*, July 5, 2015, https://archive.nytimes.com/bits.blogs.nytimes .com/2015/07/05/unicorns-a-fitting-word-for-its-time-and-place/.

30. Kevin Roose, "Farewell, Millennial Lifestyle Subsidy," *New York Times*, June 8, 2021, https://www.nytimes.com/2021/06/08/technology/farewell -millennial-lifestyle-subsidy.html.

31. Lisa B. Kahn, "The long-term labor market consequences of graduating from college in a bad economy," *Labour Economics* 17, no. 2 (2010): https://www.sciencedirect.com/science/article/pii/S0927537109001018.

32. Philip Oreopoulos, Till von Wachter, and Andrew Heisz, "The Short- and Long-Term Career Effects of Graduating in a Recession," *American Economic Journal: Applied Economics* 4, no. 1 (2012): 1–29, http://www .jstor.org/stable/41419422.

33. R. D. Goodwin et al., "Trends in anxiety among adults in the United States, 2008–2018: Rapid increases among young adults," *J Psychiatr Res* 130 (November 2020), https://doi.org/10.1016/j.jpsychires.2020.08.014.

34. Donald Trump, "Tweets of August 7, 2015," American Presidency Project, University of California, Santa Barbara, August 7, 2015, https://www .presidency.ucsb.edu/documents/tweets-august-7-2015.

35. Donald Trump, "Tweets of August 2, 2016," American Presidency Project, University of California, Santa Barbara, August 2, 2016, https:// www.presidency.ucsb.edu/documents/tweets-august-2-2016.

36. Donald Trump, "Remarks at the South Florida Fair Expo Center in West Palm Beach, Florida," American Presidency Project, University of California, Santa Barbara, October 13, 2016, https://www.presidency .ucsb.edu/documents/remarks-the-south-florida-fair-expo-center-west -palm-beach-florida.

37. Tommy Leung, Erica Chenoweth, Nathan Perkins, et al., "The Trump years launched the biggest sustained protest movement in U.S. history. It's not over," *Washington Post*, February 8, 2021, https://www .washingtonpost.com/politics/2021/02/08/trump-years-launched -biggest-sustained-protest-movement-us-history-its-not-over/.

38. Eli Rosenberg, "Protest Grows 'Out of Nowhere' at Kennedy Airport After Iraqis Are Detained," *New York Times*, January 28, 2017, https:// www.nytimes.com/2017/01/28/nyregion/jfk-protests-trump-refugee -ban.html?_r=0.

39. Mary Jordan and Scott Clement, "Rallying Nation," *Washington Post*, April 6, 2018, https://www.washingtonpost.com/news/national/wp /2018/04/06/feature/in-reaction-to-trump-millions-of-americans-are -joining-protests-and-getting-political/.

40. Benjamin Wallace-Wells, "The Changing Shape of Protests in the Second Year of the Trump Era," *New Yorker*, April 5, 2018, https://www .newyorker.com/news/news-desk/the-changing-shape-of-protests-in -the-second-year-of-the-trump-era; Laurel Wamsley, "West Virginia's Teachers Walk Off the Job, Protesting Low Pay and Benefit Cuts," NPR, February 22, 2018, https://www.npr.org/sections/thetwo-way/2018/02 /22/588086091/west-virginias-teachers-walk-off-the-job-protesting -low-pay-and-benefit-cuts; and Rachel M. Cohen, "Teacher Unrest Spreads to Oklahoma," Intercept, March 6, 2018. https://theintercept .com/2018/03/06/oklahoma-teacher-strike-west-virginia/.

41. "Tereza Lee, the original Dreamer," *Economist*, February 1, 2018, https:// www.economist.com/united-states/2018/02/01/tereza-lee-the-original -dreamer.

42. Shannon Dooling, "Why The 'Original DREAMer' Remains Hopeful Amid DACA's Uncertain Future," WBUR, January 18, 2018, https://www .wbur.org/news/2018/01/18/original-dreamer.

43. "The Original DREAMer Recalls 'All Pervasive' Fear As An Undocumented Child," NPR, June 20, 2018, https://www.npr.org /transcripts/622002025.

44. Mindi Foster et al., "Can "slacktivism" work? Perceived power differences moderate the relationship between social media activism and collective action intentions through positive affect," *Cyberpsychology: Journal of Psychosocial Research on Cyberspace* 13, no. 4 (2019), https:// doi.org/10.5817/CP2019-4-6.

45. Zeynep Tufekci, "Do Protests Even Work?," *Atlantic*, June 24, 2020, https://www.theatlantic.com/technology/archive/2020/06/why-protests -work/613420/.

46. Robert Pear, "President Signs Landmark Bill On Immigration," *New York Times*, November 7, 1986, https://www.nytimes.com/1986/11/07 /us/president-signs-landmark-bill-on-immigration.html.

47. Jodi Kantor and Megan Twohey, "Harvey Weinstein Paid Off Sexual Harassment Accusers for Decades," *New York Times*, October 5, 2017,

https://www.nytimes.com/2017/10/05/us/harvey-weinstein-harassment
-allegations.html.

48. Ronan Farrow, "From Aggressive Overtures to Sexual Assault: Harvey
Weinstein's Accusers Tell Their Stories," *New Yorker*, October 10, 2017,
https://www.newyorker.com/news/news-desk/from-aggressive-overtures
-to-sexual-assault-harvey-weinsteins-accusers-tell-their-stories.

49. Abby Ohlheiser, "The woman Behind 'Me Too' Knew the Power of
the Phrase when She Created It—10 Years Ago," *Washington Post*,
October 19, 2017, https://www.washingtonpost.com/news/the-intersect
/wp/2017/10/19/the-woman-behind-me-too-knew-the-power-of-the
-phrase-when-she-created-it-10-years-ago/.

50. Christina Caron, "NBC News and MSNBC Cut Ties With Mark Halperin,"
New York Times, October 30, 2017, https://www.nytimes.com/2017/10/30
/business/media/mark-halperin-msnbc.html.

51. Cara Buckley, Jodi Kantor, and Melena Ryzik, "Louis C.K. Is Accused
by 5 Women of Sexual Misconduct," *New York Times*, November 9, 2017,
https://www.nytimes.com/2017/11/09/arts/television/louis-ck-sexual
-misconduct.html.

52. John Koblin and Michael M. Grynbaum, "Charlie Rose Fired by CBS
and PBS After Harassment Allegations," *New York Times*, Nov. 21, 2017,
https://www.nytimes.com/2017/11/21/business/media/charlie-rose-fired
-cbs.html.

53. Jim Rutenberg, Ellen Gabler, Michael M. Grynbaum, and Rachel
Abrams, "NBC Fires Matt Lauer, the Face of 'Today'," *New York Times*,
November 29, 2017, https://www.nytimes.com/2017/11/29/business
/media/nbc-matt-lauer.html.

54. Abby Ohlheiser, "The Woman Behind 'Me Too,'" *Washington Post*,
October 19, 2017 https://www.washingtonpost.com/news/the-intersect
/wp/2017/10/19/the-woman-behind-me-too-knew-the-power-of-the
-phrase-when-she-created-it-10-years-ago/.

55. "The Look of Success," Williams College '68 Center for Career Exploration,
https://www.williams.edu/career-center/the-look-of-success/.

56. Ron Alsop, "The 'Trophy Kids' Go to Work," *Wall Street Journal*,
October 21, 2008, https://www.wsj.com/articles/SB1224552193916
52725.

57. Ryan Jenkins, "How to Help Millennials Overcome Failure," *Inc.*, June 21,
2017, https://www.inc.com/ryan-jenkins/how-to-help-millennials
-overcome-failure.html.

58. Ryan Hass and Abraham Denmark, "More Pain than Gain: How the
US-China Trade War Hurt America," Brookings Institution, August 7,

2020, https://www.brookings.edu/articles/more-pain-than-gain-how-the-us-china-trade-war-hurt-america/.

59. Allison Schrager, "Men Dropping Out of the Workforce Could Be Progress," Bloomberg Opinion, February 21, 2023, https://www.bloomberg.com/opinion/articles/2023-02-21/men-s-labor-force-participation-is-dropping-are-women-the-reason.

60. Sarah M. Flood and Katie R. Genadek, "Time for Each Other: Work and Family Constraints Among Couples," *Journal of Marriage and Family* 78, no. 1 (2015): 142–164. https://pmc.ncbi.nlm.nih.gov/articles/PMC4712716/.

61. Federal Reserve Bank of St. Louis, "All-Transactions House Price Index for San Diego-Chula Vista-Carlsbad, CA (MSA)," June 19, 2024, https://fred.stlouisfed.org/series/ATNHPIUS41740Q.

62. Aaron B. Rochlen et al., " 'I'm just providing for my family: A qualitative study of stay-at-home fathers," *Psychology of Men & Masculinity* 9, no. 4 (2008), https://doi.org/10.1037/a0012510.

63. John Gramlich, "Recent surge in U.S. drug overdose deaths has hit Black men the hardest," Pew Research Center, January 19, 2022, https://www.pewresearch.org/short-reads/2022/01/19/recent-surge-in-u-s-drug-overdose-deaths-has-hit-black-men-the-hardest/.

64. M. C. Gondré-Lewis, T. Abijo, and T. A. Gondré-Lewis, "The Opioid Epidemic: a Crisis Disproportionately Impacting Black Americans and Urban Communities," *Journal of Racial and Ethnic Health Disparities* 10, no. 4 (Aug 2023), https://doi.org/10.1007/s40615-022-01384-6.

65. Jennifer Jacobs and Steven T. Dennis, "Trump Tells Sessions He Favors Death Penalty for Fentanyl Dealers," Bloomberg News, August 23, 2018 https://www.bloomberg.com/politics/articles/2018-08-23/trump-is-said-to-propose-death-penalty-for-fentanyl-dealers.

66. Gillian Tett, "Could loneliness explain why Trump won?," *Financial Times*, August 9, 2023, https://www.ft.com/content/6bbabd62-a006-403d-ba8e-03ee6d3a46e3; Astra Taylor and Leah Hunt-Hendrix, "The One Idea That Could Save American Democracy," *New York Times*, March 21, 2024, https://www.nytimes.com/2024/03/21/opinion/democracy-solidarity-trump.html.

67. "Who Is Crazier, Donald Trump or North Korea's Kim Jong-Un?," editorial, *Mercury News*, August 10, 2017, https://www.mercurynews.com/2017/08/09/editorial-who-is-crazier-donald-trump-or-north-koreas-kim-jong-un/.

68. Miles Taylor, "I Am Part of the Resistance Inside the Trump Administration," *New York Times*, September 5, 2018, https://www

.nytimes.com/2018/09/05/opinion/trump-white-house-anonymous
-resistance.html.

69. Steven Kurutz, "There Will Be Blood-Red Trees," *New York Times*, November 30, 2018, https://www.nytimes.com/2018/11/30/fashion/white
-house-christmas-decorations.html.

70. Richard Sima, "Why we're already losing our pandemic memories," *Washington Post*, March 13, 2023, https://www.washingtonpost.com
/wellness/2023/03/13/brain-memory-pandemic-covid-forgetting/.

71. Scott A. Small, "We Will Forget Much of the Pandemic. That's a Good Thing," *New York Times*, March 9, 2022, https://www.nytimes.com/2022
/03/09/opinion/pandemic-memory.html.

72. Mark Oppenheimer, "America Forgot the 1918 Flu. Will We Also Forget Covid?," *Wall Street Journal*, January 21, 2023, https://www.wsj
.com/articles/america-forgot-the-1918-flu-will-we-also-forget-covid
-11674277262.

73. Mark Zuckerberg, "Founder's Letter, 2021," Meta, October 28, 2021, https://about.fb.com/news/2021/10/founders-letter/.

74. Mohamad Moslimani and Jeffrey S. Passel, "What the data says about immigrants in the U.S.," Pew Research Center, July 22, 2024, https://
www.pewresearch.org/short-reads/2024/07/22/key-findings-about-us
-immigrants/.

75. Jeanne Batalova, "Frequently Requested Statistics on Immigrants and Immigration in the United States," Migration Policy Institute, March 13, 2024, https://www.migrationpolicy.org/article/frequently-requested
-statistics-immigrants-and-immigration-united-states-2024.

76. Laurence Benenson, "Fact Sheet: Deferred Action for Childhood Arrivals (DACA)," Naitonal Immigration Forum, May 21, 2024, https://
immigrationforum.org/article/fact-sheet-on-deferred-action-for
-childhood-arrivals-daca/.

77. "Official Obituary of Brittany Marie Wheeler," https://www
.grfuneralhome.com/obituary/Brittany-Wheeler.

78. RAND, "More Than 40 Percent of Americans Know Someone Who Died of Drug Overdose: 13 Percent Say Deaths Have Disrupted Their Lives," February 21, 2024, https://www.rand.org/news/press/2024/02/21.html.

79. Jeneen Interlandi, "48 Million Americans Live With Addiction: Here's How to Get Them Help That Works.," *New York Times*, December 13, 2023, https://www.nytimes.com/2023/12/13/opinion/addiction-policy
-treatment-opioid.html.

BIBLIOGRAPHY

"Ad Questions John Kerry's Duty in Vietnam." *Fox News*, August 6, 2004. https:// www.foxnews.com/story/ad-questions-john-kerrys-duty-in-vietnam.

Adams, James Truslow. *The Epic of America*. New York: Blue Ribbon Books, 1941.

Akerlof, George A., Janet L. Yellen, and Michael L. Katz. "An Analysis of out-of-Wedlock Childbearing in the United States." *The Quarterly Journal of Economics* 111, no. 2 (1996): 277–317. https://doi.org/10.2307/2946680. http://www.jstor.org/stable/2946680.

Alliance Chronicle 2004–2005. Alliance High School yearbook, page 56. https://www.alliancememory.org/digital/collection/p16335coll4/id/36196 /rec/15.

———. *Alliance Chronicle 2004–2005*. Alliance High School yearbook, page 121. https://www.alliancememory.org/digital/collection/p16335coll4/id /36261/rec/15.

"All Presidents Are Deporters in Chief." Editorial, *New York Times*, July 13, 2019. https://www.nytimes.com/2019/07/13/opinion/sunday/trump -deportations-immigration.html.

Andersen, Kurt. "The Best Decade Ever? The 1990s, Obviously." *New York Times*, February 6, 2015. https://www.nytimes.com/2015/02/08/opinion /sunday/the-best-decade-ever-the-1990s-obviously.html.

"Anthony Perez." https://www.legacy.com/obituaries/name/anthony-perez -obituary?pid=132278&view=guestbook&page=4.

Arshad, M., J. A. Stanley, and N. Raz. "Adult Age Differences in Subcortical Myelin Content Are Consistent with Protracted Myelination and Unrelated to Diffusion Tensor Imaging Indices." [English]. no. 1095–9572 (Electronic).

Ashcroft, Attorney General John. "Prepared Remarks for the US Mayors Conference." News release, October 25, 2001, https://www.justice.gov /archive/ag/speeches/2001/agcrisisremarks10_25.htm.

Baker, Peter. "Mourning 'Compassionate Conservatism' Along with Its Author." *New York Times*, February 10, 2023. https://www.nytimes .com/2023/02/10/us/politics/michael-gerson-memorial-compassionate -conservatism.html.

Ballard, Jamie. "How Much Power Do Americans Think the President Has on the Economy?" *Economist and YouGov*, September 13, 2020. https://today.yougov.com/politics/articles/31891-economy-presidents-poll-data.

——. "Millennials Are the Loneliest Generation." *YouGov*, July 30, 2019, 2019. https://today.yougov.com/society/articles/24577-loneliness-friendship-new-friends-poll-survey.

Balzarini, Rhonda N., Christoffer Dharma, Taylor Kohut, et al. "Demographic Comparison of American Individuals in Polyamorous and Monogamous Relationships." *Journal of Sex Research* 56, no. 6 (July–August 2019): 681–94.

Bejan, Adrian. "Why the Days Seem Shorter as We Get Older." *European Review* 27, no. 2 (2019): 187–94. https://doi.org/10.1017/S1062798718000741. https://www.cambridge.org/core/product/2CB8EC9B0B30537230C7442B826E42F1.

Bologna, Caroline. "What Happened to the 'Going-out Top'?" *HuffPost*, March 16, 2023. https://www.huffingtonpost.co.uk/entry/going-out-top-what-happened_l_608836cee4b04620270016e1.

Brazile, Donna, and Tucker Carlson. *Crossfire*. Aired August 6, 2004, on CNN. https://transcripts.cnn.com/show/cf/date/2004-08-06/segment/00.

Brookings Institute. "How Big Is the Prospective Budget Surplus?" 2000, https://www.brookings.edu/articles/how-big-is-the-prospective-budget-surplus/.

Brooks, Khristopher J. "It's Taking Americans Much Longer in Life to Buy Their First Home." *CBS News*, August 15, 2023, 2023. https://www.cbsnews.com/news/average-homebuyer-age-millennial-data-realtor/.

Bruni, Frank, and Richard W. Stevenson. "Bush Tax Cuts Are Assailed as Too Little or Too Much." *New York Times*, December 2, 1999. https://www.nytimes.com/1999/12/02/us/bush-tax-cuts-are-assailed-as-too-little-or-too-much.html.

Bureau of Labor Statistics. "Employee Tenure in 2022." Updated September 22, 2022, https://www.bls.gov/news.release/tenure.nr0.htm.

——. "Highlights of Women's Earnings in 2020." *BLS Reports*, September 2021. https://www.bls.gov/opub/reports/womens-earnings/2020/#:~:text=(See%20table%201.),chart%204%20and%20table%2019.).

——. "Job Availability during a Recession." *Issues in Labor Statistics*, March 2010. https://www.bls.gov/opub/btn/archive/job-availability-during-a-recession-an-examination-of-the-number-of-unemployed-persons-per-job-opening.pdf.

——. "Unemployment Level - Persons Who Completed Temporary Jobs [Lnu03026637]." June 15, 2024. https://fred.stlouisfed.org/series/LNU03026637.

Burns, Maggie Haberman, and Alexander Burns. "Donald Trump's Presidential Run Began in an Effort to Gain Stature." *New York Times*, March 12, 2016. https://www.nytimes.com/2016/03/13/us/politics/donald -trump-campaign.html.

Bush, George W. "Address to a Joint Session of Congress and the American People." September 20, 2001. https://georgewbush-whitehouse.archives .gov/news/releases/2001/09/20010920-8.html.

———. "President's Remarks at the 2004 Republican National Convention." September 2, 2004. https://georgewbush-whitehouse.archives.gov/news /releases/2004/09/20040902-2.html.

———. "President Calls for Expanding Opportunities to Home Ownership." *Remarks by the President on Homeownership*, June 17, 2002. https:// georgewbush-whitehouse.archives.gov/news/releases/2002/06/text /20020617-2.html.

———. "Remarks by President Bush and Senator Kerry in Second 2004 Presidential Debate." October 9, 2004. https://georgewbush-whitehouse .archives.gov/news/releases/2004/10/text/20041009-2.html.

———. "Remarks by the President at Bush-Cheney 2004 Luncheon." https:// georgewbush-whitehouse.archives.gov/news/releases/2003/12/20031205 -1.html.

Byock, Satya Doyle. *Quarterlife: The Search for Self in Early Adulthood*. London: Penguin Books, 2024.

Cachero, Paulina. "Lots of Us Homeowners Want to Move. They Just Have Nowhere to Go." *Bloomberg News*, July 30, 2023. https://www.bloomberg .com/news/articles/2023-07-30/housing-market-is-stuck-as-homeowners -with-low-mortgage-rates-stay-put.

Calmes, Jackie. "GOP Front-Runner Defends Tax Plan as Both Parties Take Shots at Bush." *Wall Street Journal*, December 2, 1999. https://www.wsj .com/articles/SB94409523462381176.

"Campus Attitudes Towards Politics and Public Service (Capps) Survey." Fall 2001. https://iop.harvard.edu/youth-poll/2nd-edition-fall-2001.

Carmichael, Sarah Green. "Millennials Are Actually Workaholics, According to Research." *Harvard Business Review*, August 17, 2016. https://hbr.org /2016/08/millennials-are-actually-workaholics-according-to-research.

Carpenter, Scott. "Us Housing Market Is So Stressful That Buyers Are Left in Tears." *Bloomberg News*, June 2, 2022. https://www.bloomberg.com/news /articles/2022-06-02/buying-a-home-americans-say-stress-of-purchase -process-is-making-them-cry.

CDC. "Injuries and Violence Are Leading Causes of Death." https://www .cdc.gov/injury/wisqars/animated-leading-causes.html.

Center for American Women and Politics (CAWP). "Gender Gap: Voting Choices in Presidential Elections." https://cawp.rutgers.edu/gender-gap -voting-choices-presidential-elections.

Chenoweth, Erica, and Tommy Leung, Nathan Perkins, Jeremy Pressman, Jay Ulfelder. "The Trump Years Launched the Biggest Sustained Protest Movement in U.S. History. It's Not Over." *Washington Post*, February 8, 2021. https://www.washingtonpost.com/politics/2021/02/08/trump-years -launched-biggest-sustained-protest-movement-us-history-its-not-over/.

Chishti, Muzaffar, Sarah Pierce, and Jessica Bolter. "The Obama Record on Deportations: Deporter in Chief or Not?" Migration Policy Institute, January 26, 2017. https://www.migrationpolicy.org/article/obama-record -deportations-deporter-chief-or-not.

Clement, Mary Jordan, and Scott Clement. "Rallying Nation." *Washington Post*, April 6, 2018. https://www.washingtonpost.com/news/national/wp /2018/04/06/feature/in-reaction-to-trump-millions-of-americans-are -joining-protests-and-getting-political/.

CNN. "Britney Spears: 'Trust Our President in Every Decision.'" *CNN Transcript*, September 4, 2003. https://edition.cnn.com/2003/SHOWBIZ /Music/09/03/cnna.spears/.

"CNN Crossfire Ad." https://www.youtube.com/watch?v=-WDlqqy9JFk.

Comscore. "Comscore Reports May 2011 U.S. Mobile Subscriber Market Share." July 5, 2011. https://www.comscore.com/Insights/Press-Releases/2011/7 /comScore-Reports-May-2011-US-Mobile-Subscriber-Market-Share.

Congressional Budget Office. "Employment during the 2001–2003 Recovery." August 2005. https://www.cbo.gov/sites/default/files/109th-congress -2005-2006/reports/08-05-jobs.pdf.

"Contents." *Alliance Chronicle 2004–2005*, 2004. https://www .alliancememory.org/digital/collection/p16335coll4/id/36313/rec/15.

Cottom, Tressie McMillan. "We Weren't Wrong to Love 'The Cosby Show.'" *New York Times*, February 14, 2022. https://www.nytimes.com/2022/02 /14/opinion/cosby-show-documentary.html.

"Counting Their Chickens." *Economist*, February 4, 1999. https://www .economist.com/united-states/1999/02/04/counting-their-chickens.

Crossfire. "Jon Stewart's America." October 15, 2004. https://transcripts.cnn .com/show/cf/date/2004-10-15/segment/01.

Cutler, David M., and J. Travis Donahoe. "Thick Market Externalities and the Persistence of the Opioid Epidemic." *National Bureau of Economic Research Working Paper Series* no. 32055 (2024). https://doi.org/10.3386/ w32055. http://www.nber.org/papers/w32055.

Davies, James C. "Toward a Theory of Revolution." *American Sociological Review* 27, no. 1 (February 1962): 5–19. https://louischauvel.org/DAVIES2089714.pdf.

Day, Liz, Samantha Stark, and Joe Coscarelli. "Britney Spears Quietly Pushed for Years to End Her Conservatorship." *New York Times*, June 22, 2021. https://www.nytimes.com/2021/06/22/arts/music/britney-spears-conservatorship.html.

Diaz, Alex. "Rare Photos Show Fresh-Faced Britney Spears Cuddling up to Justin Timberlake at Her 18th Birthday Party." *Daily Mail*, February 22, 2021. https://www.dailymail.co.uk/news/article-9286589/Rare-photos-Britney-Spears-cuddling-Justin-Timberlake-18th-birthday-party.html.

Digiday. *Digiday*, June 15, 2015. https://digiday.com/marketing/early-onset-nostalgia-surge-cola-mad-libs-renaissance/.

DiIulio, John J., Jr. "Biden, Trump, and the 4 Categories of White Votes." Brookings Institute, April 15, 2024. https://www.brookings.edu/articles/biden-trump-and-the-4-categories-of-white-votes/.

Dimock, Michael. "How America Changed during Barack Obama's Presidency." Pew Research Center, January 10, 2017. https://www.pewresearch.org/social-trends/2017/01/10/how-america-changed-during-barack-obamas-presidency/.

Doherty, Carroll, and Hannah Hartig. "Two Decades Later, the Enduring Legacy of 9/11." Pew Research Center, September 2, 2021. https://www.pewresearch.org/politics/2021/09/02/two-decades-later-the-enduring-legacy-of-9-11/.

Dondorp, Arjen M., Sue J. Lee, and M. A. Faiz et al. "The Relationship between Age and the Manifestations of and Mortality Associated with Severe Malaria." *Clinical Infectious Diseases* 47, no. 2 (July 2008): 151–157. https://doi.org/10.1086/589287.

Dooling, Shannon. "Why the 'Original Dreamer' Remains Hopeful Amid DACA's Uncertain Future." WBUR, January 18, 2018. https://www.wbur.org/news/2018/01/18/original-dreamer.

Ducharme, Jamie. "Why So Many Women Are Waiting Longer to Have Kids." *TIME*, April 10, 2024. https://time.com/6965267/women-having-kids-later/.

Duffy, Bobby. *Generations: Does When You're Born Shape Who You Are?* London: Atlantic Books, 2021.

Dutta, Soumitra, and Matthew Fraser. "Barack Obama and the Facebook Election." *U.S. News and World Report*. https://www.usnews.com/opinion/articles/2008/11/19/barack-obama-and-the-facebook-election.

Egner, Jeremy, Dave Itzkoff, and Kathryn Shattuck. "Jon Stewart and 'The Daily Show': 9 Essential Moments." *New York Times*, August 4, 2015. https://www.nytimes.com/interactive/2015/08/04/arts/television/jon -stewart-daily-show-9-essential-moments.html.

"Election 2024: Exit Polls." CNN. https://edition.cnn.com/election/2024/ exit-polls/national-results/general/president/20.

Engelberg, Stephen. "Terrorism's New (and Very Old) Face; It's Not the Kind of War the West Fights Well." *New York Times*, September 12, 1998. https://www.nytimes.com/1998/09/12/arts/terrorism-s-new-and-very-old -face-it-s-not-the-kind-of-war-the-west-fights-well.html.

Flood, Sarah M., and Katie R. Genadek. "Time for Each Other: Work and Family Constraints Among Couples." *Journal of Marriage and Family* 78, no. 1 (2015): 142–164. https://pmc.ncbi.nlm.nih.gov/articles/PMC4712716/.

Foster, Mindi, Eden Hennessey, Benjamin Blankenship, and Abigail Stewart. "Can "Slacktivism" Work? Perceived Power Differences Moderate the Relationship between Social Media Activism and Collective Action Intentions through Positive Affect." *Cyberpsychology: Journal of Psychosocial Research on Cyberspace* 13 (11/07 2019). https://doi.org/10 .5817/CP2019-4-6.

Fraser, Matthew, and Soumitra Dutta. "Obama's Win Means Future Elections Must Be Fought Online." *Guardian*, November 7, 2008. https://www.theguardian.com/technology/2008/nov/07/barackobama -uselections2008.

Friedman, Vanessa. "How Can I Update My Millennial Style?" *New York Times*, February 12, 2024. https://www.nytimes.com/2024/02/12/style /millennial-gen-z-style.html.

Fry, Richard, Carolina Aragão, Kiley Hurst, and Kim Parker. "In a Growing Share of U.S. Marriages, Husbands and Wives Earn About the Same." *Pew Research Center*, April 13, 2023. https://www.pewresearch.org/social -trends/2023/04/13/in-a-growing-share-of-u-s-marriages-husbands-and -wives-earn-about-the-same/.

Fuchs, Chris. "'Original Dreamer' Still Fights for Undocumented Immigrants 16 Years After First Dream Act." *NBC News*, March 30, 2017. https:// www.nbcnews.com/news/asian-america/original-dreamer-still-fights -undocumented-immigrants-16-years-after-first-n740491.

"Full Text: George Bush's Victory Speech." *Guardian*, November 4, 2004. https://www.theguardian.com/world/2004/nov/04/uselections2004.usa17.

Gabler, Ellen, Jim Rutenberg, Michael M. Grynbaum, and Rachel Abrams. "NBC Fires Matt Lauer, the Face of 'Today'." *New York Times*, November 29,

2017. https://www.nytimes.com/2017/11/29/business/media/nbc-matt-lauer.html.

"Gallup Daily: Obama Job Approval." Gallup. https://news.gallup.com/poll/113980/Gallup-Daily-Obama-Job-Approval.aspx.

Galston, William A., and Rashawn Ray. "Did the 1994 Crime Bill Cause Mass Incarceration?" *Brookings*, August 28, 2020. https://www.brookings.edu/articles/did-the-1994-crime-bill-cause-mass-incarceration/.

Garber, Megan. "'The Revolution Begins Here': MSNBC's First Broadcast, July 1996." *Atlantic*, July 16, 2012. https://www.theatlantic.com/technology/archive/2012/07/the-revolution-begins-here-msnbcs-first-broadcast-july-1996/259855/.

Garza, Alicia. *The Purpose of Power: How to Build Movements for the 21st Century*. London : Black Swan, 2021.

Goldstein, Jessica M. "How 'Mr. Brightside' Became a Generation's Anthem." *New York Times*, December 6, 2023. https://www.nytimes.com/2023/12/06/arts/music/mr-brightside-killers.html.

Gonzalez, Sarah. "No One Expected Obama Would Deport More People Than Any Other U.S. President." WNYC, January 19, 2017. https://www.wnyc.org/story/no-one-thought-barack-obama-would-deport-more-people-any-other-us-president/.

"Google Trends: Fail 2004-Present." https://trends.google.com/trends/explore?date=all&geo=US&q=fail&hl=en.

"Great Telecoms Crash." *Economist*, July 18, 2002. https://www.economist.com/leaders/2002/07/18/the-great-telecoms-crash.

Greenfield, Rebecca. "How Much Did All of Those AOL CDs Cost?" *Atlantic*, December 28, 2010. https://www.theatlantic.com/technology/archive/2010/12/how-much-did-all-of-those-aol-cds-cost/68600/.

Grynbaum, Michael M., and Jim Rutenberg "How MSNBC's Leftward Tilt Delivers Ratings, and Complications." *New York Times*, May 15, 2024. https://www.nytimes.com/2024/05/15/business/media/nbc-msnbc-trump-biden.html.

Hamermesh, Daniel S. "Life Satisfaction, Loneliness and Togetherness, with an Application to Covid-19 Lock-Downs." *Journal of Public Economics* 193 (Nov. 2020): 104346

Hansen, Helena, Jules Netherland, David L Herzberg. *Whiteout: How Racial Capitalism Changed the Color of Opioids in America*. Oakland: University of California Press, 2023.

Hanson, Melanie. "College Enrollment & Student Demographic Statistics." January 10, 2024. https://educationdata.org/college-enrollment-statistics.

"Happy Birthday Britney: Spears Celebrates 18 in Style." MTV News, 1999, https://www.mtv.com/news/tud77i/happy-birthday-britney-spears-celebrates-18-in-style.

Henry, William A., III. "Shaking up the Networks." *TIME*, August 9, 1982. https://content.time.com/time/subscriber/printout/0,8816,925663,00.html.

Herman, Judith Lewis. *Trauma and Recovery*. [rev. ed.]. London: Pandora, 2001.

Heron, M. "Deaths: Leading Causes for 2017." [English]. *National Vital Statistics Reports* 68, no. 6 (Jun 2019): 1–77.

Hill, Amelia. "Thumbs Are the New Fingers for the Gameboy Generation." *Guardian*, March 24, 2002. https://www.theguardian.com/uk/2002/mar/24/mobilephones.games.

Hines, Matt. "Jon Stewart 'Crossfire' Feud Ignites Net Frenzy." CNET, May 5, 2006. https://www.cnet.com/culture/jon-stewart-crossfire-feud-ignites-net-frenzy/.

Hirschberger, G. "Collective Trauma and the Social Construction of Meaning." [English]. *Frontiers in Psychology* 9 (2018): 1441. https://doi.org/10.3389/fpsyg.2018.01441.

Hoffower, Hillary. "Are You a Geriatric Millennial? It Depends on How Comfortable You Are with Tiktok, and Whether You Remember Myspace." *Business Insider*, September 15, 2021. https://www.businessinsider.com/typical-geriatric-millennial-age-digital-skills-communication-2021-7.

Horowitz, Joy. "Snookums! Steve Urkel Is a Hit." *New York Times*, April 17, 1991. https://www.nytimes.com/1991/04/17/news/snookums-steve-urkel-is-a-hit.html.

Howe, Neil, and William Strauss. *Millennials Rising: The Next Great Generation*. New York: Vintage Books, 2000.

"How Pew Research Center Will Report on Generations Moving Forward." Pew Research Center, May 22, 2023, https://www.pewresearch.org/short-reads/2023/05/22/how-pew-research-center-will-report-on-generations-moving-forward/.

Hunt-Hendrix, Leigh, and Astra Taylor. "The One Idea That Could Save American Democracy." *New York Times*, March 21, 2024. https://www.nytimes.com/2024/03/21/opinion/democracy-solidarity-trump.html.

Igielnik, Ruth, Scott Keeter, and Hannah Hartig. "Behind Biden's 2020 Victory." *Pew Research Center*. https://www.pewresearch.org/politics/2021/06/30/behind-bidens-2020-victory/.

"Interview with Barack Obama." *Larry King Live*, March 19, 2007. https://transcripts.cnn.com/show/lkl/date/2007-03-19/segment/01.

Ipsos. "US Millennials Are Most Likely to Identify as 'Working Class.'"
March 16, 2016. https://www.ipsos.com/en-uk/us-millennials-are-most
-likely-identify-working-class.

Jacobe, Dennis. "More Than Half Still Say U.S. Is in Recession or Depression."
Gallup, April 28, 2011. https://news.gallup.com/poll/147299/half-say
-recession-depression.aspx.

Jensen, Elizabeth, and Eben Shapiro. "Fox Launches Its News Channel,
but Manhattanites Can't Get It." *Wall Street Journal*, October 8, 1996.
https://www.wsj.com/articles/SB844732515488228500.

Kaplan, Jonathan. "Bank of America 2023 Homebuyer Insights Report."
December 4, 2023. https://institute.bankofamerica.com/content/dam/bank
-of-america-institute/economic-insights/uneven-housing-market.pdf.

Kapp, Lawrence, and Charles A. Henning. "Recruiting and Retention:
An Overview of Fy2006 and Fy2007 Results for Active and Reserve
Component Enlisted Personnel." Every CRS Report, February 7, 2008.
https://www.everycrsreport.com/files/20080207_RL32965_04f747950f4
d6da0b22fec0a1953e44dc6e73a7a.pdf.

Kessler, Glenn. "When Did Mitch McConnell Say He Wanted to Make Obama
a One-Term President?" *Washington Post*, January 11, 2017. https://www
.washingtonpost.com/news/fact-checker/wp/2017/01/11/when-did-mitch
-mcconnell-say-he-wanted-to-make-obama-a-one-term-president/.

Kiley, Jocelyn, and Carroll Doherty. "A Look Back at How Fear and False
Beliefs Bolstered U.S. Public Support for War in Iraq." Pew Research
Center, March 14, 2023. https://www.pewresearch.org/politics/2023/03/14
/a-look-back-at-how-fear-and-false-beliefs-bolstered-u-s-public-support
-for-war-in-iraq/.

Kimmel, Michael S. *Manhood in America: A Cultural History*. New York;
London: Free Press, 1996.

Kirkpatrick, David D. "Rally against Gay Marriage Draws Thousands to Capital."
New York Times, October 16, 2004. https://www.nytimes.com/2004/10/16/us
/rally-against-gay-marriage-draws-thousands-to-capital.html.

Klein, Ezra. "Dan Savage on Polyamory, Chosen Family and Better Sex."
Podcast audio. *The Ezra Klein Show*. January 10, 2023. https://www
.nytimes.com/2023/01/10/opinion/ezra-klein-podcast-dan-savage.html?

———. "The Men—and Boys—Are Not Alright." *New York Times*, March 10,
2023. https://www.nytimes.com/2023/03/10/opinion/ezra-klein-podcast
-richard-reeves.html.

Klein, Naomi. "Disowned by the Ownership Society." *Nation*, February 18,
2008. https://www.thenation.com/article/archive/disowned-ownership
-society/.

Kleinfield, N. R. "For Girls Only: Glimpse of Workaday World." *New York Times*, April 29, 1993. https://www.nytimes.com/1993/04/29/us/for-girls -only-glimpse-of-workaday-world.html.

Knowlton, Brian. "Iraq War Justified, Bush Insists Again." *New York Times*, October 7, 2004. https://www.nytimes.com/2004/10/07/world/americas /iraw-war-justified-bush-insists-again.html.

Kolomatsky, Michael. "The Gen-Z Advantage in Housing." *New York Times*, April 25, 2024. https://www.nytimes.com/2024/04/25/realestate/the-gen -z-advantage-in-housing.html.

Kurutz, Steven. "There Will Be Blood-Red Trees." *New York Times*, November 30, 2018. https://www.nytimes.com/2018/11/30/fashion/white -house-christmas-decorations.html.

LaFrance, Adrienne. "How Generations Get Their Names." *Atlantic*, February 3, 2016. https://www.theatlantic.com/technology/archive/2016 /02/how-generations-get-their-names/459720/.

Langdon, David S. Terence M. McMenamin, and Thomas J. Krolik. "U.S. Labor Market in 2001: Economy Enters a Recession." *Monthly Labor Review*, February 2002. https://www.bls.gov/opub/mlr/2002/02/art1full.pdf.

Lee, Linda. "Attack of the 90-Foot Teen-Agers." *New York Times*, November 9, 1997. https://www.nytimes.com/1997/11/09/style/attack-of-the-90-foot -teen-agers.html.

Lee, Tereza. "The Original DREAMer Recalls 'All Pervasive' Fear As An Undocumented Child." Interview by Mary Louise Kelly and Dick Durbin. NPR, June 20, 2018. https://www.npr.org/transcripts/622002025.

Looney, Adam, and Michael Greenstone. "Unemployment and Earnings Losses: A Look at Long-Term Impacts of the Great Recession on American Workers." Brookings Institution, November 4, 2011. https:// www.brookings.edu/articles/unemployment-and-earnings-losses -a-look-at-long-term-impacts-of-the-great-recession-on-american -workers/.

Marquis, Christopher, and Philip Shenon. "Panel Finds No Qaeda-Iraq Tie; Describes a Wider Plot for 9/11." *New York Times*, June 17, 2004. https:// www.nytimes.com/2004/06/17/politics/panel-finds-no-qaedairaq-tie -describes-a-wider-plot-for-911.html.

"Martial Arts Studios in the US: Market Size, Industry Analysis, Trends, and Forecasts." IBISWorld, December 2024. https://www.ibisworld.com /united-states/number-of-businesses/martial-arts-studios/4187/.

Martin, Emmie. "Millennials Agree on the Best Way to Invest—but They're Wrong." CNBC, July 18, 2019. https://www.cnbc.com/2019/07 /18/millennials-say-real-estate-is-the-best-long-term-investment.html.

McKinley, Jesse. "Out for a Night in Search of the In." *New York Times*, May 28, 2000. https://www.nytimes.com/2000/05/28/style/out-for-a -night-in-search-of-the-in.html.

McLean, Bethany, and Joseph Nocera. *All the Devils Are Here: The Hidden History of the Financial Crisis*. London: Viking, 2010.

Menand, Louis. "It's Time to Stop Talking About "Generations". *New Yorker*, October 11, 2021. https://www.newyorker.com/magazine/2021/10/18/its -time-to-stop-talking-about-generations.

Mifflin, Lawrie. "At the New Fox News Channel, the Buzzword Is Fairness, Separating News from Bias." *New York Times*, October 7, 1996. https:// www.nytimes.com/1996/10/07/business/at-the-new-fox-news-channel -the-buzzword-is-fairness-separating-news-from-bias.html.

"Millennial." Encyclopedia Britannica, Updated February 1, 2024, https:// www.britannica.com/topic/millennial.

Miller, Hugo. "Blackberry Stands by Hardware as Sales Slip to 2007 Level." Bloomberg News, December 18, 2013. https://www.bloomberg.com/news /articles/2013-12-18/blackberry-s-chen-stands-by-hardware-as-sales-slip -to-2007-level.

"Modest Declines in Positive Views of 'Socialism' and 'Capitalism' in U.S." Pew Research Center, September 19, 2022. https://www.pewresearch.org /politics/2022/09/19/modest-declines-in-positive-views-of-socialism-and -capitalism-in-u-s.

Montei, Amanda. "Can a Sexless Marriage Be a Happy One?" *New York Times Magazine*, April 17, 2024. https://www.nytimes.com/2024/04/17 /magazine/sexless-marriage.html.

National Association of Realtors. "The Average Age of First-time U.S. Homeowners Is 38, an All-time High." November 5, 2024. https://www .nar.realtor/newsroom/in-the-news/the-average-age-of-first-time-u-s -homebuyers-is-38-an-all-time-high-cnbc;

"NBC Christmas in Rockefeller Center." NBC, 1999, https://www.youtube .com/watch?v=4Ml5U6-fSfo.

Newport, Frank. "Seventy-Two Percent of Americans Support War against Iraq." Gallup, March 24, 2003. https://news.gallup.com /poll /8038/seventytwo-percent-americans-support-war-against-iraq .aspx.

Obama, Barack. "Transcript: Obama's Speech against the Iraq War." October 2, 2002. https://www.npr.org/2009/01/20/99591469/transcript -obamas-speech-against-the-iraq-war.

Office of the Inspector General. "The September 11 Detainees: A Review of the Treatment of Aliens Held on Immigration Charges in Connection

with the Investigation of the September 11 Attacks." June 2003. https://
oig.justice.gov/sites/default/files/archive/special/0306/press.htm.

"Official Obituary of Brittany Marie Wheeler." https://www.grfuneralhome
.com/obituary/Brittany-Wheeler.

Onion, Rebecca. "Against Generations." Aeon, May 19, 2015. https://aeon
.co/essays/generational-labels-are-lazy-useless-and-just-plain-wrong.

"Original Dreamer Recalls 'All Pervasive' Fear as an Undocumented Child."
NPR, June 20, 2018. https://www.npr.org/transcripts/622002025.

Parachini, John V., and David E. Mosher. "Rereading the Duelfer Report:
Iraqi Insurgents and Weapons of Mass Destruction." *New York Times*,
November 15, 2004. https://www.nytimes.com/2004/11/15/opinion
/rereading-the-duelfer-report-iraqi-insurgents-and-weapons-of-mass
.html.

Pear, Robert. "President Signs Landmark Bill on Immigration." *New York
Times*, November 7, 1986. https://www.nytimes.com/1986/11/07/us
/president-signs-landmark-bill-on-immigration.html.

Pew Research Center. "Public Trust in Government: 1958–2023."
September 19, 2023. https://www.pewresearch.org/politics/2023/09/19
/public-trust-in-government-1958-2023/.

"Poll: Bush Approval Rating 92 Percent." ABC News, October 10, 2001.
https://abcnews.go.com/Politics/story?id=120971&page=1.

Powell, Alvin. "How Friends Helped Fuel the Rise of a Relentless Enemy."
Harvard Gazette, May 3, 2024. https://news.harvard.edu/gazette
/story/2024/05/how-relationships-have-fueled-the-u-s-opioid-crisis
-epidemic/.

Preston, Jennifer, and Brian Stelter. "Turning to Social Networks for News."
New York Times, May 2, 2011. https://www.nytimes.com/2011/05/03
/business/media/03media.html.

Reeves, Richard. *Of Boys and Men: Why the Modern Male Is Struggling, Why
It Matters, and What to Do About It.* Brookings Institution Press, 2022.

Riedel, Bruce. "9/11 and Iraq: The Making of a Tragedy." Brookings
Institution, September 17, 2021. https://www.brookings.edu/articles/9
-11-and-iraq-the-making-of-a-tragedy/.

Rodríguez, Jesús A. "The Supreme Court Case That Created the
'Dreamer' Narrative." *Politico*, October 31, 2021. https://www.politico
.com/news/magazine/2021/10/31/dreamers-undocumented-youth
-forever-children-516354.

Rogers, Robert P. *An Economic History of the American Steel Industry.*
Routledge Explorations in Economic History, 42. London: Routledge,
2009.

Rojas, Rick, Larry Gordon, and Christopher Goffard. "Osama Bin Laden's Death Removes a Cloud That Enveloped a Generation." *Los Angeles Times*, May 4, 2011. https://www.latimes.com/local/la-xpm-2011-may-04-la-me -bin-laden-generation-20110504-story.html.

Romero, Simon. "The Right Connections; the Simple BlackBerry Allowed Contact When Phones Failed." *New York Times*, September 20, 2001. https://www.nytimes.com/2001/09/20/technology/the-right-connections -the-simple-blackberry-allowed-contact-when-phones-failed.html.

Rose, Matthew, and John J. Flalka. "Even with More Play-by-Play, Truth Remains Elusive in Iraq." *Wall Street Journal*, March 31, 2003. https:// www.wsj.com/articles/SB104905933387235OO.

Rosenberg, Eli. "Protest Grows 'Out of Nowhere' at Kennedy Airport after Iraqis Are Detained." *New York Times*, January 28, 2017. https://www.nytimes.com /2017/01/28/nyregion/jfk-protests-trump-refugee-ban.html?_r=0.

Rosenblatt, Kalhan. "Millennial Nostalgia Sells. Just Ask These Influencers Making Their Livings Off It." *NBC News*, September 16, 2022. https://www .nbcnews.com/pop-culture/pop-culture-news/millennial-nostalgia-sells -just-ask-influencers-making-livings-rcna47736.

Rutenberg, Jim. "War or No, News on Cable Already Provides the Drama." *New York Times*, January 15, 2003. https://www.nytimes.com/2003/01/15 /business/media-business-advertising-war-no-cable-already-provides -drama.html.

Sanger, David E. "The Struggle for Iraq: The White House; Bush Backs Away from His Claims About Iraq Arms." *New York Times*, January 28, 2004. https://www.nytimes.com/2004/01/28/world/struggle-for-iraq-white -house-bush-backs-away-his-claims-about-iraq-arms.html.

———. "Talks and Turmoil: The Overview; President Chides World Trade Body in Stormy Seattle." *New York Times*, December 2, 1999. https://www .nytimes.com/1999/12/02/world/talks-turmoil-overview-president-chides -world-trade-body-stormy-seattle.html.

Saraiva, Catarina, and Olivia Rockeman. "Millennials Are Running out of Time to Build Wealth." *Bloomberg News*, June 3, 2021, 2021. https:// www.bloomberg.com/features/2021-millennials-are-running-out-of -time/.

Saucier, Jeremy K. "Mobilizing the Imagination: Army Advertising and the Politics of Culture in Post-Vietnam America." PhD diss., University of Rochester, 2010. http://hdl.handle.net/1802/12399.

Savage, Dan. "Episode 1." *Savage Love Podcast*, October 26, 2006. https:// savage.love/lovecast/2006/10/26/welcome-to-the-very-first-savage-love -podcast-in-this-episode-the-woes-of/.

Schlesinger, Jacob M., and Greg Hitt. "Bush Supports Constitutional Ban on Gay Marriage." *Wall Street Journal*, February 25, 2004. https://www .wsj.com/articles/SB107763526982637731.

Schmitt, Eric. "Bush Says Plan for Immigrants Could Expand." *New York Times*, July 27, 2001. https://www.nytimes.com/2001/07/27/us/bush-says -plan-for-immigrants-could-expand.html.

Seelye, Katharine Q. "Fiscal Year Ends with U.S. Surplus, First in 3 Decades." *New York Times*, October 1, 1998. https://www.nytimes.com/1998/10/01 /us/fiscal-year-ends-with-us-surplus-first-in-3-decades.html.

Senate Congressional Record Vol. 147, No. 110.

Seward, Zachary M. "Rim Renames Itself BlackBerry: Here's How That Name Came to Be." *Quartz*, January 30, 2013. https://qz.com/49115/rim -renames-itself-blackberry-heres-how-that-name-came-to-be.

Sherman, Gabriel. "Chasing Fox." *New York*, October 1, 2010. https://nymag .com/news/media/68717/.

———. *The Loudest Voice in the Room: How the Brilliant, Bombastic Roger Ailes Built Fox News—and Divided a Country.* New York: Random House, 2014.

Simon, Ruth, and James R. Haggerty. "As Prices Rise, Homeowners Go Deep in Debt to Buy Real Estate." *Wall Street Journal*, May 23, 2005. https:// www.wsj.com/articles/SB111680569071440252.

Smialek, Jeanna. "Are We in a Productivity Boom? For Clues, Look to 1994." February 21, 2024. https://www.nytimes.com/2024/02/21/business /economy/economy-productivity-increase.html.

Spratt, Vicky. "Why Are Millennials the Most Nostalgic Generation Ever?" *Grazia*, March 28, 2016. https://graziadaily.co.uk/life/opinion/millennials -nostalgic-generation-ever/.

Stein, Joel. "The Me Me Me Generation." *TIME*, May 20, 2013, 2013. https:// time.com/247/millennials-the-me-me-me-generation/.

Stopera, Dave. "These 13 Trivia Questions Will Finally Separate the Millennials from the Gen X'ers." *BuzzFeed*, July 8, 2019, 2019. https:// www.buzzfeed.com/daves4/youll-only-pass-this-quiz-is-youre-under -30-year-1.

"The Story of DACA and the Original Dreamer with Tereza Lee." Divided Families Podcast, September 8, 2021. https://dividedfamiliespodcast. medium.com/the-story-of-daca-and-the-original-dreamer-with-tereza -lee-136738d7809e.

Sussman, Dalia, and James Dao. "For Obama, Big Rise in Poll Numbers after Bin Laden Raid." *New York Times*, May 4, 2011. https://www.nytimes.com /2011/05/05/us/politics/05poll.html.

Szalavitz, M., and K. K. Rigg. "The Curious (Dis)Connection between the Opioid Epidemic and Crime." [English]. no. 1532-2491 (Electronic).

Taylor, Paul. "Nonmarital Births: As Rates Soar, Theories Abound." *Washington Post*, January 21, 1991. https://www.washingtonpost.com /archive/politics/1991/01/22/nonmarital-births-as-rates-soar-theories -abound/9bcc65f3-6c64-4012-b2da-fbe6eeaf0090/.

"Tereza Lee, an Original Dreamer." *Hyphen Magazine*, September 17, 2012. https://hyphenmagazine.com/blog/2012/9/17/tereza-lee-original-dreamer.

"Tereza Lee, the Original Dreamer." *Economist*, February 1, 2018. https://www .economist.com/united-states/2018/02/01/tereza-lee-the-original-dreamer.

"Text from Debate among Republicans." *New York Times*, December 14, 1999. https://archive.nytimes.com/www.nytimes.com/library/politics /camp/121499wh-gop-debate-text.html.

"Text of Bush's Victory Speech." *Wall Street Journal*, December 14, 2000. https://www.wsj.com/articles/SB976764797598003263.

Thaliath, Catherine. "Why Are Millennials So Risk-Averse?" *Take On Payments*, January 22, 2019. https://www.atlantafed.org/blogs/take-on -payments/2019/01/22/why-are-millennials-so-risk-averse.

Tierney, John. "What Is Nostalgia Good For? Quite a Bit, Research Shows." *New York Times*, July 8, 2013. https://www.nytimes.com/2013/07/09 /science/what-is-nostalgia-good-for-quite-a-bit-research-shows.html.

Tocqueville, Alexis de. *Democracy in America*. Edited by Harvey C. Mansfield and Delba Winthrop. Chicago: University of Chicago, 2000. https://press .uchicago.edu/Misc/Chicago/805328chap13.html.

Tufekci, Zeynep. "Do Protests Even Work?" *Atlantic*, June 24, 2020. https:// www.theatlantic.com/technology/archive/2020/06/why-protests-work /613420/.

———. *Twitter and Tear Gas : The Power and Fragility of Networked Protest*. New Haven: Yale University Press, 2017.

Twenge, Jean M. *Generation Me: Why Today's Young Americans Are More Confident. Assertive. Entitled—and More Miserable Than Ever Before*, updated edition. New York: Atria Books, 2014.

Uchitelle, Louis. "Spending Stalls and Businesses Slash U.S. Jobs." *New York Times*, October 25, 2008. https://www.nytimes.com/2008/10/26 /business/26layoffs.html.

"Unemployment Rate [Unrate]." Retrieved from FRED, Federal Reserve Bank of St. Louis, https://fred.stlouisfed.org/series/UNRATE.

US Government Accountability Office. "Drug Misuse: Most States Have Good Samaritan Laws and Research Indicates They May Have Positive Effects." Mar 29, 2021. https://www.gao.gov/products/gao-21-248.

U.S. Census Bureau. "Homeownership Rate in the United States." May 21, 2024. https://fred.stlouisfed.org/series/RHORUSQ156N.

Verhovek, Sam Howe, and Steven Greenhouse. "National Guard Is Called to Quell Trade-Talk Protests; Seattle Is under Curfew after Disruptions." *New York Times*, December 1, 1999. https://www.nytimes.com/1999/12/01/world/national-guard-called-quell-trade-talk-protests-seattle-under-curfew-after.html.

Wallace-Wells, Benjamin. "The Changing Shape of Protests in the Second Year of the Trump Era." *New Yorker*, April 5, 2018. https://www.newyorker.com/news/news-desk/the-changing-shape-of-protests-in-the-second-year-of-the-trump-era.

Wessel, David. "The Fed Starts to Show Concern at Signs of a Bubble in Housing." *Wall Street Journal*, May 19, 2005. https://www.wsj.com/articles/SB111645643190837423.

"What Are the Current Swing States, and How Have They Changed over Time?" USAFacts, June 16, 2023. https://usafacts.org/articles/what-are-the-current-swing-states-and-how-have-they-changed-over-time/.

Whitaker, Nancy. "Workers Get the Bad News." *Alliance Review*, February 9, 2002.

Whitehouse, Mark. "As Data Point to Slowdown, Housing Market May Land Harder Than Economists Predict." *Wall Street Journal*, August 7, 2006. https://www.wsj.com/articles/SB115491028400528328.

Whittemore, Hank. *CNN: The Inside Story*. Boston: Little, Brown and Company, 1990.

Young, Julie. "Profile of Tereza Lee." Korean American Story, November 16, 2017. https://koreanamericanstory.org/written/profile-of-tereza-lee/.

Zeleny, Jeff. "For a High-Tech President, a Hard-Fought E-Victory." *New York Times*, January 22, 2009. https://www.nytimes.com/2009/01/23/us/politics/23berry.html.

Zhao, Sarah. "Subprime Lending." American Predatory Lending, Duke University. https://predatorylending.duke.edu/wp-content/uploads/sites/9/2021/10/Subprime-Lending-Products.pdf.

Zillow. "Today's First-Time Homebuyers Older, More Often Single." Zillow, August 17, 2015. https://zillow.mediaroom.com/2015-08-17-Todays-First-Time-Homebuyers-Older-More-Often-Single.

Zumbrun, Josh. "A Millennial Puzzle: More Diverse but More Segregated." *Wall Street Journal*, May 19, 2023. https://www.wsj.com/articles/a-millennial-puzzle-more-diverse-but-more-segregated-f8db5ae2.

ABOUT THE AUTHOR

Charlie Wells is an award-winning staff editor and reporter at Bloomberg News. He writes about how the economy, society, technology, and politics influence everyday life and is a regulator contributor to Bloomberg television and radio. Before Bloomberg, he spent five years at the *Wall Street Journal* and then four years at the *Economist*. Like his subjects, he's a Millennial whose life turned out a little bit differently than he once imagined it would.